PRAISE FOR
THE WRITER'S WORLD

"A brilliant publishing enterprise. One of the best elements in American culture is a genuine, welcoming interest in writing from other languages. Beginning with essential writers from Ireland, Mexico, and Poland, the series fills a vital need. Edward Hirsch is absolutely the right general editor to guide the series. In a time of clouds, anxieties, disasters, and blunders regarding our place among the nations, here is a beacon."
—ROBERT PINSKY

"These handsome, beautifully written, and thoughtfully edited volumes could not come at a more opportune moment. Even as our political borders are growing more rigid and fiercely defended, these welcome books remind us of the ways in which literature will always cross the most seemingly impermeable barrier and leap the highest wall."
—FRANCINE PROSE

"What an inspired way to engage other cultures: through the meditations of writers on the subject that they know best—writing. And what we discover in the essays collected in The Writer's World is that for all of our seeming differences and genuine divisions, we are bound by words, which in every language offer windows through which to glimpse the heart of the matter: what it means to be alive."
—CHRISTOPHER MERRILL

"The Writer's World is a wonderfully intriguing and exciting series. Each book is like a conference of great writers and thinkers brought together to consider matters essential to culture and society. There's nothing like it."
—C. K. WILLIAMS

NINETEENTH-CENTURY AMERICAN WRITERS
on Writing

Nineteenth-Century American Writers on Writing features essays, letters, poems, prose, and excerpts of interviews by fifty-seven writers of the century, including Ralph Waldo Emerson, Edgar Allan Poe, Herman Melville, Fanny Fern, Ulysses S. Grant, William James, and Frances Harper. Each of these writers confronted what it meant for a literature to be defined as "American" during a century rocked by the industrial revolution, civil war, and the emergence of a global politics. Each of these writers had to form a community of writers in a country that did not necessarily support them, and each of them had to figure out what individual self-reliance meant in terms of the relatively new nation they spoke to, for, and about.

CONTRIBUTORS

Henry Adams
Louisa May Alcott
Ambrose Bierce
William Wells Brown
William Cullen Bryant
John Burroughs
George Washington
  Cable
John Jay Chapman
Mary Boykin Chesnut
Charles Chesnutt
Lydia Maria Child
Kate Chopin
James Fenimore
  Cooper
Stephen Crane
John De Forest
Emily Dickinson
Frederick Douglass
Paul Laurence Dunbar
Ralph Waldo Emerson
Fanny Fern (Sara Willis
  Parton)

Harold Frederic
Margaret Fuller
Hamlin Garland
Ulysses S. Grant
Frances Ellen Watkins
  Harper
Francis (Bret) Harte
Nathaniel Hawthorne
Lafcadio Hearn
Thomas Wentworth
  Higginson
Julia Ward Howe
William Dean Howells
Helen Hunt Jackson
Harriet Jacobs
Alice James
Henry James
William James
Sarah Orne Jewett
Sidney Lanier
Emma Lazarus
Abraham Lincoln

Henry Wadsworth
  Longfellow
James Russell Lowell
Herman Melville
John Neal
Frank Norris
Francis Parkman
Edgar Allan Poe
Edwin Arlington
  Robinson
Harriet Beecher Stowe
Celia Thaxter
Henry David Thoreau
Henry Timrod
Mark Twain
Edith Wharton
Walt Whitman
John Greenleaf
  Whittier
Constance Fenimore
  Woolson

THE WRITER'S WORLD
Edward Hirsch, SERIES EDITOR

The Writer's World features writers from around the globe discussing what it means to write, and to be a writer, in many different parts of the world. The series collects a broad range of material and provides access for the first time to a body of work never before gathered in English. Edward Hirsch, the series editor, is internationally acclaimed as a poet and critic. He is the president of the John Simon Guggenheim Memorial Foundation.

Chinese Writers on Writing (2010)
EDITED BY Arthur Sze

Hebrew Writers on Writing (2008)
EDITED BY Peter Cole

Irish Writers on Writing (2007)
EDITED BY Eavan Boland

Mexican Writers on Writing (2007)
EDITED BY Margaret Sayers Peden

Nineteenth-Century American Writers on Writing (2010)
EDITED BY Brenda Wineapple

Polish Writers on Writing (2007)
EDITED BY Adam Zagajewski

Trinity University Press gratefully acknowledges the generous support of the following Patrons of the Writer's World:

Sarah Harte and John Gutzler
Mach Family Fund, Joella and Steve Mach

NINETEENTH-CENTURY AMERICAN WRITERS

on *Writing*

EDITED BY
Brenda Wineapple

TRINITY UNIVERSITY PRESS
San Antonio, Texas

Published by Trinity University Press
San Antonio, Texas 78212

The book's preface appears in modified form as "Voices of a Nation" in the *American Scholar* 79, no. 3 (Summer 2010).

Cover design by Kristina Kachele Design, LLC
Book design by BookMatters, Berkeley
Cover illustration: *Cloud Shadows*, by Winslow Homer, 1890. Courtesy of the Spencer Museum of Art, University of Kansas, William Bridges Thayer Memorial, 1928.1781.

The paper used in this publication meets the minimum requirements of the American National Standard for Information Sciences—Permanence of Paper for Printed Library Materials, ANSI z39.48-1992.

Library of Congress Cataloging-in-Publication Data

Nineteenth-century American writers on writing / edited by Brenda Wineapple.
    p.   cm. — (The writer's world)
SUMMARY: "Features essays, letters, poems, prose, and excerpts of interviews by fifty-seven leading writers who had to figure out what self-reliance meant for them individually within the larger context of a relatively new country where the literature was becoming defined as American"—*Provided by publisher.*
Includes bibliographical references and index.
ISBN 978-1-59534-068-9 (alk. paper) — ISBN 978-1-59534-069-6 (pbk. : alk. paper)
   1. American literature—19th century.   2. Authorship—Literary collections.
3. National characteristics in literature.   4. Authors, American—19th century—
Psychology.   5. United States—Intellectual life—19th century.   I. Wineapple, Brenda.
PS535.N57 2010
810.8'0357—dc22   2010030570

14 13 12 11 10 5 4 3 2 1

Contents

Preface

Henry David Thoreau once famously said that Americans lead lives of quiet desperation, that flitting circumstances cause our distraction, and that despite Christianity and candles, we sit in the dark. There, in a nutshell, is the conundrum of the nineteenth-century American writer who frowned on the country's aesthetic lassitude, its getting and spending, its fundamental malaise—and yet wanted, above all, to create a language commensurate with a luminous, moral vision of national freedom; what could be more American?

"The mind of this country, taught to aim at low objects, eats upon itself," Ralph Waldo Emerson, America's spiritual cheerleader, complained. The writer, the American writer, would be different. "We will walk on our own feet; we will work with our own hands," Emerson continued, "we will speak our own minds." But though Emerson's call for self-reliance is one of the commonplaces of American literature, not until I began systematically assembling material for this volume did I understand how the nineteenth-century American authors, who frequently meditated on craft or style, also anguished about what self-reliance, to them as writers, truly meant.

Partly this is because they were trying to become masters in their own house; and by the end of the nineteenth century, they mostly were. Think of their range: the oratory of Ralph Waldo Emerson or of Sojourner Truth, the prose of jingle-man Edgar Allan Poe, the vatic humor of Melville; the cool ironies of Henry Adams, the wit of Fanny Fern, the buzzing epithets of William James, the dialect verse of Frances Harper. Yet though distinctive, these writers each had to figure out what self-reliance might mean for them individually—and in terms of a larger, national vocation.

One solution was recourse to the spread-eagle: "The spirit of Literature and the spirit of Democracy are one," claimed John O'Sullivan, editor of the *United States Magazine and Democratic Review*, a political and literary journal. In 1842 O'Sullivan and his contemporaries were still reeling from the insult hurled at them more than twenty years earlier, in 1820, when the clever British clergyman Sydney Smith taunted Americans by asking, with a sneer, "In the four quarters of the globe, who reads an American book?" As it happens, American authors were asking the very same thing.

What's more, "What *is* an American book?" they wanted to know. Typically conscientious and New Englandy, as Emily Dickinson would say, the Reverend William Ellery Channing rushed into the breach to define what this new national literature might be. "We mean the expression of a nation's mind in writing," Channing said. But what is a nation's mind? A mind distinctly and uniquely identified as American? One democratic American mind for all? The language of Channing's entreaty, like that of Emerson's rousing "American Scholar," which it anticipates, is romantic, heuristic, hopelessly nationalistic. "In going down into the secrets of his own mind," says Emerson of the true American Scholar, "he has descended into the secrets of all minds."

That is, Americans need only think for themselves to realize that, within themselves, they contained all the divinity, power, creativity, and imagination needed for any task, particularly writing. "If the single man plant himself indomitably on his instincts, and there abide, the huge world will come round to him. Patience,—patience," Emerson counseled with confidence. But his advice hints yet again at the rift, in American nineteenth-century culture, between the artist who creates and the selfsame public that sporadically and indifferently consumes those creations.

That the American mind cannot live on thought alone was made amply clear in Stephen Longfellow's advice to his son Henry, who confided to his father that he wanted to write for his career. "There is not wealth & munificence enough in this country to afford sufficient encouragement & patronage to merely literary men," the father replied. "And as you have not had the fortune, (I will not say good or ill) to be born rich, you must adopt a profession which will afford you a subsistence as well as reputation."

Money. American writers might sometimes have a room of their own—think of Thoreau's cabin in the woods—but money was a problem, sometimes even an obsession. (Savvy creature that he was, Thoreau knew this and slyly called *Walden*'s first chapter "Economy.") Making the writer's life even more difficult was the absence of international copyright. Novelist John De Forest, who coined the nagging phrase "the great American novel"—nagging, because no one seemed able to write it—explained in 1868 that this great American novel "will not soon be wrought unless more talent can be enlisted in the work, and we are sure that this sufficient talent can hardly be obtained without the encouragement of an international copyright." In other words, without such a copyright, American publishers could, and did, effectively pirate British books, selling them far more cheaply than books written by Americans, who expected and needed to be paid. It wasn't until 1891 that Congress enacted the International Copyright Act.

But as students of America know, Nature (real and imagined) quickly became the preferred refuge of the American artist, nature untrammeled and free and thus set apart from the new nation's materialistic passions. Nature is America's backyard, vast and seemingly limitless, and if the nineteenth century is about anything, it's about making that backyard—those long and lovely democratic vistas of Whitman—even bigger. "I take *space* to be the central fact to man born in America," poet Charles Olson would later say. Not surprisingly, much of nineteenth-century American writing is the bravura literature of exploration. Consider the great historians Prescott and Parkman, who interpret Cortéz and the Oregon trail, or Elisha Kent Kane, explorer of the Arctic and seeker of an open polar sea, or later John Muir, who reads glaciers, avalanches, and torrents, which he calls "the pens with which Nature produces written characters most like our own."

For these writers, Nature also comes to suggest the down-to-earth, the real, the concrete, and the unpretentious, which are presumably the most American. "The haughty soul of man has always scorned simplicity," declared a roundly democratic Lydia Maria Child. Of course the shunning of affectation for the sake of effect is itself an affectation—and central to an American argot. "I do not pretend to write English—that is, I do not pretend to write what the English themselves call English," John Neal exclaimed. "I do not, and I hope to God that I never shall write what is now worshipped under the name of classical English." Instead, as Emerson succinctly put it, "my book should smell of pines."

Many American writers (though not all) advocated what New Englanders had called the "plain style" and aspired to direct address and a clarity of language, although a few early American writers culled their style from the cadence of the religious sermon or the colloquialism of the southwestern humorists and the lingo of the frontier. These writers were looking for an idiom elastic enough to represent each singular individual and yet, somehow, to include and symbolize all Americans. "What I assume you shall assume," Whitman sings. "For every atom belonging to me as good belongs to you." In 1867 Thomas Wentworth Higginson, a Northern white man, published the "Negro Spirituals" he had scrupulously transcribed while serving in South Carolina as the leader of the first federally authorized regiment of black troops. "The present writer has been a faithful student of the Scottish ballads, and had always envied Sir Walter the delight of tracing them out amid their own heather," Higginson wrote. "It was a strange enjoyment, therefore, to be suddenly brought into the midst of a kindred world." Citing James Russell Lowell's cracker-barrel *Biglow Papers* as Yankee precedent, in case he needed one, Higginson sought to extend the language to include "kindred" worlds, for at stake was the question yet again not just of how to "write" American but of who might be one.

Both real and a pose, *vide* Emily Dickinson, who said candor was her only wile, sincerity is the hallmark of this style. In myriad introductions to slave narratives where, like Harriet Jacobs, the author contends that she wrote her book herself, the author not only authenticates the veracity of her individual experience but offers something more broadly democratic: what I assume, you can assume; what I write, even as a former slave, you can feel. Oddly, though, it is General Ulysses S. Grant's clear-headed and deeply moving *Personal Memoirs* that best epitomizes the plain style. "I have entered upon the task with the sincere desire to avoid doing injustice to any one," Grant said with typical understatement. He wrote those memoirs when ill and far down on his luck, which brings us back to Stephen Longfellow's advice to his son, those books that smell of pine notwithstanding. One writes to write; but one needs to pay the bills.

The imposture of sincerity animates some of our most unusual fictional characters—and their creators. Consider Natty Bumppo, a rough-and-ready and fundamentally anti-intellectual American wandering in an almost primeval New World forest as concocted by James Fenimore Cooper, America's first commercial author, who spent a good deal of energy figuring out how to compete (often litigiously) in the not very fictitious literary marketplace. In this, Cooper anticipates Mark Twain. Capitalist par excellence, Twain invents the youthful hero Huck Finn, who, dismayed by civilized life, seeks freedom in the form of an unbounded territory out west. Thoreau, too: at Walden Pond, he casts his line into the invisible, plumbing the depths of spirit and solitude, though he marches back to the village of Concord from his woodsy hut so his mother can wash his clothes. And the consumptive, impoverished war correspondent Henry Timrod celebrates in his ode "Ethnogenesis" the fantasy of a new Confederate nation founded on nature—that is, cotton, or the "snow of Southern summers"—which will somehow rescue the agrarian South from the fanatical, industrial, money-grubbing North.

"What I feel most moved to write, that is banned,—it will not pay," Herman Melville complained to Nathaniel Hawthorne. "Yet, altogether, write the other way I cannot. So the product is a final hash, and all my books are botches." The conflict between the wish to escape an increasingly bourgeois American life in nature and the necessity of making ends meet inevitably demoralized many nineteenth-century writers. Knocking against an increasingly conventional marketplace that demanded the predictable (or those cheap British imports), Louisiana novelist George Washington Cable balked. The artist "shall stand before kings," he said, "he shall not stand before Sunday-school library committees." Louisa May Alcott, who churned out successful popular stories, sharply satirized the public's demand for them. Referring to Jo March, the writer-heroine of *Little Women*, Alcott notes that Jo's "story was as full of desperation and despair as her limited acquaintance with those uncomfortable emotions enabled her to make it, and having located it in Lisbon, she wound up with an earthquake, as a striking and appropriate denouement." Earthquakes didn't happen in sunny America.

But these writers, whatever their means, wished to influence public opinion; they were, in effect, crusaders. Literature is born of imagination, yes, but of ethics too. Partly, this is the Puritan heritage of conscience, reflected equally in Thoreau's imperatives about writing and in those pronouncements of authors stylistically unlike him, such as Harriet Beecher Stowe, Helen Hunt Jackson, and Charles Chesnutt, who consider writing an endeavor steeped in high moral purpose. What better way to assuage guilt, particularly if you were a genteel scribbling woman who wasn't supposed to write at all? "It may be truly said that I write with my heart's blood," said Stowe, author of the wildly popular and influential *Uncle Tom's Cabin*. "This crushing of my own heart might enable me to work out some great good to others." And the hopeful novelist Chesnutt, the son of free blacks, noted when he launched his career, that "the object of my writings would be not so much the elevation of the colored people as the elevation of the whites."

At no time was the issue of moral purpose more pressing than in the years following the bloody Civil War, whose massive casualties included the idealism (and messianism) of the early part of the century. Yet as the nation redefined itself, as democracy became theoretically more inclusive, up sprang the so-called realistic writing of Ambrose Bierce and Hamlin Garland and Bret Harte and even Henry James, authors committed to what the influential William Dean Howells demanded over and over: "to do the best he can with the material he has chosen, to make the truest possible picture of life." Realism was America's new signature.

Actually, realism hearkens back to the nitty-gritty of the captivity or the slave narrative—Hannah Duston braining her Indian captors, the beating of Frederick Douglass's aunt Hester—and certainly gimlet-eyed women writing before the war, like Fanny Fern or Rebecca Harding Davis, with her "trespass vision" (Tillie Olsen's term), were nothing if not realists. Nonetheless, after the war, a generation of writers for whom Howells was a powerful spokesperson yearned to write of what they saw, however small or everyday, as they saw it. Nothing more. That was democracy. But ironically realism also springs from the increasingly Romantic notion that art evolves according to its own being, with the artist merely its medium or conduit. As John Burroughs pointed out, readers "fancy that in the works of Thoreau or Jefferies some new charm or quality of nature is disclosed, that something hidden in field or wood is brought to light. They do not see that what they are in love with is the mind or spirit of the writer himself. Thoreau does not interpret nature, but nature interprets him."

And the work itself? "Each novel has a law of its own, which it seems to create for itself," said Howells, who did not always practice what he preached. "Almost from the beginning it has its peculiar temperament and quality, and if you happen to be writing that novel you feel that you must respect its law." Naturally, there were unbelievers such as sentimentalists committed to moral uplift like the popular F. Marion Crawford or "naturalists" like Frank Norris who labeled realism a buttoned-up, uncrafted approach to literature in which mechanical fidelity to life's trivia was its sole raison d'être.

Rejecting this paint-by-the-numbers realism, which undermined their devotion to and sense of their craft, writers like Kate Chopin, with a touch of annoyance, explained that picturesque subjects were not automatically the stuff of art. "I have been taken to spots supposed to be alive with local color. I have been introduced to excruciating characters with frank permission to use them as I liked, but never, in any single instance, has such material been of the slightest service." Chopin, Jewett, Crane, Cable, Sidney Lanier, and Lafcadio Hearn concern themselves with not just imagination but its material counterpart, form. "I have had to rewrite pages fifty times," Hearn told a friend. "It is like a groping for something you know is inside the stuff, but the exact shape of which you don't know." And when advising a friend, Sarah Orne Jewett astutely remarked, "I think we must know what good work is, before we can do good work of our own, and so I say, study work that the best judges have called good and see why it is good; whether it is in that particular story, the reticence or the bravery of speech, the power of suggestion that is in it, or the absolute clearness and finality of revelation; whether it sets you thinking, or whether it makes you see a landscape with a live human figure living its life in the foreground."

"Preaching is fatal to art in literature," said Stephen Crane. To this group, even Thoreau begins to seem didactic. "Truth," Crane noted, was being true to one's own point of view. "I have tried to observe closely, and to set down what I have seen in the simplest and most concise way." Sincerity now meant devotion to craft. It also stood for integrity of vision—the ability to take what one sees and shape it into an expressive, formal whole. When Henry James advised Edith Wharton to "*do New York*," he was not talking about Zolaesque or photographic realism; rather, he was telling her to write what she knew as boldly, as capaciously, as creatively as she could.

After Emerson and Thoreau, probably no one in America meditated on the act of writing more than Henry James, whose letters and essays and novels take composition as their perpetual subject. And no one comes closer to healing the divide between craft and mission, or what was bandied about as "the novel with a purpose," than James. To him, personal vision always trumps subject matter, whether one wrote about American forests or the peoples who lived there, whether about runaway slaves or huddled masses. "Therefore, if I should certainly say to a novice, 'Write from experience, and experience only,'" he counseled in his essay "The Art of Fiction," "I should feel that this was a rather tantalizing monition if I were not careful immediately to add, 'Try to be one of the people on whom nothing is lost!'"

> It goes without saying that you will not write a good novel unless you possess the sense of reality; but it will be difficult to give you a recipe for calling that sense into being. Humanity is immense and reality has a myriad forms; the most one can affirm is that some of the flowers of fiction have the odour of it, and others have not; as for telling you in advance how your nosegay should be composed, that is another affair. It is equally excellent and inconclusive to say that one must write from experience; to our supposititious aspirant such a declaration might savour of mockery. What kind of experience is intended, and where does it begin and end? Experience is never limited and it is never complete; it is an immense sensibility, a kind of huge spider-web, of the finest silken threads, suspended in the chamber of consciousness and catching every air-borne particle in its tissue. It is the very atmosphere of the mind; and when the mind is imaginative—much more when it happens to be that of a man of genius—it takes to itself the faintest hints of life, and it converts the very pulses of the air into revelations.

"How slowly our literature grows up!" Hawthorne had groaned in 1845. Could he have read James, who read Hawthorne with such delight and profit, he might have felt that an American literature was, indeed, growing up and perhaps growing wise to boot. Though naysayers accused Henry James of denuding American literature, rendering it bloodlessly detached from the everyday, he actually broadened its definition much as his friend Howells and *their* friend Crane had tried to do, by making it alive to the possibilities of that mind on whom nothing is lost—not the struggle for survival, not the need for time and money—and which in the end makes literature a place far broader than the borders of nation.

As for the marketplace, it endured and trimmed the sales of far too many, including James, and many a writer groaned and groused about its philistine stranglehold. But it could not curtail or stop an artist, not for very long. True, Hearn left the country, as did Crane and Frederic and James and Woolson and Wharton. Nothing becomes America like the leaving of it; and said the American wit Thomas Gold Appleton, "When good Americans die, they go to Paris." Then again, American literature had always spoken the language of exploration.

Though "realism" itself became an embattled term in the second half of the nineteenth century, just as "transcendentalism" had before it, these are categories that, on final examination, have little relevance when we barge into the writer's study to listen to him or her talk about the act of getting words onto paper. Writers write. They search all day for a word, pull out their hair, rewrite what they'd laboriously composed the night before; they find and lose editors, publishers, money, loved ones, and sleep. And if we eavesdropped on all their conversations about leaky pens and elusive readers, we would have a shelf of volumes rather than this idiosyncratic one.

This is a quirky anthology. All anthologies are. Many writers have been excluded largely because they spoke too little on the craft of writing or not as eloquently as they had about other matters. As a consequence, we do not hear from Rebecca Harding Davis or Charlotte Forten or even Oliver Wendell Holmes and Richard Henry Dana, and yet I have included Abraham Lincoln, one of the nation's most brilliant orators whose urgent, concise, economic style makes way for Twain and later for Sherwood Anderson and even Gertrude Stein, effecting a revolution in literature as well as politics. I have also chosen some writers whom we might consider "minor" but who cogently bundle together questions of writing, Americanness, social mission, and craft, which is what most of these writers, I have discovered, want to talk about. And while we do not hear from Washington Irving, a major figure—for though he lived into the nineteenth century, he represents an earlier ethos—we find Edith Wharton and Edwin Arlington Robinson and John Jay Chapman, who lived into the twentieth, for to me, they are nineteenth-century writers burdened and blessed with the same self-consciousness, the same sense of vocation, and the same troublesome goal, the making of a national literature.

An editor's choice is, in the final analysis, always personal. I have tried to select passages from the journals, poems, letters, or novels of writers that may be unfamiliar and fresh. But I didn't necessarily avoid old chestnuts, like Emerson's "The Poet." For as I read through these writers and pondered what they were saying, I realized that they were really talking to one another, and I wanted to include that conversation. What we discover when we look at American writers are women and men imbued with a generosity of spirit; they read one another, support one another, admire and criticize and urge one another forward. The greatest instance of this is perhaps Melville's dedication of *Moby-Dick* to Hawthorne, but there are other examples: the literary friendships of Emerson and Fuller, Jewett and Cather, Jackson and Dickinson, James and Wharton, Frederic and Crane, Twain and Grant, Chapman and Emerson, and Howells and just about everyone.

This generosity of spirit extends to us. American literature in the nineteenth century speaks in the twenty-first in terms we have not yet abandoned for all our sophistication, technology, globalism, and panache. Like it or not, and despite their many varied voices, American writers cannot untangle those knotty, annoying questions about what it means to be an American, to feel American, to compose American, whether for oneself or for others, whether in America or not. Doubtless for all our sakes, it's better that they cannot.

Brenda Wineapple
New York City

Acknowledgments

Many thanks to the friends and colleagues who generously assisted me with advice or suggestions: Christopher Bram, Rochelle Gurstein, Frances Kiernan, Richard Kopley, Geoffrey O'Brien, Benjamin Taylor, Pierre Walker, and Greg Zacharias. I'm also indebted to the Union College Summer Internship program and to Patricia O'Toole at Columbia University's School of the Arts for providing two fine research assistants, Leonardo Villoreal and Elizabeth Redden; so, too, many thanks to Abigail Rabinowitz and Kim Tingley. I'm likewise indebted to Trent Duffy.

My beloved friends David Alexander and Richard Howard were, as ever, a steady source of literary refreshment. And so too Edward Hirsch, who originally brought me this project, and the good people associated with Trinity University Press: Barbara Ras, Sarah Nawrocki, Daniel Simon, and Tom Payton.

A nod, too, to my dear father, who loved writing. He'd have gotten a kick out of this book.

Never least or last is my husband, Michael Dellaira, special in all things.

James Fenimore Cooper

(1789–1851)

In 1895, in his hilarious essay "Fenimore Cooper's Literary Offenses," Mark Twain put the kibosh on the prolific novelist Cooper, who had been the best-known writer of his time: "Now I feel sure, deep down in my heart, that Cooper wrote about the poorest English that exists in our language, and that the English in *Deerslayer* is the very worst that even Cooper ever wrote." Cooper hadn't any more invention than a horse, he added, and *The Deerslayer* is nothing but a literary delirium tremens: "It has no invention; it has no order, system, sequence, or result; it has no lifelikeness, no thrill, no stir, no seeming of reality; its characters are confusedly drawn, and by their acts and words they prove that they are not the sort of people the author claims that they are; its humor is pathetic; its pathos is funny; its conversations are—oh! indescribable; its love-scenes odious; its English a crime against the language."

Today, few read Cooper, and the fault is partly Twain's, partly Cooper's, but mostly ours, for as the first American novelist he did bring to life the rich forest inhabited by Natty Bumppo, the lake still called Glimmerglass (Otsego Lake in upstate New York), the imponderable sense of the sea, which he had traveled young. And in many ways, both he and Washington Irving should be considered the first professional authors in America. But reviewers weren't easy on Cooper, as they aren't on any writer, and, a litigious man, he often sued those editors whose politics differed from his and, seemingly because of this, decried his work. Writing, not the courts, is the best revenge, and the second excerpt, below, from *Home as Found* (1838), skewers the pretensions of the literary world and its love of appearance, going so far as to anticipate Melville's satiric tirade against the publishing world in his novel *Pierre*.

FROM *NOTIONS OF THE AMERICANS*

You ask me to write freely on the subject of the literature and the art of the United States. The subjects are so meager as to render it a task that would require no small portion of talent necessary to figure in either, in order to render them of interest. Still, as the request has come in so urgent a form, I will oblige you.

[. . .] As respects authorship, there is not much to be said. Compared to the books that are written and read, those of native origin are few indeed. The principal reason of this poverty of original writers, is owing to the circumstance that men are not yet driven to their wits for bread.

FROM *HOME AS FOUND*

The invitation had been to a "literary fête" and Mademoiselle Viefville was too much of a Frenchwoman to be totally disconcerted at a little scenic effect on the occasion of a fête of any sort. Supposing she was now a witness of an American ceremony for the first time, for the want of representation in the country had been rather a subject of animadversion with her, she advanced steadily towards the mistress of the house, bestowing smile for smile, this being a part of the programme at which a Parisienne was not easily outdone. Eve followed, as usual, sola; Grace came next; then Sir George; then John Effingham; the captain bringing up the rear. There had been a friendly contest for the precedency between the two last, each desiring to yield it to the other on the score of merit; but the captain prevailed, by declaring that "he was navigating an unknown sea, and that he could do nothing wiser than to sail in the wake of so good a pilot as Mr. John Effingham."

As Hajjis of approved experience, the persons who led the advance in this little procession were subjects of a proper attention and respect; but as the admiration of mere vulgar travelling would in itself be vulgar, care was taken to reserve the condensed feeling of the company for the celebrated English writer and wit, who was known to bring up the rear. This was not a common house in which dollars had place, or belles rioted, but the temple of genius; and every one felt an ardent desire to manifest a proper homage to the abilities of the established foreign writer, that should be in exact proportion to their indifference to the twenty thousand a year of John Effingham, and to the nearly equal amount of Eve's expectations.

The personal appearance of the honest tar was well adapted to the character he was thus called on so unexpectedly to support. His hair had long been getting gray; but the intense anxiety of the chase, of the wreck, and of his other recent adventures, had rapidly but effectually increased this mark of time, and his head was now nearly as white as snow. The hale, fresh red of his features, which was in truth the result of exposure, might very well pass for the tint of port; and his tread, which had always a little of the quarter-deck swinging about it, might quite easily be mistaken by a tyro for the human frame staggering under a load of learning. Unfortunately for those who dislike mystification, the captain had consulted John Effingham on the subject of the toilette, and that kind and indulgent friend had suggested the propriety of appearing in black small-clothes for the occasion, a costume that he often wore himself of an evening. Reality, in this instance, then, did not disappoint expectation, and the burst of applause with which the captain was received, was accompanied by a general murmur in commendation of the admirable manner in which he "looked the character."

"What a Byronic head," whispered the author of "The Transformed" to D.O.V.E.; "and was there ever such a curl of the lip, before, to mortal man?"

The truth is, the captain had thrust his tobacco into "an aside," as a monkey is known to empocher a spare nut or a lump of sugar.

"Do you think him Byronic? To my eye the cast of his head is Shake-spearian, rather. Though I confess there is a little of Milton about the forehead!"

"Pray," said Miss Annual to Lucius Junius Brutus, "which is commonly thought to be the best of his works? That on a—a—a,—or that on e—e—e?"

Now, so it happened, that not a soul in the room, but the lion himself, had any idea what books he had written, and he knew only of some fif-teen or twenty log-books. It was generally understood that he was a great English writer, and this was more than sufficient.

"I believe the world generally prefers the a—a—a," said Lucius Junius Brutus; "but the few give a decided preference to the e—e—e."

"Oh! out of all question preferable!" exclaimed half a dozen in hearing. "With what a classic modesty he pays his compliments to Mrs. Legend," observed S. R. P. "One can always tell a man of real genius by his tenue!"

"He is so English!" cried Florio. "Ah! they are the only people after all!" This Florio was one of those geniuses who sigh most for the things that they least possess. By this time Captain Truck had got through with listening to the compliments of Mrs. Legend, when he was seized upon by a circle of rabid literati, who badgered him with questions concerning his opinions, notions, inferences, experiences, associations, sensations, senti-ments, and intentions, in a way that soon threw the old man into a profuse perspiration. Fifty times did he wish, from the bottom of his soul—that soul which the crowd around him fancied dwelt so high in the clouds—that he was seated quietly by the side of Mrs. Hawker, who, he mentally swore, was worth all the literati in Christendom. But fate had decreed otherwise,

John Neal

(1793–1876)

A native of Portland, Maine, and a Quaker, John Neal was one of the first
and loudest proponents of an American literature without frills—a literature
of democratic spunk—and he practiced what he preached in a spate of sensa-
tionalistic novels intended to shock the complacent anglophile bourgeoisie.
(He was also the first to praise Edgar Allan Poe.) "It is American books that
are wanted of America; not English books;—nor books made in America,
by Englishmen, or by writers, who are a sort of bastard English," Neal had
proclaimed, reeling from Sydney Smith's gibe in the pages of the *Edinburgh
Review* (1820), "Who reads an American book?" ("I have but one other
request to make," Neal once said. "Let these words be engraven hereafter on
my tombstone: 'Who reads an American Book?'") He influenced Nathaniel
Hawthorne early on, and though largely forgotten today, Neal's writings in
British magazines (where he disguised himself as an Englishman) promoted
the work and ways of his home through the series of editorials and reviews
written in a plain style, with natural diction, and oiled with the native idiom
not popular, and certainly not approved, until much later in the century.

The excerpt below is taken from the preface to Neal's novel *Rachel Dyer:
A North American Story* (1828), and by anticipating Poe's angry criticisms of
American literature and the sonorities of Whitman, it helps explain Neal's

mission for an American literature by outlining, in exhortatory prose, how
and why he began to rail and write as he did.

FROM *RACHEL DYER: A NORTH AMERICAN STORY*

[. . .] Would you know what more than any other thing—more than all other
things determined me at last? I was an American. I had heard the insolent
question of a Scotch Reviewer, repeated on every side of me by native
Americans—"Who reads an American Book?" I could not bear this—I
could neither eat nor sleep till my mind was made up. I reasoned with
myself—I strove hard—but the spirit within me would not be rebuked.
Shall I go forth said I, in the solitude of my own thought, and make war
alone against the foe—for alone it must he made, or there will be no hope
of success. There must be but one head, one heart in the plan—the secret
must not even be guessed at by another—it must be single and simple,
one that like the wedge in mechanics, or in the ancient military art, must
have but one point, and that point must be of adamant. Being so it may be
turned aside: A thousand more like itself may be blunted or shivered; but
if at last, any one of the whole should make any impression whatever upon
the foe, or effect any entrance whatever into the sanctity and strength of
his tremendous phalanx, then, from that moment, the day is our own. Our
literature will begin to wake up, and our pride of country will wake up with
it. Those who follow will have nothing to do but keep what the forlorn
hope, who goes to irretrievable martyrdom if he fail, has gained.

Moreover—who was there to stand by the native American that should
go out, haply with a sling and a stone, against a tower of strength and the
everlasting entrenchments of prejudice? Could he hope to find so much as
one of his countrymen, to go with him or even to bear his shield? Would the
Reviewers of America befriend him? No—they have not courage enough to
fight their own battles manfully. No—they would rather flatter than strike.
They negotiate altogether too much—where blows are wanted, they give
words. And the best of our literary champions, would they? No; they would
only bewail his temerity, if he were the bold headlong creature he should

be to accomplish the work; and pity his folly and presumption, if he were any thing else.

After all however, why should they be reproached for this? They have gained their little reputation hardly. "It were too much to spend that little"—so grudgingly acquiesced in by their beloved countrymen—"rashly." No wonder they fight shy. It is their duty—considering what little they have at stake—their little all. There is Washington Irving now; he has obtained the reputation of being—what?—why at the best, of being the American Addison, in the view of Englishmen. And is this a title to care much for? Would such a name, though Addison stood far higher in the opinion of the English themselves, than he now does, or ever again will, be enough to satisfy the ambition of a lofty minded, original thinker? Would such a man falter and reef his plumage midway up the altitude of his blinding and brave ascent, to be called the American Addison, or even what in my view were ten thousand times better, the American Goldsmith? No—up to the very key stone of the broad blue firmament! he would say. or back to the vile earth again: ay, lower than the earth first! Understand me however. I do not say this lightly nor disparagingly. I love and admire Washington Irving. I wish him all the reputation he covets, and of the very kind he covets. Our paths never did, never will cross each other. And so with Mr. Cooper; and a multitude more, of whom we may rightfully be proud. They have gained just enough popular favor to make them afraid of hazarding one jot or tittle of it, by stepping aside into a new path. No one of these could avail me in my design. They would have everything to lose, and nothing to gain by embarking in it. While I—what had I to lose—nay what have I to lose? I am not now, I never have been, I never shall be an author by trade. The opinion of the public, is not the breath of life to me; for if the truth must be told, I have to this hour very little respect for it—so long as it is indeed the opinion of the public—of the mere multitude, the careless, unthinking judgment of the mob, unregulated by the wise and thoughtful.

To succeed as I hoped, I must put everything at hazard. It would not do for me to imitate anybody. Nor would it do for my country. Who would care for the *American* Addison where he could have the English by asking for it? Who would languish, a twelvemonth after they appeared, for Mr. Cooper's imitations of Sir Walter Scott, or Charles Brockden Brown's imitations of

Godwin? Those, and those only, who after having seen the transfiguration
of Raphael, (or that of Talma,) or Domenichino's St. Jerome, would walk
away to a village painting room, or a provincial theatre, to pick their teeth
and play the critic over an imitation of the one or a copy of the other. At
the best, all such things are but imitations. And what are imitations? Sheer
mimicry—more or less exalted to be sure; but still mimicry—wherever the
copies of life are copied and not life itself: a sort of high-handed, noon-day
plagiarism—nothing more. People are never amazed, nor carried away, nor
uplifted by imitations. They are pleased with the ingenuity of the artist—
they are delighted with the closeness of the imitation—but that is all. The
better the work is done, the worse they think of the workman. [. . .]

Yes—to succeed, I must imitate nobody—I must *resemble* nobody; for
with your critic, resemblance in the unknown to the known, is never anything but adroit imitation. To succeed therefore, I must be unlike all that
have gone before me. That were no easy matter; nor would be it so difficult
as men are apt to believe. Nor is it necessary that I should do *better* than
all who have gone before me. I should be more likely to prosper, in the
long run, by worse original productions—with a poor story told in poor
language, (if it were original in spirit and character) than by a much better
story told in much better language, if after the transports of the public
were over, they should be able to trace a resemblance between it and Walter
Scott, or Oliver Goldsmith, or Mr. Addison.

So far so good. There was, beyond a doubt, a fair chance in the great
commonwealth of literature, even though I should not achieve a miracle,
nor prove myself both wiser and better, than all the authors who had gone
before me. And moreover, might it not be possible—*possible*, I say—for the
mob are a jealous guardian of sepulchres and ashes, and high-sounding
names, particularly where a name will save them the trouble of judging
for themselves, or do their arguments for them in the shape of a perpetual
demonstration, whatever may be the nature of the controversy in which
they are involved—might it not be possible then, I say, that, as the whole
body of mankind have been growing wiser and wiser, and better and better,
since the day when these great writers flourished, who are now ruling "our
spirits from their urns," that authors may have improved with them?—that
they alone of the whole human race, by some possibility, may not have

remained altogether stationary age after age—while the least enquiring and the most indolent of human beings—the very multitude—have been steadily advancing both in knowledge and power? And if so, might it not be possible for some improvements to be made, some discoveries, even yet in style and composition, by launching forth into space. True, we might not be certain of finding a new world, like Columbus, nor a new heaven, like Tycho Brahe; but we should probably encounter some phenomena in the great unvisited moral sky and ocean; we should at least find out, after a while—which would of itself be the next greatest consolation for our trouble and anxiety, after that of discovering a new world or a new system—that there remained no new world nor system to be discovered; that they who should adventure after us, would have so much the less to do for all that we had done; that they must follow in our steps; that if our health and strength had been wasted in a prodigious dream, it would have the good effect of preventing any future waste of health and strength on the part of others in any similar enterprise.

Islands and planets may still be found, we should say, and they that find them, are welcome to them; but continents and systems cannot be beyond where we have been: and if there be any within it, why—they are neither continents nor systems.

But then, after all, there was one plain question to be asked, which no honest man would like to evade, however much a mere dreamer might wish to do so. It was this. After all my fine theory—what are my chances of success? And if successful, what have I to gain? I chose to answer the last question first. Gain!—of a truth, it were no easy matter to say. Nothing here, nothing now—certainly nothing in America, till my bones have been canonized; for my countrymen are a thrifty, calculating people—they give nothing for the reputation of a man, till they are sure of selling it for more than they give. Were they visited by saints and prophets instead of gifted men, they would never believe that they were either saints or prophets, till they had been starved to death—or lived by a miracle—by no visible means; or until their cast-off clothes, bones, hair and teeth, or the furniture of the houses wherein they were starved, or the trees under which they had been chilled to death, carved into snuff-boxes or walking-sticks, would sell for as much as that sympathy had cost them, or as much as it would come to,

to build a monument over—I do not say over their unsheltered remains, for
by that time there would be but little or no remains of them to be found,
unmingled with the sky and water, earth and air about them, save perhaps
in here and there a museum or college where they might always be bought
up, however, immortality and all—for something more than compound
interest added to the original cost—but to build a monument or a shed over
the unappropriated stock, with certain privileges to the manufacturer of
the walking-sticks and snuff-boxes aforesaid, so long as any of the material
remained; taking care to provide with all due solemnity, perhaps by an act
of the legislature, for securing the monopoly to the sovereign State itself.

Thus much perhaps I might hope for from my own people. But what
from the British? They were magnanimous, or at least they would bear to
be told so; and telling them so in a Simple, off-hand, ingenuous way, with
a great appearance of Sincerity, and as if one had been carried away by a
sudden impulse, to speak a forbidden truth, or surprised into a prohibited
expression of feeling by some spectacle of generosity, in spite of his consti-
tutional reserve and timidity and caution, would be likely to pay well. But
I would do no such thing. I would flatter nobody—no people—no nation. I
would lie to nobody—neither to my own countrymen, nor to the British—
unless I were better paid for it, than any of my countrymen were ever yet
paid either at home or abroad.

No—I choose to see for myself, by putting the proof touch like a hot
iron to their foreheads, whether the British are indeed a magnanimous
people. But then, if I do all this, what are my chances of reward, even with
the British themselves? That was a fearful question to be sure. The British
are a nation of writers. Their novel-writers are as a cloud. True—true—but
they still want something which they have not. They want a real American
writer—one with courage enough to write in his native tongue. *That* they
have not, even at this day. *That* they never had. Our best writers are English
writers, not American writers. They are English in every thing they do,
and in every thing they say, as authors—in the structure and moral of their
stories, in their dialogue, speech and pronunciation, yea in the very characters they draw. Not so much as one true Yankee is to be found in any of
our native books: hardly so much as one true Yankee phrase. Not so much
as one true Indian, though you hardly take up a story on either side of the

water now, without finding a red-man stowed away in it; and what sort of a red-man? Why one that uniformly talks the best English the author is capable of—more than half the time perhaps out-Ossianing Ossian.

I have the modesty to believe that in some things I am unlike all the other writers of my country—both living and dead; although there are not a few, I dare say who would be glad to hear of my bearing a great resemblance to the latter. For my own part I do not pretend to write English—that is, I do not pretend to write what the English themselves call English—I do not, and I hope to God—I say this reverently, although one of their Reviewers may be again puzzled to determine "whether I am swearing or praying" when I say so—that I never shall write what is now worshipped under the name of classical English. It is no natural language—it never was—it never will be spoken alive on this earth: and therefore, ought never to be written. We have dead languages enough now; but the deadest language I ever met with or heard of, was that in use among the writers of Queen Anne's day.

At last I came to the conclusion—that the chances were at least a thousand to one against me. A thousand to one said I, to myself, that I perish outright in my headlong enterprise. But then, if I do not perish—if I triumph, what a triumph it will be! If I succeed, I shall be rewarded well—if the British are what they are believed to be—in fair proportion to the toil and peril I have encountered. At any rate, whether I fail or not, I shall be, and am willing to be, one of the first hundred to carry the war into the very camp, yea among the very household gods of the enemy. And if I die, I will die with my right arm consuming in the blaze of their altars—like Mutius Scaevola.

But enough on this head. The plan took shape, and you have the commencement now before you, reader. I have had several objects in view at the same time, all subordinate however to that which I first mentioned, in the prosecution of my wayward enterprise. One was to show to my countrymen that there are abundant and hidden sources of fertility in their own beautiful brave earth, waiting only to be broken up; and barren places to all outward appearance, in the northern, as well as the southern Americas— yet teeming below with bright sail—where the plough-share that is driven through them with a strong arm, will come out laden with rich mineral and followed by running water: places where—if you but lay your ear to the scented ground, you may hear the perpetual gush of innumerable fountains pouring their subterranean melody night and day among the minerals and rocks, the iron and the gold: places where the way-faring man, the pilgrim or the wanderer through what he may deem the very deserts of literature, the barren-places of knowledge, will find the very roots of the withered and blasted shrubbery, which like the traveller in Peru, he may have accidentally uptorn in his weary and discouraging ascent, and the very bowels of the earth into which he has torn his way, heavy with a brightness that may be coined, like the soil about the favorite hiding places of the sunny-haired Apollo.

William Cullen Bryant

(1794–1878)

Born in Cummington, Massachusetts, Bryant was early encouraged to imitate his father, a distinguished medical practitioner who sat in the state legislature, but he was also encouraged in his poetry. "Thanatopsis," arguably his most well-known poem, was begun when Bryant was only seventeen, and when published, it was hailed as real American poetry. After Bryant's marriage, the death of his father, and the publication of several other poems, he moved to New York, where he was editor of the *New York Review* and *Atheneum Magazine* and then, famously and forcefully, of the antislavery and Democratic *Evening Post*. Flags flew at half-mast when he died.

A beloved and strong editor and a beloved poet of nature and quiet, Bryant did not explore the terrors we associate with Dickinson or write with the formal expansiveness of Whitman. Yet, though soothing, his poems and his belief in poetry were rock hard. In his popular *Lectures on Poetry* (delivered in 1826), he was as clear as Thoreau about poetry's aim: "The truth is, that poetry which does not find its way to the heart is scarcely deserving of the name; it may be brilliant and ingenious, but it soon wearies the attention." And for all his years as one of the strongest and most influential editors in America during one of the nation's most tumultuous periods, Bryant never forgot what poetry meant to him, or what it could do. Must do. This is the subject of "Green River" (1820), his simple meditation on nature, poetry, and business.

from "Green River"

When breezes are soft and skies are fair,
I steal an hour from study and care,
And hie me away to the woodland scene,
Where wanders the stream with waters of green,
As if the bright fringe of herbs on its brink
Had given their stain to the waves they drink;
And they, whose meadows it murmurs through,
Have named the stream from its own fair hue.

Yet pure its waters—its shallows are bright
With colored pebbles and sparkles of light,
And clear the depths where its eddies play,
And dimples deepen and whirl away,
And the plane-tree's speckled arms o'ershoot
The swifter current that mines its root,
Through whose shifting leaves, as you walk the hill,
The quivering glimmer of sun and rill
With a sudden flash on the eye is thrown,
Like the ray that streams from the diamond-stone.
Oh, loveliest there the spring days come,
With blossoms, and birds, and wild-bees' hum;
The flowers of summer are fairest there,
And freshest the breath of the summer air;
And sweetest the golden autumn day
In silence and sunshine glides away.

Yet, fair as thou art, thou shunnest to glide,
Beautiful stream! by the village side;
But windest away from haunts of men,
To quiet valley and shaded glen;
And forest, and meadow, and slope of hill,
Around thee, are lonely, lovely, and still,

Lonely—save when, by thy rippling tides,
From thicket to thicket the angler glides;
Or the simpler comes, with basket and book,
For herbs of power on thy banks to look;
Or haply, some idle dreamer, like me,
To wander, and muse, and gaze on thee,
Still—save the chirp of birds that feed
On the river cherry and seedy reed,
And thy own wild music gushing out
With mellow murmur of fairy shout,
From dawn to the blush of another day,
Like traveller singing along his way.

That fairy music I never hear,
Nor gaze on those waters so green and clear,
And mark them winding away from sight,
Darkened with shade or flashing with light,
While o'er them the vine to its thicket clings,
And the zephyr stoops to freshen his wings,
But I wish that fate had left me free
To wander these quiet haunts with thee,
Till the eating cares of earth should depart,
And the peace of the scene pass into my heart;
And I envy thy stream, as it glides along
Through its beautiful banks in a trance of song.

Though forced to drudge for the dregs of men,
And scrawl strange words with the barbarous pen,
And mingle among the jostling crowd,
Where the sons of strife are subtle and loud—
I often come to this quiet place,
To breathe the airs that ruffle thy face,
And gaze upon thee in silent dream,
For in thy lonely and lovely stream
An image of that calm life appears
That won my heart in my greener years.

Lydia Maria Child

(1802–1880)

"Over the river and through the wood, / To grandfather's house we go" strikes us today as a greeting-card epigram, and though we remember it, we forget its author, Lydia Maria Child. In the nineteenth century, she represented all the literary forms—and reforms—that the era offered: a crusade against slavery, religious bigotry, and the unequal treatment afforded women and Native Americans. Child wrote rational polemic, historical fiction, children's literature, a domestic advice book (that went into thirty-three printings), journalism, and poetry. "In the simplest things I write, whether for children or grown people, I always try to sow some seeds for freedom, truth, and humanity," she told a friend. With a sense that she could—see the first excerpt below—she wrote prolifically and fervently, not separating her sense of mission from her sense of what literature was and could do. Some of her work now seems dated or quaint, but her excellent "Letters from New York," published in the *Boston Courier* (1841–43), were the ancestors of such journalistic essays by women like Janet Flanner, who wrote her stylish "Letter from Paris" for the *New Yorker* in the twentieth century. Here, in one of them, Child defines "transcendentalism" with a pith not ordinarily associated with such a reformer as she; but in point of fact, Child wrote with—and valued—a clarity and a precision she did not always find in her peers.

FROM *LETTERS OF LYDIA MARIA CHILD*

To Convers Francis

1838

I know not how it is, but my natural temperament is such that when I wish to do anything I seem to have an instinctive faith that I can do it; whether it be cutting and making a garment, or writing a Greek novel. The sort of unconsciousness of danger arising from this is in itself strength. Whence came it? I did not acquire it. But the "whence? how? whither?" of our inward life must always be answered, "From a mystery; in a mystery; to a mystery."

FROM *LETTERS FROM NEW YORK*

APRIL 24, 1844

You ask me what is transcendentalism, and what do transcendentalists believe? It is a question difficult, nay, impossible, to answer; for the minds so classified are incongruous individuals, without any creed. The name is in fact applied to everything new, strange, and unaccountable. If a man is a non-conformist to established creeds and opinions, and expresses his dissent in a manner ever so slightly peculiar, he is called a transcendentalist. It is indeed amusing to see how easily one may acquire this title. A southern lady lately said to a friend of mine, "I knew you were a transcendentalist the first half hour I heard you talk." "How so?" inquired my friend. "Oh, it is easy enough to be seen by your peculiar phrases." "Indeed! I had thought my language was very plain and natural. Pray what transcendental phrase have I used?" "The first time I ever saw you, you spoke of a person at the North as unusually gifted; and I have often since heard you use other transcendental expressions." [. . .]

"Transcendental muslins" I have often seen advertised in the Bowery; but I have rarely met with transcendentalism in any other form, in this city. I did once, out of pure mischief, send a politician and an active man of business to a house, where I knew they would encounter three or four of these disciples, who occasionally ride a pretty high horse. When they came back, I asked with a sober face, what they had talked about. They said they did not know; but being unmercifully urged to tell something that was said, the politician at last answered: "One of them divided man into three states; the disconscious, the conscious, and the unconscious. The disconscious is the state of a pig; the conscious is the baptism by water; and the unconscious is the baptism by fire." "How did the conversation impress your mind?" said I, restraining a smile. "Why, after I had heard them talk a few minutes," replied he, "I'll be hanged if I knew whether I had any mind."

Ralph Waldo Emerson

(1803–1882)

"The aim of the author is not to tell truth—," Ralph Waldo Emerson wrote
in his journals, "that he cannot do, but to suggest it." Born in 1803 to a long
line of preachers, Ralph Waldo Emerson left the Unitarian Church, which
itself had abandoned hard-line Congregationalism, in order to find the
suggestive truths encapsulated in the divine nature, inner and outer, of the
universe. "We but half express ourselves, and are ashamed of that divine
idea which each of us represents," he writes in his essay "Self-Reliance." And
self-expression takes its form in action, deed, knowledge—and writing.

Over six feet tall, with bright blue eyes, a craggy nose, and high cheek-
bones, Emerson became the darling of the lecture circuit. Audiences loved
him; many still do. Generations of readers—and not just Americans—interpret personally, and misinterpret, his call for self-reliance, autonomy, and
immanence, often reducing, alas, his insistence on self-expression as permission to say or do anything. Yet his individualistic grit was the fruit of gnarled
despair: two of his brothers had died young, another was mentally ill, and his
first wife succumbed to tuberculosis before the couple had been married two
years. But after his remarriage in 1835, Emerson moved to Concord with his
second wife, Lydia, whom Emerson renamed Lydian, adding the "n" to her
name to make it more euphonious, and there he wrote the transcendentalist

bible, *Nature* (1836). For despite personal sorrow, the death of a son, and the advent of a terrible war, he staked his life on light—and language: "The maker of a sentence launches out into the infinite and builds a road into Chaos and old Night, and is followed by those who hear him with something of wild, creative delight."

Emerson's power, his force, his influence cannot be underestimated. Nor can his adamantine definition of how one writes best: "Put the argument into a concrete shape, an image," he writes in his essay "Eloquence," "some hard phrase, round and solid as a ball, which they can see and handle and carry home with them,—and the cause is half won."

Or, take this, from his description of Montaigne in *Representative Men* (1850): "The sincerity and marrow of the man reaches to his sentences. I know not anywhere the book that seems less written. It is the language of conversation transferred to a book. Cut these words, and they would bleed; they are vascular and alive. One has the same pleasure in it that he feels in listening to the necessary speech of men about their work, when any unusual circumstance gives momentary importance to the dialogue. For blacksmiths and teamsters do not trip in their speech; it is a shower of bullets. It is Cambridge men who correct themselves and begin again at every half sentence, and, moreover, will pun, and refine too much, and swerve from the matter to the expression."

The following excerpts include some of Emerson's remarks from his journals and essays as well as a passage, albeit one of his best known, from "The Poet."

FROM *Journal and Miscellaneous Notebooks*

[1836]

How hard to write the truth. [. . .] Write it down, & it is gone.

from "Tantalus"

1844

For no man can write any thing, who does not think that what he writes is for the time the history of the world; or do any thing well, who does not esteem his work to be of greatest importance. My work may be of none, but I must not think it of none, or I shall not do it with impunity.

from "Circles"

1840

Our moods do not believe in each other. To-day I am full of thoughts, and can write what I please. I see no reason why I should not have the same thought, the same power of expression, to-morrow. What I write, whilst I write it, seems the most natural thing in the world; but yesterday I saw a dreary vacuity in this direction in which now I see so much; and a month hence, I doubt not, I shall wonder who he was that wrote so many continuous pages.

from "The Poet"

1844

[. . .] The poet is representative. He stands among partial men for the complete man, and apprises us not of his wealth, but of the common-wealth. The young man reveres men of genius, because, to speak truly, they are more himself than he is. They receive of the soul as he also receives, but they more. Nature enhances her beauty, to the eye of loving men, from their belief that the poet is beholding her shows at the same time. He is isolated among his contemporaries, by truth and by his art, but with this consolation in his pursuits, that they will draw all men sooner or later. For all men live by truth, and stand in need of expression. In love, in art, in avarice, in politics, in labor, in games, we study to utter our painful secret. The man is only half himself, the other half is his expression.

Notwithstanding this necessity to be published, adequate expression is rare. I know not how it is that we need an interpreter; but the great majority of men seem to be minors, who have not yet come into possession of their own, or mutes, who cannot report the conversation they have had with nature. There is no man who does not anticipate a supersensual utility in the sun, and stars, earth, and water. These stand and wait to render him a peculiar service. But there is some obstruction, or some excess of phlegm in our constitution, which does not suffer them to yield the due effect. Too feeble fall the impressions of nature on us to make us artists. Every touch should thrill. Every man should be so much an artist, that he could report in conversation what had befallen him. Yet, in our experience, the rays or appulses have sufficient force to arrive at the senses, but not enough to reach the quick, and compel the reproduction of themselves in speech. The poet is the person in whom these powers are in balance, the man without impediment, who sees and handles that which others dream of, traverses the whole scale of experience, and is representative of man, in virtue of being the largest power to receive and to impart.

For the Universe has three children, born at one time, which reappear, under different names, in every system of thought, whether they be called cause, operation, and effect; or, more poetically, Jove, Pluto, Neptune; or, theologically, the Father, the Spirit, and the Son; but which we will call here, the Knower, the Doer, and the Sayer. These stand respectively for the love of truth, for the love of good, and for the love of beauty. These three are equal. Each is that which he is essentially, so that he cannot be surmounted or analyzed, and each of these three has the power of the others latent in him, and his own patent.

The poet is the sayer, the namer, and represents beauty. He is a sovereign, and stands on the centre. For the world is not painted, or adorned, but is from the beginning beautiful; and God has not made some beautiful things, but Beauty is the creator of the universe. Therefore the poet is not any permissive potentate, but is emperor in his own right. Criticism is infested with a cant of materialism, which assumes that manual skill and activity is the first merit of all men, and disparages such as say and do not, overlooking the fact, that some men, namely, poets, are natural sayers, sent into the world to the end of expression, and confounds them with those whose province is action, but who quit it to imitate the sayers. But Homer's words are as costly and admirable to Homer, as Agamemnon's victories are to Agamemnon. The poet does not wait for the hero or the sage, but, as they act and think primarily, so he writes primarily what will and must be spoken, reckoning the others, though primaries also, yet, in respect to him, secondaries and servants; as sitters or models in the studio of a painter, or as assistants who bring building materials to an architect.

For poetry was all written before time was, and whenever we are so finely organized that we can penetrate into that region where the air is music, we hear those primal warblings, and attempt to write them down, but we lose ever and anon a word, or a verse, and substitute something of our own, and thus miswrite the poem. The men of more delicate ear write down these cadences more faithfully, and these transcripts, though imperfect, become the songs of the nations. For nature is as truly beautiful as it is good, or as it is reasonable, and must as much appear, as it must be done, or be known. Words and deeds are quite indifferent modes of the divine energy. Words are also actions, and actions are a kind of words.

The sign and credentials of the poet are, that he announces that which no man foretold. He is the true and only doctor; he knows and tells; he is the only teller of news, for he was present and privy to the appearance which he describes. He is a beholder of ideas, and an utterer of the necessary and causal. For we do not speak now of men of poetical talents, or of industry and skill in metre, but of the true poet. I took part in a conversation the other day, concerning a recent writer of lyrics, a man of subtle mind, whose head appeared to be a music-box of delicate tunes and rhythms, and whose skill, and command of language, we could not sufficiently praise. But when the question arose, whether he was not only a lyrist, but a poet, we were obliged to confess that he is plainly a contemporary, not an eternal man. He does not stand out of our low limitations, like a Chimborazo under the line, running up from the torrid base through all the climates of the globe, with belts of the herbage of every latitude on its high and mottled sides; but this genius is the landscape-garden of a modern house, adorned with fountains and statues, with well-bred men and women standing and sitting in the walks and terraces. We hear, through all the varied music, the ground-tone of conventional life. Our poets are men of talents who sing, and not the children of music. The argument is secondary, the finish of the verses is primary.

For it is not metres, but a metre-making argument, that makes a poem,—a thought so passionate and alive, that, like the spirit of a plant or an animal, it has an architecture of its own, and adorns nature with a new thing. The thought and the form are equal in the order of time, but in the order of genesis the thought is prior to the form. The poet has a new thought: he has a whole new experience to unfold; he will tell us how it was with him, and all men will be the richer in his fortune. For, the experience of each new age requires a new confession, and the world seems always waiting for its poet. I remember, when I was young, how much I was moved one morning by tidings that genius had appeared in a youth who sat near me at table. He had left his work, and gone rambling none knew whither, and had written hundreds of lines, but could not tell whether that which was in him was therein told: he could tell nothing but that all was changed,—man, beast, heaven, earth, and sea. How gladly we listened! how credulous! Society seemed to be compromised. We sat in the aurora of a sunrise which was to put out all the stars. Boston seemed to be at twice the distance it had the night before, or was much farther than that. Rome,—what was Rome? Plutarch and Shakespeare were in the yellow leaf, and Homer no more should be heard of. It is much to know that poetry has been written this very day, under this very roof, by your side. What! that wonderful spirit has not expired! these stony moments are still sparkling and animated! I had fancied that the oracles were all silent, and nature had spent her fires, and behold! all night, from every pore, these fine auroras have been streaming. Every one has some interest in the advent of the poet, and no one knows how much it may concern him. We know that the secret of the world is profound, but who or what shall be our interpreter, we know not. A mountain ramble, a new style of face, a new person, may put the key into our hands. Of course, the value of genius to us is in the veracity of its report. Talent may frolic and juggle; genius realizes and adds. Mankind, in good earnest, have availed so far in understanding themselves and their work, that the foremost watchman on the peak announces his news. It is the truest word ever spoken, and the phrase will be the fittest, most musical, and the unerring voice of the world for that time. [. . .]

The Universe is the externalisation of the soul. Wherever the life is, that bursts into appearance around it. Our science is sensual, and therefore superficial. The earth, and the heavenly bodies, physics, and chemistry, we sensually treat, as if they were self-existent; but these are the retinue of that Being we have. "The mighty heaven," said Proclus, "exhibits, in its transfigurations, clear images of the splendor of intellectual perceptions; being moved in conjunction with the unapparent periods of intellectual natures." Therefore, science always goes abreast with the just elevation of the man, keeping step with religion and metaphysics; or, the state of science is an index of our self-knowledge. Since everything in nature answers to a moral power, if any phenomenon remains brute and dark, it is that the corresponding faculty in the observer is not yet active.

No wonder, then, if these waters be so deep, that we hover over them with a religious regard. The beauty of the fable proves the importance of the sense; to the poet, and to all others; or, if you please, every man is so far a poet as to be susceptible of these enchantments of nature: for all men have the thoughts whereof the universe is the celebration. I find that the fascination resides in the symbol. Who loves nature? Who does not? Is it only poets, and men of leisure and cultivation, who live with her? No; but also hunters, farmers, grooms, and butchers, though they express their affection in their choice of life, and not in their choice of words. The writer wonders what the coachman or the hunter values in riding, in horses, and dogs. It is not superficial qualities. When you talk with him, he holds these at as slight a rate as you. His worship is sympathetic; he has no definitions, but he is commanded in nature, by the living power which he feels to be there present. No imitation, or playing of these things, would content him; he loves the earnest of the northwind, of rain, of stone, and wood, and iron. A beauty not explicable, is dearer than a beauty which we can see to the end of. It is nature the symbol, nature certifying the supernatural, body overflowed by life, which he worships, with coarse, but sincere rites.

The inwardness, and mystery, of this attachment, drives men of every class to the use of emblems. The schools of poets, and philosophers, are not more intoxicated with their symbols, than the populace with theirs. In our political parties, compute the power of badges and emblems. See the great ball which they roll from Baltimore to Bunker hill! In the political processions, Lowell goes in a loom, and Lynn in a shoe, and Salem in a ship. Witness the cider-barrel, the log-cabin, the hickory-stick, the palmetto, and all the cognizances of party. See the power of national emblems. Some

stars, lilies, leopards, a crescent, a lion, an eagle, or other figure, which
came into credit God knows how, on an old rag of bunting, blowing in the
wind, on a fort, at the ends of the earth, shall make the blood tingle under
the rudest, or the most conventional exterior. The people fancy they hate
poetry, and they are all poets and mystics!

Beyond this universality of the symbolic language, we are apprised of
the divineness of this superior use of things, whereby the world is a temple,
whose walls are covered with emblems, pictures, and commandments of
the Deity, in this, that there is no fact in nature which does not carry the
whole sense of nature; and the distinctions which we make in events, and in
affairs, of low and high, honest and base, disappear when nature is used as a
symbol. Thought makes every thing fit for use. The vocabulary of an omni-
scient man would embrace words and images excluded from polite conversation. What would be base, or even obscene, to the obscene, becomes
illustrious, spoken in a new connexion of thought. The piety of the Hebrew
prophets purges their grossness. The circumcision is an example of the
power of poetry to raise the low and offensive. Small and mean things serve
as well as great symbols. The meaner the type by which a law is expressed,
the more pungent it is, and the more lasting in the memories of men: just
as we choose the smallest box, or case, in which any needful utensil can
be carried. Bare lists of words are found suggestive, to an imaginative and
excited mind; as it is related of Lord Chatham, that he was accustomed to
read in Bailey's Dictionary, when he was preparing to speak in Parliament.
The poorest experience is rich enough for all the purposes of expressing
thought. Why covet a knowledge of new facts? Day and night, house and
garden, a few books, a few actions, serve us as well as would all trades and
all spectacles. We are far from having exhausted the significance of the few
symbols we use. We can come to use them yet with a terrible simplicity. It
does not need that a poem should be long. Every word was once a poem.
Every new relation is a new word. Also, we use defects and deformities to a
sacred purpose, so expressing our sense that the evils of the world are such
only to the evil eye. In the old mythology, mythologists observe, defects are
ascribed to divine natures, as lameness to Vulcan, blindness to Cupid, and
the like, to signify exuberances.

For, as it is dislocation and detachment from the life of God, that makes

things ugly, the poet, who re-attaches things to nature and the Whole,—
re-attaching even artificial things, and violations of nature, to nature,
by a deeper insight,—disposes very easily of the most disagreeable facts.
Readers of poetry see the factory-village, and the railway, and fancy that
the poetry of the landscape is broken up by these; for these works of art
are not yet consecrated in their reading; but the poet sees them fall within
the great Order not less than the beehive, or the spider's geometrical web.
Nature adopts them very fast into her vital circles, and the gliding train of
cars she loves like her own. Besides, in a centred mind, it signifies nothing
how many mechanical inventions you exhibit. Though you add millions,
and never so surprising, the fact of mechanics has not gained a grain's
weight. The spiritual fact remains unalterable, by many or by few particulars; as no mountain is of any appreciable height to break the curve of the
sphere. A shrewd country-boy goes to the city for the first time, and the
complacent citizen is not satisfied with his little wonder. It is not that he
does not see all the fine houses, and know that he never saw such before,
but he disposes of them as easily as the poet finds place for the railway.
The chief value of the new fact, is to enhance the great and constant fact of
Life, which can dwarf any and every circumstance, and to which the belt of
wampum, and the commerce of America, are alike.

The world being thus put under the mind for verb and noun, the poet
is he who can articulate it. For, though life is great, and fascinates, and
absorbs,—and though all men are intelligent of the symbols through which
it is named,—yet they cannot originally use them. We are symbols, and
inhabit symbols; workman, work, and tools, words and things, birth and
death, all are emblems; but we sympathize with the symbols, and, being
infatuated with the economical uses of things, we do not know that they
are thoughts. The poet, by an ulterior intellectual perception, gives them
a power which makes their old use forgotten, and puts eyes, and a tongue,
into every dumb and inanimate object. He perceives the independence of
the thought on the symbol, the stability of the thought, the accidency and
fugacity of the symbol. As the eyes of Lynceaus were said to see through
the earth, so the poet turns the world to glass, and shows us all things in
their right series and procession. For, through that better perception, he
stands one step nearer to things, and sees the flowing or metamorphosis;

perceives that thought is multiform; that within the form of every creature is a force impelling it to ascend into a higher form; and, following with his eyes the life, uses the forms which express that life, and so his speech flows with the flowing of nature. All the facts of the animal economy, sex, nutriment, gestation, birth, growth, are symbols of the passage of the world into the soul of man, to suffer there a change, and reappear a new and higher fact. He uses forms according to the life, and not according to the form. This is true science. The poet alone knows astronomy, chemistry, vegetation, and animation, for he does not stop at these facts, but employs them as signs. He knows why the plain, or meadow of space, was strewn with these flowers we call suns, and moons, and stars; why the great deep is adorned with animals, with men, and gods; for, in every word he speaks he rides on them as the horses of thought.

By virtue of this science the poet is the Namer, or Language-maker, naming things sometimes after their appearance, sometimes after their essence, and giving to every one its own name and not another's, thereby rejoicing the intellect, which delights in detachment or boundary. The poets made all the words, and therefore language is the archives of history, and, if we must say it, a sort of tomb of the muses. For, though the origin of most of our words is forgotten, each word was at first a stroke of genius, and obtained currency, because for the moment it symbolized the world to the first speaker and to the hearer. The etymologist finds the deadest word to have been once a brilliant picture. Language is fossil poetry. As the limestone of the continent consists of infinite masses of the shells of animalcules, so language is made up of images, or tropes, which now, in their secondary use, have long ceased to remind us of their poetic origin. But the poet names the thing because he sees it, or comes one step nearer to it than any other. This expression, or naming, is not art, but a second nature, grown out of the first, as a leaf out of a tree. What we call nature, is a certain self-regulated motion, or change; and nature does all things by her own hands, and does not leave another to baptise her, but baptises herself; and this through the metamorphosis again. [. . .]

The poet also resigns himself to his mood, and that thought which agitated him is expressed, but alter idem, in a manner totally new. The expression is organic, or, the new type which things themselves take when liberated. As, in the sun, objects paint their images on the retina of the eye, so they, sharing the aspiration of the whole universe, tend to paint a far more delicate copy of their essence in his mind. Like the metamorphosis of things into higher organic forms, is their change into melodies. Over everything stands its daemon, or soul, and, as the form of the thing is reflected by the eye, so the soul of the thing is reflected by a melody. The sea, the mountain-ridge, Niagara, and every flower-bed, pre-exist, or super-exist, in pre-cantations, which sail like odors in the air, and when any man goes by with an ear sufficiently fine, he overhears them, and endeavors to write down the notes, without diluting or depraving them. And herein is the legitimation of criticism, in the mind's faith, that the poems are a corrupt version of some text in nature, with which they ought to be made to tally. A rhyme in one of our sonnets should not be less pleasing than the iterated nodes of a sea-shell, or the resembling difference of a group of flowers. The pairing of the birds is an idyl, not tedious as our idyls are; a tempest is a rough ode, without falsehood or rant: a summer, with its harvest sown, reaped, and stored, is an epic song, subordinating how many admirably executed parts. Why should not the symmetry and truth that modulate these, glide into our spirits, and we participate the invention of nature?

This insight, which expresses itself by what is called Imagination, is a very high sort of seeing, which does not come by study, but by the intellect being where and what it sees, by sharing the path, or circuit of things through forms, and so making them translucid to others. The path of things is silent. Will they suffer a speaker to go with them? A spy they will not suffer; a lover, a poet, is the transcendency of their own nature,—him they will suffer. The condition of true naming, on the poet's part, is his resigning himself to the divine aura which breathes through forms, and accompanying that.

It is a secret which every intellectual man quickly learns, that, beyond the energy of his possessed and conscious intellect, he is capable of a new energy (as of an intellect doubled on itself), by abandonment to the nature of things; that, beside his privacy of power as an individual man, there is a great public power, on which he can draw, by unlocking, at all risks, his human doors, and suffering the ethereal tides to roll and circulate through him: then he is caught up into the life of the Universe, his speech is thunder, his thought is law, and his words are universally intelligible as the plants and animals. The poet knows that he speaks adequately, then, only when he speaks somewhat wildly, or, "with the flower of the mind;" not with the intellect, used as an organ, but with the intellect released from all service, and suffered to take its direction from its celestial life; or, as the ancients were wont to express themselves, not with intellect alone, but with the intellect inebriated by nectar. As the traveller who has lost his way, throws his reins on his horse's neck, and trusts to the instinct of the animal to find his road, so must we do with the divine animal who carries us through this world. For if in any manner we can stimulate this instinct, new passages are opened for us into nature, the mind flows into and through things hardest and highest, and the metamorphosis is possible.

This is the reason why bards love wine, mead, narcotics, coffee, tea, opium, the fumes of sandal-wood and tobacco, or whatever other species of animal exhilaration. All men avail themselves of such means as they can, to add this extraordinary power to their normal powers; and to this end they prize conversation, music, pictures, sculpture, dancing, theatres, travelling, war, mobs, fires, gaming, politics, or love, or science, or animal intoxication, which are several coarser or finer quasi-mechanical substitutes for the true nectar, which is the ravishment of the intellect by coming nearer to the fact. These are auxiliaries to the centrifugal tendency of a man, to his passage out into free space, and they help him to escape the custody of that body in which he is pent up, and of that jail-yard of individual relations in which he is enclosed. Hence a great number of such as were professionally expressors of Beauty, as painters, poets, musicians, and actors, have been more than others wont to lead a life of pleasure and indulgence; all but the few who received the true nectar; and, as it was a spurious mode of attaining freedom, as it was an emancipation not into the heavens, but into the freedom of baser places, they were punished for that advantage they won, by a dissipation and deterioration. But never can any advantage be taken of nature by a trick. The spirit of the world, the great calm presence of the creator, comes not forth to the sorceries of opium or of wine. The sublime vision comes to the pure and simple soul in a clean and chaste body. That is not an inspiration which we owe to narcotics, but some counterfeit excitement and fury. Milton says, that the lyric poet may drink wine and live generously, but the epic poet, he who shall sing of the gods, and their descent unto men, must drink water out of a wooden bowl. For poetry is not "Devil's wine," but God's wine. It is with this as it is with toys. We fill the hands and nurseries of our children with all manner of dolls, drums, and horses, withdrawing their eyes from the plain face and sufficing objects of nature, the sun, and moon, the animals, the water, and stones, which should be their toys. So the poet's habit of living should be set on a key so low and plain, that the common influences should delight him. His cheerfulness should be the gift of the sunlight; the air should suffice for his inspiration, and he should be tipsy with water. That spirit which suffices quiet hearts, which seems to come forth to such from every dry knoll of sere grass, from every pine-stump, and half-imbedded stone, on which the dull March sun shines, comes forth to the poor and hungry, and such as are of simple taste. If thou fill thy brain with Boston and New York, with fashion and covetousness, and wilt stimulate thy jaded senses with wine and French coffee, thou shalt find no radiance of wisdom in the lonely waste of the pinewoods.

If the imagination intoxicates the poet, it is not inactive in other men. The metamorphosis excites in the beholder an emotion of joy. The use of symbols has a certain power of emancipation and exhilaration for all men. We seem to be touched by a wand, which makes us dance and run about happily, like children. We are like persons who come out of a cave or cellar into the open air. This is the effect on us of tropes, fables, oracles, and all poetic forms. Poets are thus liberating gods. Men have really got a new sense, and found within their world, another world, or nest of worlds; for, the metamorphosis once seen, we divine that it does not stop. [. . .]

The poets are thus liberating gods. The ancient British bards had for the title of their order, "Those who are free throughout the world." They are free, and they make free. An imaginative book renders us much more service at first, by stimulating us through its tropes, than afterward, when we arrive at the precise sense of the author. I think nothing is of any value in books, excepting the transcendental and extraordinary. If a man is inflamed and carried away by his thought, to that degree that he forgets the authors and the public, and heeds only this one dream, which holds him like an insanity, let me read his paper, and you may have all the arguments and histories and criticism. All the value which attaches to Pythagoras, Paracelsus, Cornelius Agrippa, Cardan, Kepler, Swedenborg, Schelling, Oken, or any other who introduces questionable facts into his cosmogony, as angels, devils, magic, astrology, palmistry, mesmerism, and so on, is the certificate we have of departure from routine, and that here is a new witness. That also is the best success in conversation, the magic of liberty, which puts the world, like a ball, in our hands. How cheap even the liberty then seems; how mean to study, when an emotion communicates to the intellect the power to sap and upheave nature: how great the perspective! nations, times, systems, enter and disappear, like threads in tapestry of large figure and many colors; dream delivers us to dream, and, while the drunkenness lasts, we will sell our bed, our philosophy, our religion, in our opulence.

There is good reason why we should prize this liberation. The fate of the poor shepherd, who, blinded and lost in the snow-storm, perishes in a drift within a few feet of his cottage door, is an emblem of the state of man. On the brink of the waters of life and truth, we are miserably dying. The inaccessibleness of every thought but that we are in, is wonderful. What if you come near to it,—you are as remote, when you are nearest, as when you are farthest. Every thought is also a prison; every heaven is also a prison. Therefore we love the poet, the inventor, who in any form, whether in an ode, or in an action, or in looks and behavior, has yielded us a new thought. He unlocks our chains, and admits us to a new scene.

This emancipation is dear to all men, and the power to impart it, as it must come from greater depth and scope of thought, is a measure of intellect. Therefore all books of the imagination endure, all which ascend to that truth, that the writer sees nature beneath him, and uses it as his exponent. Every verse or sentence, possessing this virtue, will take care of its own immortality. The religions of the world are the ejaculations of a few imaginative men.

But the quality of the imagination is to flow, and not to freeze. The poet did not stop at the color, or the form, but read their meaning; neither may he rest in this meaning, but he makes the same objects exponents of his new thought. Here is the difference betwixt the poet and the mystic, that the last nails a symbol to one sense, which was a true sense for a moment, but soon becomes old and false. For all symbols are fluxional; all language is vehicular and transitive, and is good, as ferries and horses are, for conveyance, not as farms and houses are, for homestead. Mysticism consists in the mistake of an accidental and individual symbol for an universal one. The morning-redness happens to be the favorite meteor to the eyes of Jacob Behmen, and comes to stand to him for truth and faith; and he believes should stand for the same realities to every reader. But the first reader prefers as naturally the symbol of a mother and child, or a gardener and his bulb, or a jeweller polishing a gem. Either of these, or of a myriad more, are equally good to the person to whom they are significant. Only they must be held lightly, and be very willingly translated into the equivalent terms which others use. And the mystic must be steadily told,—All that you say is just as true without the tedious use of that symbol as with it. Let us have a little algebra, instead of this trite rhetoric,—universal signs, instead of these village symbols,—and we shall both be gainers. The history of hierarchies seems to show, that all religious error consisted in making the symbol too stark and solid, and, at last, nothing but an excess of the organ of language. [. . .]

I look in vain for the poet whom I describe. We do not, with sufficient plainness, or sufficient profoundness, address ourselves to life, nor dare we chaunt our own times and social circumstance. If we filled the day with bravery, we should not shrink from celebrating it. Time and nature yield us many gifts, but not yet the timely man, the new religion, the reconciler, whom all things await. Dante's praise is, that he dared to write his autobiography in colossal cipher, or into universality. We have yet had no genius in America, with tyrannous eye, which knew the value of our incomparable materials, and saw, in the barbarism and materialism of the times, another carnival of the same gods whose picture he so much admires in Homer; then in the middle age; then in Calvinism. Banks and tariffs, the newspaper and caucus, methodism and unitarianism, are flat and dull to dull people, but rest on the same foundations of wonder as the town of Troy, and the temple of Delphos, and are as swiftly passing away. Our logrolling, our stumps and their politics, our fisheries, our Negroes, and Indians, our boasts, and our repudiations, the wrath of rogues, and the pusillanimity of

honest men, the northern trade, the southern planting, the western clearing, Oregon, and Texas, are yet unsung. Yet America is a poem in our eyes;
its ample geography dazzles the imagination, and it will not wait long for
metres. [. . .]

Doubt not, O poet, but persist. Say, "It is in me, and shall out." Stand
there, baulked and dumb, stuttering and stammering, hissed and hooted,
stand and strive, until, at last, rage draw out of thee that dream-power
which every night shows thee is thine own; a power transcending all limit
and privacy, and by virtue of which a man is the conductor of the whole
river of electricity. Nothing walks, or creeps, or grows, or exists, which
must not in turn arise and walk before him as exponent of his meaning.
Comes he to that power, his genius is no longer exhaustible. All the creatures, by pairs and by tribes, pour into his mind as into a Noah's ark, to
come forth again to people a new world. This is like the stock of air for
our respiration, or for the combustion of our fireplace, not a measure of
gallons, but the entire atmosphere if wanted. And therefore the rich poets,
as Homer, Chaucer, Shakespeare, and Raphael, have obviously no limits
to their works, except the limits of their lifetime, and resemble a mirror
carried through the street, ready to render an image of every created thing.

Nathaniel Hawthorne

(1804–1864)

When a friend gave Emerson a copy of Hawthorne's sketch "Footsteps on the Sea-Shore," Emerson remarked with some aspersion that "there was no inside to it." And though Emerson liked Hawthorne the more he knew him, never an easy thing to do, he long remained equivocal about the work. "N. Hawthorn's reputation as a writer is a very pleasing fact," Emerson wrote in his own journals, "because his writing is not good for anything, and this is a tribute to the man."

For his part, Hawthorne described Emerson as "a great searcher for facts; but they seem to melt away and become unsubstantial in his grasp." Hawthorne preferred "the narrow but earnest cushion thumper of puritanical times," he half-joked, to the "cold, lifeless, vaguely liberal clergyman of our own day."

Hawthorne was the untranscendentalist, the man with cat's-eyes, as Henry James said, who could see in the dark and was ambivalent about most things, especially writing. When his youngest daughter, Rose, began to scribble tales, he stood over her, "dark as a prophetic flight of birds," she recalled; "'Never let me hear of your writing stories!'" he growled. Never did he forget, even at the end of his life, that for a very long time, he had been, as Poe called him, "*the* example, par excellence, in this country, of the privately admired and publicly unappreciated man of genius."

In other words, Hawthorne embeds a tragic vision—that our ends seldom match our aims—in a deft prose where expectation is inevitably disappointed by human history. This is the subject of *The Marble Faun* (1860), set in a Rome heaped with history's fragments—chipped statues, cracked columns: "You look through a vista of century beyond century—through much shadow, and a little sunshine," Hawthorne writes, "through barbarism and civilization, alternating with one another, [. . .] until, in the distance, you behold the obelisks, with their unintelligible inscriptions, hinting at a Past infinitely more remote than history can define. Your own life is as nothing, when compared with that immeasurable distance; but still you demand a gleam of sunshine, instead of a speck of shadow, on the stop or two that will bring you to your rest."

For a writer like Hawthorne, the long view stretches out to a horizon that simultaneously entices and appalls, as Emily Dickinson said of him, and Hawthorne delineates that horizon in graceful sentences which reveal for a consoling moment the best that humans can do and asks us, over and over, what it means to be alive, to live with others and feel apart; to love passionately and never forget; to hope too long, plot secrets, grow old, feel scared, and still believe in the written word. "My theory is," he told a friend, "that there is less indelicacy in speaking out your highest, deepest, tenderest emotions to the world at large, than to almost any individual. You may be mistaken in the individual; but you cannot be mistaken in thinking that, somewhere among your fellow-creatures, there is a heart that will receive yours into itself."

Though Hawthorne insisted he was not "one of those supremely hospitable people, who serve up their own hearts delicately fried, with brainsauce, as a tidbit for their beloved public," he nonetheless wrote frequently about what it means to be a writer, and what writing means, whether in his definition of the romancer in the famous "The Custom-House" essay that introduces *The Scarlet Letter* (1850) or in the equally famous preface to *The House of the Seven Gables* (1851), or in the "Fragmentary Sentences" chapter of *The Marble Faun* (1860)—or in his notes for his last, incomplete book, excerpted here.

But that was toward the end of his life. Far earlier, he wrote satiric tales about the hazards of authorship that explain the frustrations of a young author bursting with talent whom no one reads or publishes. This is the subject of the very contemporary and satiric story "The Devil in Manuscript" (1835), from which the first excerpt is taken.

FROM "THE DEVIL IN MANUSCRIPT"

On a bitter evening of December, I arrived by mail in a large town, which was then the residence of an intimate friend, one of those gifted youths who cultivate poetry and the belles-lettres, and call themselves students at law. My first business, after supper, was to visit him at the office of his distinguished instructor. As I have said, it was a bitter night, clear starlight, but cold as Nova Zembla,—the shop-windows along the street being frosted, so as almost to hide the lights, while the wheels of coaches thundered equally loud over frozen earth and pavements of stone. There was no snow, either on the ground or the roofs of the houses. The wind blew so violently, that I had but to spread my cloak like a main-sail, and scud along the street at the rate of ten knots, greatly envied by other navigators, who were beating slowly up, with the gale right in their teeth. One of these I capsized, but was gone on the wings of the wind before he could even vociferate an oath.

After this picture of an inclement night, behold us seated by a great blazing fire, which looked so comfortable and delicious that I felt inclined to lie down and roll among the hot coals. The usual furniture of a lawyer's office was around us,—rows of volumes in sheepskin, and a multitude of writs, summonses, and other legal papers, scattered over the desks and tables. But there were certain objects which seemed to intimate that we had little dread of the intrusion of clients, or of the learned counsellor himself, who, indeed, was attending court in a distant town. A tall, decanter-shaped bottle stood on the table, between two tumblers, and beside a pile of blotted manuscripts, altogether dissimilar to any law documents recognized in our courts. My friend, whom I shall call Oberon,—it was a name of fancy and friendship between him and me,—my friend Oberon looked at these papers with a peculiar expression of disquietude.

"I do believe," said he, soberly, "or, at least, I could believe, if I chose, that there is a devil in this pile of blotted papers. You have read them, and know what I mean,—that conception in which I endeavored to embody the character of a fiend, as represented in our traditions and the written records of witchcraft. Oh, I have a horror of what was created in my own brain, and shudder at the manuscripts in which I gave that dark idea a sort of material existence! Would they were out of my sight!"

"And of mine, too," thought I.

"You remember," continued Oberon, "how the hellish thing used to suck away the happiness of those who, by a simple concession that seemed almost innocent, subjected themselves to his power. Just so my peace is gone, and all by these accursed manuscripts. Have you felt nothing of the same influence?"

"Nothing," replied I, "unless the spell be hid in a desire to turn novelist, after reading your delightful tales."

"Novelist!" exclaimed Oberon, half seriously. "Then, indeed, my devil has his claw on you! You are gone! You cannot even pray for deliverance! But we will be the last and only victims; for this night I mean to burn the manuscripts, and commit the fiend to his retribution in the flames."

"Burn your tales!" repeated I, startled at the desperation of the idea.

"Even so," said the author, despondingly. "You cannot conceive what an effect the composition of these tales has had on me. I have become ambitious of a bubble, and careless of solid reputation. I am surrounding myself with shadows, which bewilder me, by aping the realities of life. They have drawn me aside from the beaten path of the world, and led me into a strange sort of solitude,—a solitude in the midst of men,—where nobody wishes for what I do, nor thinks nor feels as I do. The tales have done all this. When they are ashes, perhaps I shall be as I was before they had existence. Moreover, the sacrifice is less than you may suppose, since nobody will publish them."

"That does make a difference, indeed," said I.

"They have been offered, by letter," continued Oberon, reddening with vexation, "to some seventeen booksellers. It would make you stare to read their answers; and read them you should, only that I burnt them as fast as they arrived. One man publishes nothing but school-books; another has five novels already under examination."

"What a voluminous mass the unpublished literature of America must be!" cried I.

"Oh, the Alexandrian manuscripts were nothing to it!" said my friend. "Well, another gentleman is just giving up business, on purpose, I verily believe, to escape publishing my book. Several, however, would not absolutely decline the agency, on my advancing half the cost of an edition, and giving bonds for the remainder, besides a high percentage to themselves, whether the book sells or not. Another advises a subscription."

"The villain!" exclaimed I.

"A fact!" said Oberon. "In short, of all the seventeen booksellers, only one has vouchsafed even to read my tales; and he—a literary dabbler himself, I should judge—has the impertinence to criticise them, proposing what he calls vast improvements, and concluding, after a general sentence of condemnation, with the definitive assurance that he will not be concerned on any terms."

"It might not be amiss to pull that fellow's nose," remarked I.

"If the whole 'trade' had one common nose, there would be some satisfaction in pulling it," answered the author. "But, there does seem to be one honest man among these seventeen unrighteous ones; and he tells me fairly, that no American publisher will meddle with an American work,—seldom if by a known writer, and never if by a new one,—unless at the writer's risk."

"The paltry rogues!" cried I. "Will they live by literature, and yet risk nothing for its sake? But, after all, you might publish on your own account."

"And so I might," replied Oberon. "But the devil of the business is this. These people have put me so out of conceit with the tales, that I loathe the very thought of them, and actually experience a physical sickness of the stomach, whenever I glance at them on the table. I tell you there is a demon in them! I anticipate a wild enjoyment in seeing them in the blaze; such as I should feel in taking vengeance on an enemy, or destroying something noxious."

I did not very strenuously oppose this determination, being privately of the opinion, in spite of my partiality for the author, that his tales would make a more brilliant appearance in the fire than anywhere else. Before proceeding to execution, we broached the bottle of champagne, which Oberon had provided for keeping up his spirits in this doleful business. We swallowed each a tumblerful, in sparkling commotion; it went bubbling down our throats, and brightened my eyes at once, but left my friend sad and heavy as before. He drew the tales towards him, with a mixture of natural affection and natural disgust, like a father taking a deformed infant into his arms.

"Pooh! Pish! Pshaw!" exclaimed he, holding them at arm's-length. "It was Gray's idea of heaven, to lounge on a sofa and read new novels. Now, what more appropriate torture would Dante himself have contrived, for the sinner who perpetrates a bad book, than to be continually turning over the manuscript?"

"It would fail of effect," said I, "because a bad author is always his own great admirer."

"I lack that one characteristic of my tribe,—the only desirable one," observed Oberon. "But how many recollections throng upon me, as I turn over these leaves! This scene came into my fancy as I walked along a hilly road, on a starlight October evening; in the pure and bracing air, I became all soul, and felt as if I could climb the sky, and run a race along the Milky Way. Here is another tale, in which I wrapt myself during a dark and dreary night-ride in the month of March, till the rattling of the wheels and the voices of my companions seemed like faint sounds of a dream, and my visions a bright reality. That scribbled page describes shadows which I summoned to my bedside at midnight: they would not depart when I bade them; the gray dawn came, and found me wide awake and feverish, the victim of my own enchantments!"

"There must have been a sort of happiness in all this," said I, smitten with a strange longing to make proof of it.

"There may be happiness in a fever fit," replied the author. "And then the various moods in which I wrote! Sometimes my ideas were like precious stones under the earth, requiring toil to dig them up, and care to polish and brighten them; but often a delicious stream of thought would gush out upon the page at once, like water sparkling up suddenly in the desert;

and when it had passed, I gnawed my pen hopelessly, or blundered on with cold and miserable toil, as if there were a wall of ice between me and my subject."

"Do you now perceive a corresponding difference," inquired I, "between the passages which you wrote so coldly, and those fervid flashes of the mind?"

"No," said Oberon, tossing the manuscripts on the table. "I find no traces of the golden pen with which I wrote in characters of fire. My treasure of fairy coin is changed to worthless dross. My picture, painted in what seemed the loveliest hues, presents nothing but a faded and indistinguishable surface. I have been eloquent and poetical and humorous in a dream,—and behold! it is all nonsense, now that I am awake."

My friend now threw sticks of wood and dry chips upon the fire, and seeing it blaze like Nebuchadnezzar's furnace, seized the champagne bottle, and drank two or three brimming bumpers, successively. The heady liquor combined with his agitation to throw him into a species of rage. He laid violent hands on the tales. In one instant more, their faults and beauties would alike have vanished in a glowing purgatory. But, all at once, I remembered passages of high imagination, deep pathos, original thoughts, and points of such varied excellence, that the vastness of the sacrifice struck me most forcibly. I caught his arm.

"Surely, you do not mean to burn them!" I exclaimed.

"Let me alone!" cried Oberon, his eyes flashing fire. "I will burn them! Not a scorched syllable shall escape! Would you have me a damned author?—To undergo sneers, taunts, abuse, and cold neglect, and faint praise, bestowed, for pity's sake, against the giver's conscience! A hissing and a laughing-stock to my own traitorous thoughts! An outlaw from the protection of the grave,—one whose ashes every careless foot might spurn, unhonored in life, and remembered scornfully in death! Am I to bear all this, when yonder fire will insure me from the whole? No! There go the tales! May my hand wither when it would write another!"

The deed was done. He had thrown the manuscripts into the hottest of the fire, which at first seemed to shrink away, but soon curled around them, and made them a part of its own fervent brightness. Oberon stood gazing at the conflagration, and shortly began to soliloquize, in the wildest strain, as if Fancy resisted and became riotous, at the moment when he would have compelled her to ascend that funeral pile. His words described objects which he appeared to discern in the fire, fed by his own precious thoughts; perhaps the thousand visions which the writer's magic had incorporated with these pages became visible to him in the dissolving heat, brightening forth ere they vanished forever; while the smoke, the vivid sheets of flame, the ruddy and whitening coals, caught the aspect of a varied scenery.

"They blaze," said he, "as if I had steeped them in the intensest spirit of genius. There I see my lovers clasped in each other's arms. How pure the flame that bursts from their glowing hearts! And yonder the features of a villain writhing in the fire that shall torment him to eternity. My holy men, my pious and angelic women, stand like martyrs amid the flames, their mild eyes lifted heavenward. Ring out the bells! A city is on fire. See!—destruction roars through my dark forests, while the lakes boil up in steaming billows, and the mountains are volcanoes, and the sky kindles with a lurid brightness! All elements are but one pervading flame! Ha! The fiend!"

I was somewhat startled by this latter exclamation. The tales were almost consumed, but just then threw forth a broad sheet of fire, which flickered as with laughter, making the whole room dance in its brightness, and then roared portentously up the chimney.

"You saw him? You must have seen him!" cried Oberon. "How he glared at me and laughed, in that last sheet of flame, with just the features that I imagined for him! Well! The tales are gone."

The papers were indeed reduced to a heap of black cinders, with a multitude of sparks hurrying confusedly among them, the traces of the pen being now represented by white lines, and the whole mass fluttering to and fro in the draughts of air. The destroyer knelt down to look at them.

"What is more potent than fire!" said he, in his gloomiest tone. "Even thought, invisible and incorporeal as it is, cannot escape it. In this little time, it has annihilated the creations of long nights and days, which I could no more reproduce, in their first glow and freshness, than cause ashes and whitened bones to rise up and live. There, too, I sacrificed the unborn children of my mind. All that I had accomplished—all that I planned for future years—has perished by one common ruin, and left only this heap of embers! The deed has been my fate. And what remains? A weary and aimless life,—a long repentance of this hour,—and at last an obscure grave, where they will bury and forget me!"

As the author concluded his dolorous moan, the extinguished embers arose and settled down and arose again, and finally flew up the chimney, like a demon with sable wings. Just as they disappeared, there was a loud and solitary cry in the street below us. "Fire!" Fire! Other voices caught up that terrible word, and it speedily became the shout of a multitude. Oberon started to his feet, in fresh excitement.

"A fire on such a night!" cried he. "The wind blows a gale, and wherever it whirls the flames, the roofs will flash up like gunpowder. Every pump is frozen up, and boiling water would turn to ice the moment it was flung from the engine. In an hour, this wooden town will be one great bonfire! What a glorious scene for my next—Pshaw!"

The street was now all alive with footsteps, and the air full of voices. We heard one engine thundering round a corner, and another rattling from a distance over the pavements. The bells of three steeples clanged out at once, spreading the alarm to many a neighboring town, and expressing hurry, confusion, and terror, so inimitably that I could almost distinguish in their peal the burden of the universal cry,—"Fire! Fire! Fire!"

"What is so eloquent as their iron tongues!" exclaimed Oberon. "My heart leaps and trembles, but not with fear. And that other sound, too,—deep and awful as a mighty organ,—the roar and thunder of the multitude on the pavement below! Come! We are losing time. I will cry out in the loudest of the uproar, and mingle my spirit with the wildest of the confusion, and be a bubble on the top of the ferment!"

From the first outcry, my forebodings had warned me of the true object and centre of alarm. There was nothing now but uproar, above, beneath, and around us; footsteps stumbling pell-mell up the public staircase, eager shouts and heavy thumps at the door, the whiz and dash of water from the engines, and the crash of furniture thrown upon the pavement. At once, the truth flashed upon my friend. His frenzy took the hue of joy, and, with a wild gesture of exultation, he leaped almost to the ceiling of the chamber.

"My tales!" cried Oberon. "The chimney! The roof! The Fiend has gone forth by night, and startled thousands in fear and wonder from their beds!

Here I stand,—a triumphant author! Huzza! Huzza! My brain has set the town on fire! Huzza!"

from "The Elixir of Life"

It may be observed, that a man no sooner sets his heart on any object, great or small, be it the lengthening out of his life interminably, or merely writing a romance about it, than his fellow beings, and fate and circumstance to back them, seem to conspire to hinder, to prevent, to throw in each his obstacle, great or small according to his power. In the original composition and organic purpose of the world, there is certainly some principle to obviate great success; some provision that nothing particularly worth doing shall ever get done; so inevitably does a mistiness settle between us and any such object, and harden into granite when we attempt to pass through it; so strongly do mocking voices call us back, or encouraging voices cease to be heard, when our sinking hearts need them most; so unaccountably, at last, when we feel as if we might grasp our life-long object by merely stretching out our hand, does it all at once put on an aspect of not being worth our grasp; by such apparently feeble impediments are our hands subtly bound; so hard is it to stir to-day, while it looks as if it would be easy to stir to-day, while it looks as if it would be easy to stir to purpose tomorrow; so strongly do petty necessities insist upon being compared with immortal desire.

Henry Wadsworth Longfellow

(1807–1882)

Exceptional among nineteenth-century American poets, Longfellow actually earned a living from his verse even though he did supplement that income with his teaching post as Smith Professor of Modern Languages at Harvard University. In his writing, his subjects were largely local, his metrics perfect, his models European, and his knowledge of poetic form virtuosic—but he also wanted to create an indigenous American literature. After composing the ballad "The Wreck of the Hesperus" in 1840, he wrote to a friend that "the national ballad is a virgin soil here in New England; and there are great materials. Besides, I have a great notion of working upon the people's feelings." He did; think of poems, once so popular, like "The Village Blacksmith" and "Paul Revere's Ride," never mind "The Song of Hiawatha" and "Evangeline." In 1854 his unprecedented and international fame, as well as his wife's wealth, allowed him to resign his position and devote himself full time to his writing. But in 1861 his beloved second wife died in a horrible accident—sealing wax fell onto her dress, which burst into flames, and Longfellow arrived too late on the scene to save her. When he could muster the strength to write again, he returned to the fine translation of Dante he had started years before.

Not everyone banged the drum as loudly as John Neal had for a distinctly "American" literature, and in the novel *Kavanagh* (1849), one of the

books that Emily Dickinson said her father did not want her or her brother to
read (the siblings hid it under the piano cover), Longfellow takes issue with
the call—even his own earlier one—for a strictly national literature. National-
ism and the meaning of literature is the subject of the excerpt included here.

FROM *KAVANAGH*

[. . .] He announced himself as Mr. Hathaway. Passing through the village,
he could not deny himself the pleasure of calling on Mr. Churchill, whom
he knew by his writings in the periodicals, though not personally. He
wished, moreover, to secure the co-operation of one already so favorably
known to the literary world, in a new Magazine he was about to establish,
in order to raise the character of American literature, which, in his opinion, the existing reviews and magazines had entirely failed to accomplish.
A daily increasing want of something better was felt by the public; and the
time had come for the establishment of such a periodical as he proposed.
After explaining in rather a florid and exuberant manner his plans and
prospects, he entered more at large into the subject of American literature,
which it was his design to foster and patronize.

"I think, Mr. Churchill," said he, "that we want a national literature
commensurate with our mountains and rivers,—commensurate with
Niagara, and the Alleghanies, and the Great Lakes!"

"Oh!"

"We want a national epic that shall correspond to the size of the country;
that shall be to all other epics what Banvard's 'Panorama of the Mississippi'
is to all other paintings,—the largest in the world!"

"Ah!"

"We want a national drama in which scope enough shall be given to our
gigantic ideas, and to the unparalleled activity and progress of our people!"

"Of course."

"In a word, we want a national literature altogether shaggy and unshorn,
that shall shake the earth, like a herd of buffaloes thundering over the
prairies!"

"Precisely," interrupted Mr. Churchill; "but excuse me!—are you not confounding things that have no analogy? Great has a very different mean-ing when applied to a river, and when applied to a literature. Large and shal-low may perhaps be applied to both. Literature is rather an image of the spiritual world, than of the physical, is it not?—of the internal, rather than the external. Mountains, lakes, and rivers are, after all, only its scenery and decorations, not its substance and essence. A man will not necessarily be a great poet because he lives near a great mountain. Nor, being a poet, will he necessarily write better poems than another, because he lives nearer Niagara."

"But, Mr. Churchill, you do not certainly mean to deny the influence of scenery on the mind?"

"No, only to deny that it can create genius. At best, it can only develop it. Switzerland has produced no extraordinary poet; nor, as far as I know, have the Andes, or the Himalaya mountains, or the Mountains of the Moon in Africa."

"But, at all events," urged Mr. Hathaway, "let us have our literature national. If it is not national, it is nothing."

"On the contrary, it may be a great deal. Nationality is a good thing to a certain extent, but universality is better. All that is best in the great poets of all countries is not what is national in them, but what is universal. Their roots are in their native soil; but their branches wave in the unpatriotic air, that speaks the same language unto all men, and their leaves shine with the illimitable light that pervades all lands. Let us throw all the windows open; let us admit the light and air on all sides; that we may look towards the four corners of the heavens, and not always in the same direction."

"But you admit nationality to be a good thing?"

"Yes, if not carried too far; still, I confess, it rather limits one's views of truth. I prefer what is natural. Mere nationality is often ridiculous. Every one smiles when he hears the Icelandic proverb, 'Iceland is the best land the sun shines upon.' Let us be natural, and we shall be national enough. Besides, our literature can be strictly national only so far as our character and modes of thought differ from those of other nations. Now, as we are very like the English,—are, in fact, English under a different sky,—I do not see how our literature can be very different from theirs. Westward from hand to hand we pass the lighted torch, but it was lighted at the old domestic fireside of England."

"Then you think our literature is never to be anything but an imitation of the English."

"Not at all. It is not an imitation, but, as some one has said, a continuation."

"It seems to me that you take a very narrow view of the subject."

"On the contrary, a very broad one. No literature is complete until the language in which it is written is dead. We may well be proud of our task and of our position. Let us see if we can build in any way worthy of our forefathers."

"But I insist upon originality."

"Yes, but without spasms and convulsions. Authors must not, like Chinese soldiers, expect to win victories by turning somersets in the air."

"Well, really, the prospect from your point of view is not very brilliant. Pray, what do you think of our national literature?"

"Simply, that a national literature is not the growth of a day. Centuries must contribute their dew and sunshine to it. Our own is growing slowly but surely, striking its roots downward, and its branches upward, as is natural; and I do not wish, for the sake of what some people call originality, to invert it, and try to make it grow with its roots in the air. And as for having it so savage and wild as you want it, I have only to say, that all literature, as well as all art, is the result of culture and intellectual refinement."

"Ah! we do not want art and refinement: we want genius,—untutored, wild, original, free."

"But, if this genius is to find any expression, it must employ art; for art is the external expression of our thoughts. Many have genius, but, wanting art, are for ever dumb. The two must go together to form the great poet, painter, or sculptor."

"In that sense, very well."

"I was about to say also that I thought our literature would finally not be wanting in a kind of universality."

"As the blood of all nations is mingling with our own, so will their thoughts and feelings finally mingle in our literature. We shall draw from the Germans, tenderness; from the Spaniards, passion; from the French, vivacity, to mingle more and more with our English solid sense. And this will give us universality, so much to be desired."

John Greenleaf Whittier

(1807–1892)

A young farm boy, virtually uneducated, grows up with the nineteenth century in rural Massachusetts, where his Quaker family serves as his main emotional and moral sustenance; he dies at the end of that century, in 1892, celebrated as one of its most famous and beloved figures: a poet who touched the heart of Americans and helped to create an "American" litera-ture; a man of faith and belief in justice for all, especially the enslaved and disenfranchised; and an abolitionist and pacifist during the nation's grueling Civil War who balanced his ecumenical love of person and place with his abolitionist anger. Today he is virtually forgotten.

Read by schoolchildren well into the twentieth century and considered, in his time, the "people's poet" because of his accessibility, Whittier is nonetheless derided by modern critics as a "Fireside" writer who, according to Edmund Wilson, wrote versified journalism. This isn't quite fair. His stirring poem "Ichabod," composed to protest Daniel Webster's support for the 1850 Fugitive Slave Law, is dense, austere, passionate. And his splendid, haunting postwar poem "Snow-Bound" (1866) has justly influenced a host of modern writers, including Robert Frost, Ezra Pound, and W. H. Auden.

Accessible though he is, Whittier's lissome sentiment is undergirded by steel. His social conscience rock solid, the poet created a homely rural scene something like Oliver Goldsmith's "Deserted Village" but with far more terror beneath its octosyllabic surface. Yet to Whittier, a long poem "unless consecrated to the sacred interests of religion and humanity would be a criminal waste of life."

In his younger years, Whittier was steadfast in his political views but in many ways insecure about his poetry and wrote fairly often about the obstacles he faced as poet: "I am not a builder in the sense of Milton's phrase of one who could 'build the lofty rhyme.'" And, as he also said of himself, "my vehicles have been of the humbler sort—merely the farm wagon and buckboard of verse." Similarly, in the poem he chose, after 1847, to reintroduce all his collected works, he writes,

> [. . .] if to me belong
> Not mighty Milton's gift divine,
> Nor Marvell's wit and graceful song,
> Still with a love as deep and strong
> As theirs, I lay, like them, my best gifts on thy shrine!

The following excerpt elaborates Whittier's self-assessment as writer. Similarly, he told Francis Henry Underwood (the man who first conceived of the *Atlantic Monthly* magazine) that he did not consider himself "one of the master singers" and doesn't pose as one. The excerpt below comes from Whittier's introduction to *The Tent on the Beach* (1867) in which he describes with certain acuity the political poetry he wrote, and how he wrote it, from the 1830s to the 1850s.

FROM *THE TENT ON THE BEACH*

> And one there was, a dreamer born,
> Who, with a mission to fulfil,
> Had left the Muses' haunts to turn
> The crank of an opinion-mill,
> Making his rustic reed of song
> A weapon in the war with wrong,

Yoking his fancy to the breaking-plough
That beam-deep turned the soil for truth to spring and grow.

Too quiet seemed the man to ride
The wingèd Hippogriff Reform;
Was his a voice from side to side
To pierce the tumult of the storm?
A silent, shy, peace-loving man,
He seemed no fiery partisan
To hold his way against the public frown,
The ban of Church and State, the fierce mob's hounding down.

For while he wrought with strenuous will
The work his hands had found to do,
He heard the fitful music still
Of winds that out of dream-land blew.
The din about him could not drown
What the strange voices whispered down;
Along his task-field weird processions swept,
The visionary pomp of stately phantoms stepped

The common air was thick with dreams,—
He told them to the toiling crowd;
Such music as the woods and streams
Sang in his ear he sang aloud;
In still, shut bays, on windy capes,
He heard the call of beckoning shapes,
And, as the gray old shadows prompted him,
To homely moulds of rhyme he shaped their legends grim.
He rested now his weary hands,
And lightly moralized and laughed,
As, tracing on the shifting sands
A burlesque of his paper-craft,
He saw the careless waves o'errun
His words, as time before had done,
Each day's tide-water washing clean away,
Like letters from the sand, the work of yesterday.

Abraham Lincoln

(1809–1865)

Abraham Lincoln needs no headnote. The sixteenth president of the United States, whose term coincided with the Civil War and whose assassination—and understandable canonization—took place just as that war ended, Lincoln embodied and surpassed all extant myths of American heroes: born in poverty, he was self-made, without privilege or advantage, and largely self-taught, largely brilliant, largely ambitious, and quite far-seeing; he schooled himself in politics and oratory, studying the law along with the Bible, Milton, and Shakespeare. Why is he included here? His trenchant wit and his eloquent oratory buoyed the entire nineteenth century, and then some, setting a standard for excellence, simplicity, and wisdom rarely surpassed, before or after. From what source did his genius spring? No one can really know, but stories about the president's love of Shakespeare trail him. Presumably, during the Battle of the Wilderness, when twenty thousand men on both sides had been killed or wounded, Lincoln groaned at the news and recovered somewhat only by reading Shakespeare's *Macbeth*. He evidently knew the opening of *Richard III* by heart, ranked *Hamlet* high, adored the humor in *Henry VI* and *The Merry Wives of Windsor*, and recited from *Richard II:*

> For you have but mistook me all this while:
> I live with bread like you, feel want,

Taste grief, need friends: subjected
thus: How can you say to me, I am a king?

This was a man, among his other virtues, who thought long and hard about the essence of writing, which he practiced so stupendously well. Unfortunately, he commented little on the art and craft of writing, but what follow are two telling remarks.

FROM "LECTURE ON DISCOVERIES AND INVENTIONS"

Writing—the art of communicating thoughts to the mind, through the eye—is the great invention of the world. Great in the astonishing range of analysis and combination which necessarily underlies the most crude and general conception of it—great, very great, in enabling us to converse with the dead, the absent, and the unborn, at all distances of time and space.

FROM COLLECTED WORKS

Some of Shakespeare's plays I have never read; while others I have gone over perhaps as frequently as any unprofessional reader. Among the latter are *Lear*, *Richard Third*, *Henry Eighth*, *Hamlet*, and especially *Macbeth*. I think nothing equals *Macbeth*.

Edgar Allan Poe

(1809–1849)

No one cared more about literature or was more impoverished, beset, and perhaps maddened by its pursuit than Edgar Allan Poe, who fought with and insulted many of the literati of his time (he famously called Longfellow a plagiarist), who fathered the modern detective story, who wrote tales of gothic horror that haunt us today and a poetry of otherworldliness that the French symbolists understood long before Americans did. Henry James, for instance, considered him puerile and provincial, although James admired Poe's *Narrative of Arthur Gordon Pym* (1838). As a critic, too, Poe was tops. "Get a bottle of visible ink, come out from the Old Manse, cut Mr. Alcott, hang (if possible) the editor of *The Dial*, and throw out of the window to the pigs all his odd numbers of *The North American Review*," he advised Nathaniel Hawthorne, whose neglect he deplored and genius he praised. He also insisted critics tackle the formal qualities of prose and poetry and in this regard considered "The Philosophy of Composition" his best specimen of analysis. So it is, and even though it is excerpted often, it cannot be read too much, for not only is it an ingenious work of imagination and criticism, but there is a humor to it often overlooked. Moreover, he "gives the sense," as William Carlos Williams said in *In the American Grain* (1953), "for the first time in America, that literature is *serious*, not a matter of courtesy but of truth." But brilliant, mercurial, untranscendental (in a transcendental age), and self-destructive, Poe, who died young and probably mad, left behind him for many years a grudging reputation in the very America that James had also called provincial.

Excerpted here, in addition to "The Philosophy of Composition" (1846), which lucidly details the decisions Poe made in writing "The Raven" (1845), are examples of his plainspoken, fearless, and hilarious denunciation of literary editors and their flatterers in the introduction to "The Literati of New York City," a controversial examination of the same, which Poe published in 1846 in the popular magazine *The Lady's Book,* as well as his brief comments on the making of good books, and a short unsarcastic paragraph written to a literary aspirant about the rewards of the literary life.

FROM "MARGINALIA"

1844

How many good books suffer neglect through the inefficiency of their beginnings! It is far better that we commence irregularly—immethodically—than that we fail to arrest attention; but the two points, method and pungency, may always be combined.

FROM "THOMAS MORE"

All novel conceptions are merely unusual combinations. The mind of man can *imagine* nothing which has not really existed. [. . .] It will be said, perhaps, that we can imagine a *griffin*, and that a griffin does not exist. Not the griffin, certainly, but its component parts. It is a mere compendium of known limbs and features—of known qualities. Thus with all which seems to be *new*—which appears to be a creation of intellect. It is resoluble into the old.

FROM "THE LITERATI OF NEW YORK"

I have endeavored to show that the cases are rare indeed in which these journals express any other sentiment about books than such as may be attributed directly or indirectly to the authors of the books. The most "popular," the most "successful" writers among us, (for a brief period, at least,) are, ninety-nine times out of a hundred, persons of mere address, perseverance, effrontery—in a word, busy-bodies, toadies, quacks. These people easily succeed in boring editors (whose attention is too often entirely engrossed by politics or other "business" matter) into the admission of favorable notices written or caused to be written by interested parties—or, at least, into the admission of some notice where, under ordinary circumstances, no notice would be given at all. In this way ephemeral "reputations" are manufactured, which, for the most part, serve all the purposes designed—that is to say, the putting money into the purse of the quack and the quack's publisher; for there never was a quack who could be brought to comprehend the value of mere fame.

Now, men of genius will not resort to these maneuvers, because genius involves in its very essence a scorn of chicanery; and thus for a time the quacks always get the advantage of them, both in respect to pecuniary profit and what appears to be public esteem.

There is another point of view, too. Your literary quacks court, in especial, the personal acquaintance of those "connected with the press." Now these latter, even when penning a voluntary, that is to say, an uninstigated notice of the book of an acquaintance, feel as if writing not so much for the eye of the public as for the eye of the acquaintance, and the notice is fashioned accordingly. The bad points of the work are slurred over, and the good ones brought out into the best light, all this through a feeling akin to that which makes it unpleasant to speak ill of one to one's face. In the case of men of genius, editors, as a general rule, have no such delicacy—for the simple reason that, as a general rule, they have no acquaintance with these men of genius, a class proverbial for shunning society.

But the very editors who hesitate at saying in print an ill word of an author personally known, are usually the most frank in speaking about him privately. In literary society, they seem bent upon avenging the wrongs self-inflicted upon their own consciences. Here, accordingly, the quack is treated as he deserves—even a little more harshly than he deserves—by way of striking a balance. True merit, on the same principle, is apt to be slightly overrated; but, upon the whole, there is a close approximation to absolute honesty of opinion; and this honesty is farther secured by the mere trouble to which it puts one in conversation to model one's countenance to a falsehood. We place on paper without hesitation a tissue of flatteries, to which in society we could not give utterance, for our lives, without either blushing or laughing outright.

For these reasons there exists a very remarkable discrepancy between the apparent public opinion of any given author's merits, and the opinion which is expressed of him orally by those who are best qualified to judge. For example, Mr. Hawthorne, the author of "Twice-Told Tales," is scarcely recognized by the press or by the public, and when noticed at all, is noticed merely to be damned by faint praise. Now, my own opinion of him is, that, although his walk is limited, and he is fairly to be charged with mannerism, treating all subjects in a similar tone of dreamy innuendo, yet in this walk he evinces extraordinary genius, having no rival either in America or elsewhere—and this opinion I have never heard gainsaid by any one literary person in the country.

That this opinion, however, is a spoken and not a written one, is referable to the facts, first, that Mr. Hawthorne is a poor man, and, second, that he is not an ubiquitous quack. Again, of Mr. Longfellow, who, although a little quacky per se, has, through his social and literary position as a man of property and a professor at Harvard, a whole legion of active quacks at his control—of him what is the apparent popular opinion? Of course, that he is a poetical phenomenon, as entirely without fault, as is the luxurious paper upon which his poems are invariably borne to the public eye. In private society he is regarded with one voice as a poet of far more than usual ability, a skillful artist and a well-read man, but as less remarkable in either capacity than as a determined imitator and a dexterous adapter of the ideas of other people. For years I have conversed with no literary person who did not entertain precisely these ideas of Professor L.; and, in fact, on all literary topics, there is in society a seemingly wonderful coincidence of opinion. The author accustomed to seclusion, and mingling for

the first time with those who have been associated with him only through
their works, is astonished and delighted at finding common to all whom he
meets, conclusions which he had blindly fancied were attained by himself
alone, and in opposition to the judgment of mankind.

In the series of papers which I now propose, my design is, in giving my
own unbiased opinion of the literati (male and female) of New York, to
give at the same time very closely, if not with absolute accuracy, that of
conversational society in literary circles. It must be expected, of course,
that, in innumerable particulars, I shall differ from the voice, that is to say,
from what appears to be the voice of the public—but this is a matter of no
consequence whatever. [. . .]

FROM "THE PHILOSOPHY OF COMPOSITION"

Nothing is more clear than that every plot, worth the name, must be elaborated to its *dénouement* before any thing be attempted with the pen. It is
only with the *dénouement* constantly in view that we can give a plot its indispensable air of consequence, or causation, by making the incidents, and
especially the tone at all points, tend to the development of the intention.

There is a radical error, I think, in the usual mode of constructing a
story. Either history affords a thesis—or one is suggested by an incident
of the day—or, at best, the author sets himself to work in the combination
of striking events to form merely the basis of his narrative—designing,
generally, to fill in with description, dialogue, or authorial comment, whatever crevices of fact, or action, may, from page to page, render themselves
apparent.

I prefer commencing with the consideration of an *effect*. Keeping originality *always* in view—for he is false to himself who ventures to dispense
with so obvious and so easily attainable a source of interest—I say to
myself, in the first place, "Of the innumerable effects, or impressions, of
which the heart, the intellect, or (more generally) the soul is susceptible,
what one shall I, on the present occasion, select?" Having chosen a novel,
first, and secondly a vivid effect, I consider whether it can best be wrought
by incident or tone—whether by ordinary incidents and peculiar tone, or
the converse, or by peculiarity both of incident and tone—afterward look-

ing about me (or rather within) for such combinations of event, or tone, as shall best aid me in the construction of the effect.

I have often thought how interesting a magazine paper might be written by any author who would—that is to say, who could—detail, step by step, the processes by which any one of his compositions attained its ultimate point of completion. Why such a paper has never been given to the world, I am much at a loss to say—but, perhaps, the authorial vanity has had more to do with the omission than any one other cause. Most writers— poets in especial—prefer having it understood that they compose by a species of fine frenzy—an ecstatic intuition—and would positively shudder at letting the public take a peep behind the scenes, at the elaborate and vacillating crudities of thought—at the true purposes seized only at the last moment—at the innumerable glimpses of idea that arrived not at the maturity of full view—at the fully matured fancies discarded in despair as unmanageable—at the cautious selections and rejections—at the painful erasures and interpolations—in a word, at the wheels and pinions—the tackle for scene-shifting—the step-ladders, and demon-traps—the cock's feathers, the red paint and the black patches, which, in ninety-nine cases out of the hundred, constitute the properties of the literary *histrio*.

I am aware, on the other hand, that the case is by no means common, in which an author is at all in condition to retrace the steps by which his conclusions have been attained. In general, suggestions, having arisen pell-mell, are pursued and forgotten in a similar manner.

For my own part, I have neither sympathy with the repugnance alluded to, nor, at any time, the least difficulty in recalling to mind the progressive steps of any of my compositions; and, since the interest of an analysis, or reconstruction, such as I have considered a *desideratum*, is quite independent of any real or fancied interest in the thing analysed, it will not be regarded as a breach of decorum on my part to show the *modus operandi* by which some one of my own works was put together. I select "The Raven" as most generally known. It is my design to render it manifest that no one point in its composition is referable either to accident or intuition—that the work proceeded step by step, to its completion with the precision and rigid consequence of a mathematical problem.

Let us dismiss, as irrelevant to the poem *per se*, the circumstance—or say

the necessity—which, in the first place, gave rise to the intention of composing *a* poem that should suit at once the popular and the critical taste.

We commence, then, with this intention.

The initial consideration was that of extent. If any literary work is too
long to be read at one sitting, we must be content to dispense with the im-
mensely important effect derivable from unity of impression—for, if two
sittings be required, the affairs of the world interfere, and every thing like
totality is at once destroyed. But since, *ceteris paribus*, no poet can afford to
dispense with *any thing* that may advance his design, it but remains to be
seen whether there is, in extent, any advantage to counterbalance the loss
of unity which attends it. Here I say no, at once. What we term a long poem
is, in fact, merely a succession of brief ones—that is to say, of brief poetical
effects. It is needless to demonstrate that a poem is such, only inasmuch as
it intensely excites, by elevating the soul; and all intense excitements are,
through a psychal necessity, brief. For this reason, at least, one half of the
"Paradise Lost" is essentially prose—a succession of poetical excitements
interspersed, *inevitably,* with corresponding depressions—the whole being
deprived, through the extremeness of its length, of the vastly important
artistic element, totality, or unity, of effect.

It appears evident, then, that there is a distinct limit, as regards length,
to all works of literary art—the limit of a single sitting—and that, although
in certain classes of prose composition, such as "Robinson Crusoe," (demanding no unity), this limit may be advantageously overpassed, it can
never properly be overpassed in a poem. Within this limit, the extent of
a poem may be made to bear mathematical relation to its merit—in other
words, to the excitement or elevation—again in other words, to the degree
of the true poetical effect which it is capable of inducing; for it is clear that
the brevity must be in direct ratio of the intensity of the intended effect:—
this, with one proviso—that a certain degree of duration is absolutely requisite for the production of any effect at all.

Holding in view these considerations, as well as that degree of excitement which I deemed not above the popular, while not below the critical,
taste, I reached at once what I conceived the proper *length* for my intended
poem—a length of about one hundred lines. It is, in fact, a hundred and
eight.

My next thought concerned the choice of an impression, or effect, to be conveyed: and here I may as well observe that, throughout the construction, I kept steadily in view the design of rendering the work *universally* appreciable. I should be carried too far out of my immediate topic were I to demonstrate a point upon which I have repeatedly insisted, and which, with the poetical, stands not in the slightest need of demonstration—the point, I mean, that Beauty is the sole legitimate province of the poem. A few words, however, in elucidation of my real meaning, which some of my friends have evinced a disposition to misrepresent. That pleasure which is at once the most intense, the most elevating, and the most pure, is, I believe, found in the contemplation of the beautiful. When, indeed, men speak of Beauty, they mean, precisely, not a quality, as is supposed, but an effect— they refer, in short, just to that intense and pure elevation of *soul—not* of intellect, or of heart—upon which I have commented, and which is experienced in consequence of contemplating "the beautiful." Now I designate Beauty as the province of the poem, merely because it is an obvious rule of Art that effects should be made to spring from direct causes—that objects should be attained through means best adapted for their attainment—no one as yet having been weak enough to deny that the peculiar elevation alluded to, is *most readily* attained in the poem. Now the object, Truth, or the satisfaction of the intellect, and the object Passion, or the excitement of the heart, are, although attainable, to a certain extent, in poetry, far more readily attainable in prose. Truth, in fact, demands a precision, and Passion, a *homeliness* (the truly passionate will comprehend me) which are absolutely antagonistic to that Beauty which, I maintain, is the excitement, or pleasurable elevation, of the soul. It by no means follows from any thing here said, that passion, or even truth, may not be introduced, and even profitably introduced, into a poem—for they may serve in elucidation, or aid the general effect, as do discords in music, by contrast—but the true artist will always contrive, first, to tone them into proper subservience to the predominant aim, and, secondly, to enveil them, as far as possible, in that Beauty which is the atmosphere and the essence of the poem.

Regarding, then, Beauty as my province, my next question referred to the *tone* of its highest manifestation—and all experience has shown that this tone is one of *sadness*. Beauty of whatever kind, in its supreme development, invariably excites the sensitive soul to tears. Melancholy is thus the most legitimate of all the poetical tones.

The length, the province, and the tone, being thus determined, I betook myself to ordinary induction, with the view of obtaining some artistic piquancy which might serve me as a key-note in the construction of the poem—some pivot upon which the whole structure might turn. In carefully thinking over all the usual artistic effects—or more properly *points,* in the theatrical sense—I did not fail to perceive immediately that no one had been so universally employed as that of the *refrain.* The universality of its employment sufficed to assure me of its intrinsic value, and spared me the necessity of submitting it to analysis. I considered it, however, with regard to its susceptibility of improvement, and soon saw it to be in a primitive condition. As commonly used, the *refrain,* or burden, not only is limited to lyric verse, but depends for its impression upon the force of monotone—both in sound and thought. The pleasure is deduced solely from the sense of identity—of repetition. I resolved to diversify, and so vastly heighten, the effect, by adhering, in general, to the monotone of sound, while I continually varied that of thought: that is to say, I determined to produce continuously novel effects, by the variation *of the application* of the *refrain*—the *refrain* itself remaining, for the most part, unvaried.

These points being settled, I next bethought me of the *nature* of my *refrain.* Since its application was to be repeatedly varied, it was clear that the *refrain* itself must be brief, for there would have been an insurmountable difficulty in frequent variations of application in any sentence of length. In proportion to the brevity of the sentence, would, of course, be the facility of the variation. This led me at once to a single word as the best *refrain.*

The question now arose as to the *character* of the word. Having made up my mind to a *refrain,* the division of the poem into stanzas was, of course, a corollary: the *refrain* forming the close to each stanza. That such a close, to have force, must be sonorous and susceptible of protracted emphasis, admitted no doubt: and these considerations inevitably led me to the long *o* as the most sonorous vowel, in connection with *r* as the most producible consonant.

The sound of the *refrain* being thus determined, it became necessary to select a word embodying this sound, and at the same time in the fullest possible keeping with that melancholy which I had predetermined as the tone of the poem. In such a search it would have been absolutely impossible to overlook the word "Nevermore." In fact, it was the very first which presented itself.

The next *desideratum* was a pretext for the continuous use of the one word "nevermore." In observing the difficulty which I had at once found in inventing a sufficiently plausible reason for its continuous repetition, I did not fail to perceive that this difficulty arose solely from the pre-assumption that the word was to be so continuously or monotonously spoken by a *human* being—I did not fail to perceive, in short, that the difficulty lay in the reconciliation of this monotony with the exercise of reason on the part of the creature repeating the word. Here, then, immediately arose the idea of a *non*-reasoning creature capable of speech; and, very naturally, a parrot, in the first instance, suggested itself, but was superseded forthwith by a Raven, as equally capable of speech, and infinitely more in keeping with the intended *tone*.

I had now gone so far as the conception of a Raven—the bird of ill omen—monotonously repeating the one word, "Nevermore," at the conclusion of each stanza, in a poem of melancholy tone, and in length about one hundred lines. Now, never losing sight of the object *supremeness*, or perfection, at all points, I asked myself—"Of all melancholy topics, what, according to the *universal* understanding of mankind, is the *most* melancholy?" Death—was the obvious reply. "And when," I said, "is this most melancholy of topics most poetical?" From what I have already explained at some length, the answer, here also, is obvious—"When it most closely allies itself to *Beauty:* the death, then, of a beautiful woman is, unquestionably, the most poetical topic in the world—and equally is it beyond doubt that the lips best suited for such topic are those of a bereaved lover."

I had now to combine the two ideas, of a lover lamenting his deceased mistress and a Raven continuously repeating the word "Nevermore"—I had to combine these, bearing in mind my design of varying, at every turn, the *application* of the word repeated; but the only intelligible mode of such combination is that of imagining the Raven employing the word in answer to the queries of the lover. And here it was that I saw at once the opportunity afforded for the effect on which I had been depending—

that is to say, the effect of the *variation of application*. I saw that I could make the first query propounded by the lover—the first query to which the Raven should reply "Nevermore"—that I could make this first query a commonplace one—the second less so—the third still less, and so on—until at length the lover, startled from his original *nonchalance* by the melancholy character of the word itself—by its frequent repetition—and by a consideration of the ominous reputation of the fowl that uttered it—is at length excited to superstition, and wildly propounds queries of a far different character—queries whose solution he has passionately at heart—propounds them half in superstition and half in that species of despair which delights in self-torture—propounds them not altogether because he believes in the prophetic or demoniac character of the bird (which, reason assures him, is merely repeating a lesson learned by rote) but because he experiences a phrenzied pleasure in so modeling his questions as to receive from the *expected* "Nevermore" the most delicious because the most intolerable of sorrow. Perceiving the opportunity thus afforded me—or, more strictly, thus forced upon me in the progress of the construction—I first established in mind the climax, or concluding query—that to which "Nevermore" should be in the last place an answer—that in reply to which this word "Nevermore" should involve the utmost conceivable amount of sorrow and despair.

Here then the poem may be said to have its beginning—at the end, where all works of art should begin—for it was here, at this point of my preconsiderations, that I first put pen to paper in the composition of the stanza:

> "Prophet," said I, "thing of evil! prophet still if bird or devil!
> By that heaven that bends above us—by that God we both adore,
> Tell this soul with sorrow laden, if within the distant Aidenn,
> It shall clasp a sainted maiden whom the angels name Lenore—
> Clasp a rare and radiant maiden whom the angels name Lenore."
> Quoth the raven—"Nevermore."

I composed this stanza, at this point, first that, by establishing the climax, I might the better vary and graduate, as regards seriousness and importance, the preceding queries of the lover—and, secondly, that I might definitely settle the rhythm, the metre, and the length and general arrangement of the stanza—as well as graduate the stanzas which were to precede, so that none of them might surpass this in rhythmical effect. Had I been able, in the subsequent composition, to construct more vigorous stanzas, I should, without scruple, have purposely enfeebled them, so as not to interfere with the climacteric effect.

And here I may as well say a few words of the versification. My first object (as usual) was originality. The extent to which this has been neglected, in versification, is one of the most unaccountable things in the world. Admitting that there is little possibility of variety in mere *rhythm,* it is still clear that the possible varieties of metre and stanza are absolutely infinite—and yet, *for centuries, no man, in verse, has ever done, or ever seemed to think of doing, an original thing.* The fact is, originality (unless in minds of very unusual force) is by no means a matter, as some suppose, of impulse or intuition. In general, to be found, it must be elaborately sought, and although a positive merit of the highest class, demands in its attainment less of invention than negation.

Of course, I pretend to no originality in either the rhythm or metre of the "Raven." The former is trochaic—the latter is octametre acatalectic, alternating with heptameter catalectic repeated in the *refrain* of the fifth verse, and terminating with tetrameter catalectic. Less pedantically—the feet employed throughout (trochees) consist of a long syllable followed by a short: the first line of the stanza consists of eight of these feet—the second of seven and a half (in effect two-thirds)—the third of eight—the fourth of seven and a half—the fifth the same—the sixth three and a half. Now, each of these lines, taken individually, has been employed before, and what originality the "Raven" has, is in their *combination into stanza;* nothing even remotely approaching this combination has ever been attempted. The effect of this originality of combination is aided by other unusual, and some altogether novel effects, arising from an extension of the application of the principles of rhyme and alliteration.

The next point to be considered was the mode of bringing together the lover and the Raven—and the first branch of this consideration was the *locale.* For this the most natural suggestion might seem to be a forest, or the fields—but it has always appeared to me that a close *circumscription of space* is absolutely necessary to the effect of insulated incident:—it has the force of a frame to a picture. It has an indisputable moral power in keeping concentrated the attention, and, of course, must not be confounded with mere unity of place.

I determined, then, to place the lover in his chamber—in a chamber rendered sacred to him by memories of her who had frequented it. The room is represented as richly furnished—this in mere pursuance of the ideas I have already explained on the subject of Beauty, as the sole true poetical thesis.

The *locale* being thus determined, I had now to introduce the bird—and the thought of introducing him through the window, was inevitable. The idea of making the lover suppose, in the first instance, that the flapping of the wings of the bird against the shutter, is a "tapping" at the door, originated in a wish to increase, by prolonging, the reader's curiosity, and in a desire to admit the incidental effect arising from the lover's throwing open the door, finding all dark, and thence adopting the half-fancy that it was the spirit of his mistress that knocked.

I made the night tempestuous, first, to account for the Raven's seeking admission, and secondly, for the effect of contrast with the (physical) serenity within the chamber.

I made the bird alight on the bust of Pallas, also for the effect of contrast between the marble and the plumage—it being understood that the bust was absolutely *suggested* by the bird—the bust of *Pallas* being chosen, first, as most in keeping with the scholarship of the lover, and, secondly, for the sonorousness of the word, Pallas, itself.

About the middle of the poem, also, I have availed myself of the force of contrast, with a view of deepening the ultimate impression. For example, an air of the fantastic—approaching as nearly to the ludicrous as was admissible—is given to the Raven's entrance. He comes in "with many a flirt and flutter."

> Not the *least obeisance made he*—not a moment stopped or stayed he,
> *But with mien of lord or lady,* perched above my chamber door.

In the two stanzas which follow, the design is more obviously carried out:—

> Then this ebony bird beguiling my sad fancy into smiling
> By the *grave and stern decorum of the countenance it wore,*

"Though thy *crest be shorn and shaven* thou," I said, "art sure no craven,
Ghastly grim and ancient Raven wandering from the nightly shore—
Tell me what thy lordly name is on the Night's Plutonian shore!"
Quoth the Raven—"Nevermore."

Much I marvelled *this ungainly fowl* to hear discourse so plainly,
Though its answer little meaning—little relevancy bore;
For we cannot help agreeing that no living human being
Ever yet was blessed with seeing bird above his chamber door—
Bird or beast upon the sculptured bust above his chamber door,
With such name as "Nevermore."

The effect of the *dénouement* being thus provided for, I immediately drop the fantastic for a tone of the most profound seriousness:—this tone commencing in the stanza directly following the one last quoted, with the line,

But the Raven, sitting lonely on that placid bust, spoke only, etc.

From this epoch the lover no longer jests—no longer sees any thing even of the fantastic in the Raven's demeanor. He speaks of him as a "grim, ungainly, ghastly, gaunt, and ominous bird of yore," and feels the "fiery eyes" burning into his "bosom's core." This revolution of thought, or fancy, on the lover's part, is intended to induce a similar one on the part of the reader—to bring the mind into a proper frame for the *dénouement*—which is now brought about as rapidly and as *directly* as possible.

With the *dénouement* proper—with the Raven's reply, "Nevermore," to the lover's final demand if he shall meet his mistress in another world—the poem, in its obvious phase, that of a simple narrative, may be said to have its completion. So far, every thing is within the limits of the accountable— of the real. A raven, having learned by rote the single word, "Nevermore," and having escaped from the custody of its owner, is driven, at midnight, through the violence of a storm, to seek admission at a window from which a light still gleams—the chamber-window of a student, occupied half in poring over a volume, half in dreaming of a beloved mistress deceased. The casement being thrown open at the fluttering of the bird's wings, the bird itself perches on the most convenient seat out of the immediate reach of the student, who, amused by the incident and the oddity of the visitor's demeanor, demands of it, in jest and without looking for a reply, its name. The raven addressed, answers with its customary word, "Nevermore"—a word which finds immediate echo in the melancholy heart of the student, who, giving utterance aloud to certain thoughts suggested by the occasion, is again startled by the fowl's repetition of "Nevermore." The student now guesses the state of the case, but is impelled, as I have before explained, by the human thirst for self-torture, and in part by superstition, to propound such queries to the bird as will bring him, the lover, the most of the luxury of sorrow, through the anticipated answer, "Nevermore." With the indulgence, to the utmost extreme, of this self-torture, the narration, in what I have termed its first or obvious phase, has a natural termination, and so far there has been no overstepping of the limits of the real.

But in subjects so handled, however skillfully, or with however vivid an array of incident, there is always a certain hardness or nakedness, which repels the artistical eye. Two things are invariably required—first, some amount of complexity, or more properly, adaptation; and, secondly, some amount of suggestiveness—some under current, however indefinite of meaning. It is this latter, in especial, which imparts to a work of art so much of that *richness* (to borrow from colloquy a forcible term) which we are too fond of confounding with *the ideal*. It is the *excess* of the suggested meaning—it is the rendering this the upper instead of the under current of the theme—which turns into prose (and that of the very flattest kind) the so called poetry of the so called transcendentalists.

Holding these opinions, I added the two concluding stanzas of the poem—their suggestiveness being thus made to pervade all the narrative which has preceded them. The under current of meaning is rendered first apparent in the lines—

> "Take thy beak from out *my heart,* and take thy form from off my door!"
> Quoth the Raven "Nevermore!"

It will be observed that the words, "from out my heart," involve the first metaphorical expression in the poem. They, with the answer, "Nevermore," dispose the mind to seek a moral in all that has been previously narrated. The reader begins now to regard the Raven as emblematical—but it is not until the very last line of the very last stanza, that the intention of making him emblematical of *Mournful and Never-ending Remembrance* is permitted distinctly to be seen:

> And the Raven, never flitting, still is sitting, still is sitting,
> On the pallid bust of Pallas just above my chamber door;
> And his eyes have all the seeming of a demon's that is dreaming,
> And the lamplight o'er him streaming throws his shadow on the floor;
> And my soul *from out that shadow* that lies floating on the floor
> Shall be lifted—nevermore.

FROM *THE WORKS OF EDGAR ALLAN POE*

To F. W. Thomas

Depend on it, after all, Thomas, literature is the most noble of professions. In fact, it is about the only one fit for a man. For my own part, there is no seducing me from the path. I shall be a Littérateur at least all of my life; nor would I abandon all the hopes which still lead me on for all the gold in California. Talking of gold and of the temptations at present held out to "poor-devil authors," did it ever strike you that all which is really valuable to a man of letters—to a poet in especial—is absolutely unpurchasable? Love, fame, the dominion of intellect, the consciousness of power, the thrilling sense of beauty, the free air of Heaven, exercise of body and mind, with the physical and moral health which result—these and such as these are really all that a poet cares for. [. . .]

Margaret Fuller

(1810–1850)

"The life of Woman must be outwardly a well-intentioned, cheerful dissimulation of her real life," Margaret Fuller wrote in *Woman in the Nineteenth Century* (1845), a book that influenced both Nathaniel Hawthorne and Louisa May Alcott and, we may assume, scores of others who understood it as a protofeminist call to consciousness. Known in her own time as an unusually ardent and wholly brilliant speaker whose "Conversations" for Boston women earned her the title of resident Sybil, Fuller exhorted her listeners and readers to think for themselves, to take risks, to question everything. "Her powers of speech throw her writing into the shade," said Emerson.

Initial editor of the magazine *The Dial*, an organ of the so-called transcendental movement, Fuller was born in 1810, read Latin at six, taught school, wrote lugubrious essays, was a semi-invalid like her mother, and suffered from migraines, which helped her to escape the dominion of her father, a four-term congressman and amateur scholar of exacting standards. She worked as Bronson Alcott's assistant at his radical Temple School in Boston, where she took on his pedagogical method, using conversation as a tool of discovery. Alcott himself said Fuller might as well have been born in Greece; certainly she was no New England woman. "Womanhood is at present too straightly-bound to give me scope," she once admitted.

In 1844 she became literary editor for Horace Greeley's *New York Tribune*, in 1845 she published *Woman in the Nineteenth Century*, and in 1846 she published her *Papers on Literature and Art*. That year she also left America for Europe as the *Tribune*'s foreign correspondent and soon met George Sand, Harriet Martineau, William Wordsworth, and Thomas Carlyle, among others. In Italy, where she was writing of the rise and fall of the Roman republic, she married Giovanni Angelo, marchese d'Ossoli, and lived for a time with the Brownings. But sailing home with her husband and child—and manuscript—in the summer of 1850, Fuller died when the ship hit a sandbar near New York harbor. Only the body of her son was recovered, although Emerson dispatched his friend Henry Thoreau to comb the beach for Fuller's lost manuscript.

As an intellectual woman who did not suffer fools, Fuller threatened many of the literary men and women who also admired her. She appears, for instance, in Hawthorne's *Blithedale Romance* (1852) as the brilliant but doomed Zenobia, and Poe, who largely preferred the effects of dead women to living ones, said that when she talked "her upper lip, as if impelled by the action of involuntary muscles, habitually uplifts itself, conveying the impression of a sneer." But talk she did, and well. Yet talk is ephemeral, and she aspired to something else, something even beyond the journalism for which she was also known.

Aware that a writer needs an audience, in this excerpt from her 1846 essay "American Literature," she too takes up the lance for a fearless national literature. Noting that timid publishers and authors are afraid of speaking the truth, she insists that "only a noble fearlessness can give wings to the mind." In the second excerpt, taken from the memoir that three friends cobbled together after her death, she speaks more personally and candidly about her own work and her fears about its worth.

FROM "AMERICAN LITERATURE"

Under present circumstances the amount of talent and labour given to writing ought to surprise us. Literature is in this dim and struggling state, and its pecuniary results exceedingly pitiful. From many well known causes it is impossible for ninety-nine out of the hundred, who wish to use the pen, to ransom, by its use, the time they need. This state of things will have to be changed in some way. No man of genius writes for money; but it is essential to the free use of his powers, that he should be able to disembarrass his life from care and perplexity. This is very difficult here; and the state of things gets worse and worse, as less and less is offered in pecuniary meed for works demanding great devotion of time and labour (to say nothing of the ether engaged) and the publisher, obliged to regard the transaction as a matter of business, demands of the author to give him only what will find an immediate market, for he cannot afford to take any thing else. This will not do! When an immortal poet was secure only of a few copyists to circulate his works, there were princes and nobles to patronize literature and the arts. Here is only the public, and the public must learn how to cherish the nobler and rarer plants, and to plant the aloe, able to wait a hundred years for its bloom, or its garden will contain, presently, nothing but potatoes and pot-herbs. We shall have, in the course of the next two or three years, a convention of authors to inquire into the causes of this state of things and propose measures for its remedy. Some have already been thought of that look promising, but we shall not announce them till the time be ripe; that date is not distant, for the difficulties increase from day to day, in consequence of the system of cheap publication, on a great scale. [. . .]

Meanwhile, the most important part of our literature, while the work of diffusion is still going on, lies in the journals, which monthly, weekly, daily, send their messages to every corner of this great land, and form, at present, the only efficient instrument for the general education of the people.

Among these, the Magazines take the lowest rank. Their object is principally to cater for the amusement of vacant hours, and, as there is not a great deal of wit or light talent in this country, they do not even this to much advantage. More wit, grace, and elegant trifling, embellish the annals of literature in one day of France than in a year of America.

The Reviews are more able. If they cannot compare, on equal terms, with those of France, England, and Germany, where, if genius be rare, at least a vast amount of talent and culture are brought to bear upon all the departments of knowledge, they are yet very creditable to a new country, where so large a portion of manly ability must be bent on making laws, making speeches, making rail-roads and canals. They are, however, much injured by a partisan spirit, and the fear of censure from their own public. This last is always slow death to a journal; its natural and only safe position is *to lead;* if, instead, it bows to the will of the multitude, it will find the ostracism of democracy far more dangerous than the worse censure of a tyranny could be. It is not half so dangerous to a man to be immured in a dungeon alone with God and his own clear conscience, as to walk the streets fearing the scrutiny of a thousand eyes, ready to veil, with anxious care, whatever may not suit the many-headed monster in its momentary mood. Gentleness is dignified, but caution is debasing; only a noble fearlessness can give wings to the mind, with which to soar beyond the common ken, and learn what may be of use to the crowd below. Writers have nothing to do but to love truth fervently, seek justice according to their ability, and then express what is in the mind; they have nothing to do with consequences, God will take care of those. The want of such noble courage, such faith in the power of truth and good desire, paralyze mind greatly in this country. Publishers are afraid; authors are afraid; and if a worthy resistance is not made by religious souls, there is danger that all the light will soon be put under bushels, lest some wind should waft from it a spark that may kindle dangerous fire.

FROM *MEMOIRS OF MARGARET FULLER OSSOLI*

When I look at my papers, I feel as if I had never had a thought that was worthy the attention of any but myself; and it is only when, on talking with people, I find I tell them what they did not know, that my confidence at all returns. My verses,—I am ashamed when I think there is 'scarce a line of poetry in them,—all rhetorical and impassioned,' as Goethe said of De Stael. However, such as they are, they have been overflowing drops from the somewhat bitter cup of my existence. How can I ever write with this impatience of detail [?] I shall never be an artist; I have no patient love of execution; I am delighted with my sketch, but if I try to finish it, I am chilled. Never was there a great sculptor who did not love to chip the marble. I have talent and knowledge enough to furnish a dwelling for friendship, but not enough to deck with golden gifts a Delphi for the world. Then a woman of tact and brilliancy, like me, has an undue advantage in conversation with men. They are astonished at our instincts. They do not see where we got our knowledge; and, while they tramp on in their clumsy way, we wheel, and fly, and dart hither and thither, and seize with ready eye all the weak points, like Saladin in the desert. It is quite another thing when we come to write and, without suggestion from another mind, to declare the positive amount of thought that is in us. Because we seemed to know all, they think we can tell all; and, finding we can tell so little, lose faith in their first opinion of us, which, nathless, was true.

These gentlemen are surprised that I write no better, because I talk so well. But I have served a long apprenticeship to the one, none to the other. I shall write better, but never, I think, so well as I talk; for then I feel inspired. The means are pleasant; my voice excites me, my pen never. I shall not be discouraged, nor take for final what they say, but sift from it the truth, and use it. I feel the strength to dispense with all illusions. I will stand steady, and rejoice in the severest probations.

What a vulgarity there seems in this writing for the multitude! We know not yet, have not made ourselves known to a single soul, and shall we address those still more unknown? [. . .] But where to find fit, though few, representatives for all we value in humanity?

Fanny Fern
(Sara Willis Parton)

(1811–1872)

"No happy woman ever writes," said the fictional Ruth Hall, Fanny Fern's alter-ego in her satiric novel of the same name. Born Sara Payson Willis in Portland, Maine, Fanny Fern took up the pen after her younger sister, her mother, her husband, and her oldest daughter died, one after another, and after she left her abusive second husband, something women did not do. To support her two remaining daughters, she was soon writing for Boston and New York newspapers under the pseudonym Fanny Fern, despite the discouragement of her more hidebound brother, the author Nathaniel P. Willis. Her first collection of essays, columns, and stories, *Fern Leaves from Fanny's Portfolio* (1853), was hugely popular, and her best-selling autobio-graphical novel, *Ruth Hall* (1854), with its barbed send-up of male arrogance and domination, particularly in the workplace, prompted Hawthorne, who was suspicious of what he called "a d—d mob of scribbling women," to say admiringly that Fern "writes as if the devil was in her; and that is the only condition under which a woman ever writes anything worth reading." As one of the highest paid writers in America, and as the country's first female columnist, Fern proffered her point of view with panache, humor, and a good deal of sass, and by 1856 was a weekly columnist exclusively for the innovative newspaperman Robert Bonner, at the *New York Ledger*, a post she held until her death. When she married the writer James Parton, eleven years her junior, she insisted on a prenuptial agreement, something unheard-of for women at the time.

The first excerpt, collected from one of Fern's columns, gives a taste of her saucy prose; in the second excerpt, she provides an unsentimental snapshot of the home life of "literary people."

FROM "A PRACTICAL BLUESTOCKING"

"Have you called on your old friend, James Lee, since your return?" said Mr. Seldon to his nephew.

"No, sir; I understand he has the misfortune to have a blue-stocking for a wife, and whenever I have thought of going there, a vision with inky fingers, frowzled hair, rumpled dress, and slip-shod heels has come between me and my old friend,—not to mention thoughts of a disorderly house, smoky puddings, and dirty-faced children. Defend me from a wife who spends her time dabbling in ink, and writing for the papers. I'll lay a wager James hasn't a shirt with a button on it, or a pair of stockings that is not full of holes. Such a glorious fellow as he used to be, too!" said Harry, soliloquizing, "so dependent upon somebody to love him. By Jove, it's a hard ease." "Harry, will you oblige me by calling there?" said Mr. Seldon with a peculiar smile. "Well, yes, if you desire it; but these married men get so metamorphosed by their wives, that it's a chance if I recognize the melancholy remains of my old friend. A literary wife!" and he shrugged his shoulders contemptuously.

FROM "LITERARY PEOPLE"

It is a difficult thing for literary people, as well as others, to tell the truth sometimes. Now here is a letter containing an article by which the writer hopes to make money; and of which my "candid opinion is asked, as soon as convenient."

Now in the first place, the article is most illegibly written; an objection sufficient to condemn it at once, with a hurried editor—and all editors are hurried—beside having always a bushel basket full of MSS. already in hand to look over. In the second place, the spelling is wofully at fault. In the third place, the punctuation is altogether missing. In the fourth place, if all these things were amended, the article itself is tame, common-place, and badly expressed. Now that is my "candid opinion" of it.

Still, I am not verdant enough to believe that the writer wished my "candid opinion" were it so condemnatory as this; and should I give it, there is great danger it would be misconstrued. The author, in his wounded self-love, might say, that, being a writer myself, I was not disposed to be impartial. Or he might go farther and say that I had probably forgotten the time when *I* commenced writing, and longed for an appreciative or encouraging word myself. Now this would pain me very much; it would also be very unjust; because when I began to write I called that person my best and truest friend who dared tell me when I was at fault in such matters. I have now in my remembrance a stranger, who often wrote me, regarding my articles, as they appeared from time to time; who criticised them unsparingly; finding fault in the plainest Saxon when he could not approve or praise. I thanked him then, I do so now; and was gratified at the singular interest he manifested in one unknown to him. I have never seen him all these years of my literary effort; but I know him to have been more truly my friend than they who would flatter me into believing better of what talent I may possess than it really merits.

This is the way I felt about friendly though unfavorable criticism. The question is, have *I* sufficient courage to risk being misunderstood, should *I*, in this instance, speak honestly and plainly. Or shall I write a very polite, non-committal answer, meaning anything, or nothing. Or shall I praise it unqualifiedly, and recommend the writer to persevere in a vocation in which I am sure he is certain to be doomed to disappoint; and all for the sake of being thought a generous, genial, kindly, sympathetic sort of person.

What shall I do?

The writer would not like to descend from his pedestal, and hear that he must begin at the foot of the ladder, and first of all, learn to spell correctly, before he can write. And that after words, must come thoughts; and that after thoughts, must come the felicitous expression of thoughts. And that, after all that, he must then look about for a market for the same.

This, you see, is a tedious process to one who wants not only immediate but *large* pecuniary results, and evidently considers himself entitled to them, notwithstanding his deference to your "candid opinion."

But what a pleasure, when the person appealed to, can conscientiously say to a writer, that he has not *over* but *under*-rated his gifts! What a pleasure, if one's opinion can be of any value to him, to be able to speak encouragingly of the present; and hopefully for the future. And surely, he who has himself waded through this initiatory "Slough of Despond," and, by one chance in a thousand, landed safely on the other side, should be the last to beckon, or lure into it, those whose careless steps, struggle they ever so blindly, may never find sure or permanent foothold.

"What did I do, after all, about *that letter?*" Well, if you insist upon cornering me, it lies unanswered on my desk, this minute: a staring monument of the moral cowardice of FANNY FERN.

Harriet Beecher Stowe

(1811–1896)

"So you're the little lady who started this big war," Abraham Lincoln reportedly said to the diminutive Harriet Beecher Stowe when he met her in 1862. Though likely apocryphal, the remark encapsulates what was then—and remains—Stowe's troublemaking contribution to literature and life: the novel *Uncle Tom's Cabin*, a whopping best-seller in 1851, which placed the antislavery movement squarely on the American table.

But for a woman writing midcentury, that table was cluttered, as the following letter to her sister attests. Born in Litchfield, Connecticut, Stowe was the daughter of Roxana Foote and the noted preacher Lyman Beecher, whose other children included domestic writer Catherine Beecher, the feminist Isabella Hooker Beecher, and the famous clergyman Henry Ward Beecher. Marrying the impoverished Reverend Calvin E. Stowe and bearing seven children left little time for writing; still, Mrs. Stowe published a book of stories in 1842 and then, upset by the passage of the Fugitive Slave Law, said she saw Uncle Tom's death in a dream.

Serialized in the *National Era*, an antislavery publication, *Uncle Tom's Cabin; or, Life Among the Lowly* was such a riveting success that the abolitionist William Lloyd Garrison soon wrote Stowe that the defenders of slavery had let him alone, at last, and instead were abusing her. Perhaps; so, too, did some of the literati of that day, who considered, as later critics did, the novel sentimental and, worse yet, propagandistic. (Hawthorne published the not-best-selling *The Scarlet Letter* in 1850, and Melville, whose *Moby-Dick* appeared the next year, was, thanks to it, considered crazy.) Regardless, neither Stowe nor her writing would disappear.

The following letter to the abolitionist Eliza Cabot Follen opens a window onto the life of a busy woman trying to make time for her writing; and it also casts light on what Stowe believed herself to be doing or, more to the point, how she wanted others to perceive her writing, particularly *Uncle Tom's Cabin*. For her, writing was a supremely moral act, and her insistence on morality in fiction would by the end of the century seem anachronistic and benighted to incipient modernists.

FROM *THE LIFE OF HARRIET BEECHER STOWE*

To Eliza Cabot Follen

ANDOVER, FEBRUARY 16, 1853

My dear Madam,—I hasten to reply to your letter, to me the more interesting that I have long been acquainted with you, and during all the nursery part of my life made daily use of your poems for children. I used to think sometimes in those days that I would write to you, and tell you how much I was obliged to you for the pleasure which they gave us all.

So you want to know something about what sort of a woman I am! Well, if this is any object, you shall have statistics free of charge. To begin, then, I am a little bit of a woman,—somewhat more than forty, about as thin and dry as a pinch of snuff; never very much to look at in my best days, and looking like a used-up article now.

I was married when I was twenty-five years old to a man rich in Greek and Hebrew, Latin and Arabic, and, alas! rich in nothing else. When I went to housekeeping, my entire stock of china for parlor and kitchen was bought for eleven dollars. That lasted very well for two years, till my brother was married and brought his bride to visit me. I then found, on review, that I had neither plates nor teacups to set a table for my father's family; wherefore I thought it best to reinforce the establishment by getting me a tea-set that cost ten dollars more, and this, I believe, formed my whole stock in trade for some years.

But then I was abundantly enriched with wealth of another sort.

I had two little, curly-headed twin daughters to begin with, and my stock in this line has gradually increased, till I have been the mother of seven children, the most beautiful and the most loved of whom lies buried near my Cincinnati residence. It was at his dying bed and at his grave that I learned what a poor slave mother may feel when her child is torn away from her. In those depths of sorrow which seemed to me immeasurable, it was my only prayer to God that such anguish might not be suffered in vain. There were circumstances about his death of such peculiar bitterness, of what seemed almost cruel suffering, that I felt that I could never be consoled for it, unless this crushing of my own heart might enable me to work out some great good to others. [. . .]

I allude to this here because I have often felt that much that is in that book ("Uncle Tom") had its root in the awful scenes and bitter sorrows of that summer. It has left now, I trust, no trace on my mind, except a deep compassion for the sorrowful, especially for mothers who are separated from their children.

During long years of struggling with poverty and sickness, and a hot, debilitating climate, my children grew up around me. The nursery and the kitchen were my principal fields of labor. Some of my friends, pitying my trials, copied and sent a number of little sketches from my pen to certain liberally paying "Annuals" with my name. With the first money that I earned in this way I bought a feather-bed! for as I had married into poverty and without a dowry, and as my husband had only a large library of books and a great deal of learning, the bed and pillows were thought the most profitable investment. After this I thought that I had discovered the philosopher's stone. So when a new carpet or mattress was going to be needed, or when, at the close of the year, it began to be evident that my family accounts, like poor Dora's, "wouldn't add up," then I used to say to my faithful friend and factotum Anna, who shared all my joys and sorrows, "Now, if you will keep the babies and attend to the things in the house for one day, I'll write a piece, and then we shall be out of the scrape." So I became an author,—very modest at first, I do assure you, and remonstrating very seriously with the friends who had thought it best to put my name to the pieces by way of getting up a reputation; and if you ever see a woodcut of me, with an immoderately long nose, on the cover of all the U.S. Almanacs, I wish you to take notice, that I have been forced into it contrary to my natural modesty by the imperative solicitations of my dear five thousand friends and the public generally. One thing I must say with regard to my life at the West, which you will understand better than many English women could.

I lived two miles from the city of Cincinnati, in the country, and domestic service, not always you know to be found in the city, is next to an impossibility to obtain in the country, even by those who are willing to give the highest wages; so what was to be expected for poor me, who had very little of this world's goods to offer?

Had it not been for my inseparable friend Anna, a noble-hearted English girl, who landed on our shores in destitution and sorrow, and clave to me as Ruth to Naomi, I had never lived through all the trials which this uncertainty and want of domestic service imposed on us both: you may imagine, therefore, how glad I was when, our seminary property being divided out into small lots which were rented at a low price, a number of poor families settled in our vicinity, from whom we could occasionally obtain domestic service. About a dozen families of liberated slaves were among the number, and they became my favorite resort in cases of emergency. If anybody wishes to have a black face look handsome, let them be left, as I have been, in feeble health in oppressive hot weather, with a sick baby in arms, and two or three other little ones in the nursery, and not a servant in the whole house to do a single turn. Then, if they could see my good old Aunt Frankie coming with her honest, bluff, black face, her long, strong arms, her chest as big and stout as a barrel, and her hilarious, hearty laugh, perfectly delighted to take one's washing and do it at a fair price, they would appreciate the beauty of black people.

My cook, poor Eliza Buck,—how she would stare to think of her name going to England!—was a regular epitome of slave life in herself; fat, gentle, easy, loving and lovable, always calling my very modest house and door-yard "The Place," as if it had been a plantation with seven hundred hands on it. She had lived through the whole sad story of a Virginia-raised slave's life. In her youth she must have been a very handsome mulatto girl. Her voice was sweet, and her manners refined and agreeable. She was raised in a good family as a nurse and seamstress. When the family became embarrassed, she was suddenly sold on to a plantation in Louisiana. She has often told me how, without any warning, she was suddenly forced into a carriage, and saw her little mistress screaming and stretching her arms from the window towards her as she was driven away. She has told me of scenes on the Louisiana plantation, and she has often been out at night by stealth ministering to poor slaves who had been mangled and lacerated by the lash. Hence she was sold into Kentucky, and her last master was the father of all her children. On this point she ever maintained a delicacy and reserve that always appeared to me remarkable. She always called him her husband; and it was not till after she had lived with me some years that I discovered the real nature of the connection. I shall never forget how sorry I felt for her, nor my feelings at her humble apology, "You know, Mrs. Stowe, slave women cannot help themselves." She had two very pretty quadroon daughters, with her beautiful hair and eyes, interesting children, whom I had instructed in the family school with my children. Time would fail to tell you all that I learned incidentally of the slave system in the history of various slaves who came into my family, and of the underground railroad which, I may say, ran through our house. But the letter is already too long.

You ask with regard to the remuneration which I have received for my work here in America. Having been poor all my life and expecting to be poor the rest of it, the idea of making money by a book which I wrote just because I could not help it, never occurred to me. It was therefore an agreeable surprise to receive ten thousand dollars as the first-fruits of three months' sale. I presume as much more is now due. Mr. Bosworth in England, the firm of Clarke & Co., and Mr. Bentley, have all offered me an interest in the sales of their editions in London. I am very glad of it, both on account of the value of what they offer, and the value of the example they set in this matter, wherein I think that justice has been too little regarded.

I have been invited to visit Scotland, and shall probably spend the summer there and in England.

I have very much at heart a design to erect in some of the Northern States a normal school, for the education of colored teachers in the United States and in Canada. I have very much wished that some permanent memorial of good to the colored race might be created out of the proceeds of a work which promises to have so unprecedented a sale. My own share of the profits will be less than that of the publishers', either English or American; but I am willing to give largely for this purpose, and I have no doubt that the publishers, both American and English, will unite with me; for nothing tends more immediately to the emancipation of the slave than the education and elevation of the free.

I am now writing a work which will contain, perhaps, an equal amount of matter with "Uncle Tom's Cabin." It will contain all the facts and documents on which that story was founded, and an immense body of facts, reports of trials, legal documents, and testimony of people now living South, which will more than confirm every statement in "Uncle Tom's Cabin."

I must confess that till I began the examination of facts in order to write this book, much as I thought I knew before, I had not begun to measure the depth of the abyss. The law records of courts and judicial proceedings are so incredible as to fill me with amazement whenever I think of them. It seems to me that the book cannot but be felt, and, coming upon the sensibility awaked by the other, do something.

I suffer exquisitely in writing these things. It may be truly said that I write with my heart's blood. Many times in writing "Uncle Tom's Cabin" I thought my health would fail utterly; but I prayed earnestly that God would help me till I got through, and still I am pressed beyond measure and above strength. This horror, this nightmare abomination! can it be in my country! It lies like lead on my heart, it shadows my life with sorrow; the more so that I feel, as for my own brothers, for the South, and am pained by every horror I am obliged to write, as one who is forced by some awful oath to disclose in court some family disgrace. Many times I have thought that I must die, and yet I pray God that I may live to see something done. I shall in all probability be in London in May: shall I see you?

It seems to me so odd and dream-like that so many persons desire to see me, and now I cannot help thinking that they will think, when they do, that God hath chosen "the weak things of this world."

If I live till spring I shall hope to see Shakespeare's grave, and Milton's mulberry-tree, and the good land of my fathers,—old, old England! May that day come!

Yours affectionately, H. B. STOWE.

Harriet Jacobs

(ca. 1813–1897)

With an epigraph from Isaiah, "Rise up, ye women that are at ease! Hear my voice, ye careless daughters! Give ear unto my speech," Harriet Jacobs's auto-biography, *Incidents in the Life of a Slave Girl, Written by Herself* (1861), is a call to arms directed to and about women. As such it is a contribution to the slave narratives more and more popular in the northern United States before and during the Civil War, which were largely about men and were directed to male audiences. But here, not only does Jacobs narrate her escape from slavery, as is to be expected, she also graphically portrays how she avoided sexual degradation and abuse at the hands of her masters—a distinctly un-Victorian theme—in such a way as to shock and move and illuminate read-ers into realizing that Books with a Moral Purpose, such as Harriet Beecher Stowe wanted to write, could in fact aspire to be something more literary, and real, than tracts. Originally published in Horace Greeley's *New York Trib-une* under the pen name Linda Brent, *Incidents* is a well-wrought narrative compellingly told by means of clever rhetorical devices.

The first excerpt is from Harriet Jacobs's letter to Amy Post, an abolition-ist friend and the woman who urged Jacobs to write her story; it reveals the difficulties Jacobs faced while writing the book, for, though committed to telling the truth, she had an ugly and distinctly immodest story to tell, which included the revelation that the father of her children was white. The second excerpt is the preface from *Incidents*, in which Jacobs is explicit about her book's intentions. When it appeared, it was introduced and edited by Lydia Maria Child. (Stowe had declined to sponsor it.) Child's introduction also appears below.

FROM AUTOGRAPH LETTER (1857)

My dear friend— [. . .] [obliterated] striven faithfully to give a true and just account of my own life in slavery—God knows I have tried to do it in a Christian spirit—there are some things that I might have made plainer I know—woman can whisper—her cruel wrongs into the ear of a very dear friend—much easier than she can record them for the world to read—I have left nothing out but what I thought—the world might believe that a Slave woman was too willing to pour out—that she might gain their sympathies I ask nothing—I have placed myself before you to be judged as a woman whether . . . [obliterated] I deserve your pity or contempt. I have another object in view—it is to come to you just as I am a poor slave Mother—not to tell you what I have heard but what I have seen—and what I have suffered—and if there is any sympathy to give—let it be given to the thousands—of Slave Mothers that are still in bondage—suffering far more than I have—let it plead for their helpless Children that they [obliterated] may enjoy the same liberties that my Children now enjoy— Say anything of me that you have had from a truthful source that you think best—ask me any question you like—in regard to the father of my Children I think I have stated all perhaps I did not tell you—that he was a member of Congress—at that time all that of this I have written—I think it would be best for you to begin with our acquaintance and the length of time that I was in your family your advice about giving the history of my life in Slavery mention that I lived at service *all the* while that I was striving to get the Book out but do not say with whom I lived as I would not use the Willis name neither would I like to have people think that I was living an Idle life—and had got this book out merely to make money— my kind friend I do not restrict you in anything for you know far better

than I do what to say I am only too happy to think that I am going to have
it from you— [. . .]

PREFACE TO *INCIDENTS IN THE LIFE OF A SLAVE GIRL*

Reader be assured this narrative is no fiction. I am aware that some of my
adventures may seem incredible; but they are, nevertheless, strictly true. I
have not exaggerated the wrongs inflicted by Slavery; on the contrary, my
descriptions fall far short of the facts. I have concealed the names of places,
and given persons fictitious names. I had no motive for secrecy on my own
account, but I deemed it kind and considerate towards others to pursue this
course. I wish I were more competent to the task I have undertaken. But I
trust my readers will excuse deficiencies in consideration of circumstances.
I was born and reared in Slavery; and I remained in a Slave State twenty-
seven years. Since I have been at the North, it has been necessary for me to
work diligently for my own support, and the education of my children. This
has not left me much leisure to make up for the loss of early opportunities
to improve myself; and it has compelled me to write these pages at irregular
intervals, whenever I could snatch an hour from household duties.

When I first arrived in Philadelphia, Bishop Paine advised me to publish
a sketch of my life, but I told him I was altogether incompetent to such an
undertaking. Though I have improved my mind somewhat since that time,
I still remain of the same opinion; but I trust my motives will excuse what
might otherwise seem presumptuous. I have not written my experiences
in order to attract attention to myself; on the contrary, it would have been
more pleasant to me to have been silent about my own history. Neither do I
care to excite sympathy for my own sufferings. But I do earnestly desire to
arouse the women of the North to a realizing sense of the condition of two
millions of women at the South, still in bondage, suffering what I suffered,
and most of them far worse. I want to add my testimony to that of abler
pens to convince the people of the Free States what Slavery really is. Only
by experience can any one realize how deep, and dark, and foul is that pit
of abominations. May the blessing of God rest on this imperfect effort in
behalf of my persecuted people!

—Linda Brent

Autograph Letter (1860)

Wayland [Massachusetts], August 13, 1860

Dear Mrs. Jacobs,

I have been busy with your M.S. ever since I saw you; and have only done one third of it. I have very little occasion to alter the language, which is wonderfully good, for one whose opportunities for education have been so limited. The events are interesting and well told; the remarks are also good, and to the purpose. But I am copying a great deal of it, for the purpose of transposing sentences and pages, so as to bring the story into continuous order, and the remarks into appropriate places. I think you will see that this renders the story much more clear and entertaining.

I should not take so much pains, if I did not consider the book unusually interesting, and likely to do much service to the Anti-Slavery cause. So you need not feel under great personal obligations. You know I would go through fire and water to help give a blow to Slavery. I suppose you will want to see the M.S. after I have exercised my bump of mental order upon it; and I will send it wherever you direct, a fortnight hence.

My object in writing at this time is to ask you to write what you can recollect of the outrages committed on the colored people, in Nat Turner's time. You say the reader would not believe what you saw "inflicted on men, women, and children, without the slightest ground of suspicion against them." What were those inflictions? Were any tortured to make them confess? and how? Were any killed? Please write down some of the most striking particulars, and let me have them to insert.

I think the last Chapter, about John Brown, had better be omitted. It does not naturally come into your story, and the M.S. is already too long. Nothing can be so appropriate to end with, as the death of your grand mother.

Mr. Child desires to be respectfully remembered to you. Very cordially your friend,

L. Maria Child.

William Wells Brown

(1814?–1884)

Born a slave in Kentucky, Brown escaped to freedom in January 1834, and
in 1847, after being hired as a Massachusetts Anti-Slavery Society lecture
agent—he was also a fine orator—he moved to Boston, where he finished
writing the *Narrative of William W. Brown, a Fugitive Slave, Written by Himself* (1847), partly to remind Americans that "while the people of the United
States boast of their freedom, they at the same time keep three millions of
their own citizens in chains; and while I am seated here in sight of Bunker
Hill Monument, writing this narrative, I am a slave, and no law, not even in
Massachusetts, can protect me from the hands of the slaveholder!" In 1849
he began a lecture tour of Britain and remained abroad until 1854, returning
to America with his novel, *Clotel; or, The President's Daughter: A Narrative
of Slave Life in the United States*, composed while the unconfirmed rumors
of Thomas Jefferson's affair with Sally Hemings were circulating. A prolific
writer and abolitionist, he also published a travelogue, wrote several plays, a
good deal of journalism, a number of books about African American history,
and he collected a series of antislavery songs. The excerpt here, from the
introduction to *Clotel*, explains how Brown began writing and implies the
deep connection between writing and identity, which for him, as for so many
others, is a means toward an end: full-fledged freedom in life and in art.

FROM *CLOTEL; OR, THE PRESIDENT'S DAUGHTER*

How do you suppose I first commenced writing? For you will understand that up to the present time I never spent a day in school in my life, for I had no money to pay for schooling, so that I had to get my learning first from one and then from another. I carried a piece of chalk in my pocket, and whenever I met a boy I would stop him and take out my chalk and get at a board fence and then commence. First I made some flourishes with no meaning, and called a boy up, and said, "Do you see that? Can you beat that writing?" Said he, "That's not writing." Well, I wanted to get so as to write my own name. I had got out of slavery with only one name. While escaping, I received the hospitality of a very good man, who had spared part of his name to me, and finally my name got pretty long, and I wanted to be able to write it. "Now, what do you call that?" said the boy, looking at my flourishes. I said, "Is not that William Wells Brown?" "Give me the chalk," says he, and he wrote out in large letters "William Wells Brown," and I marked up the fence for nearly a quarter of a mile, trying to copy, till I got so that I could write my name. Then I went on with my chalking, and, in fact, all board fences within half a mile of where I lived were marked over with some kind of figures I had made, in trying to learn how to write. I next obtained an arithmetic, and then a grammar, and I stand here to-night, without having had a day's schooling in my life.

Henry David Thoreau

(1817–1862)

Thoreau was obsessed with writing—what it is, what it can do, how one does it—and perhaps no one else in the nineteenth century better or more unselfconsciously expressed what one goes through when one writes. In his journal, for example, he writes in the imperative mode, exhorting himself, convincing himself, impelling himself forward, instructing himself: "If thou art a writer," he says, "write as if thy time were short" (January 23, 1852). "The arrow had best not be loosely shot," he adds in another passage. "The writer must direct his sentences as carefully and leisurely as the marksman his rifle. [. . .] He must not merely seem to speak the truth. He must really speak it" (January 26, 1852). Must: what he must do, needs be done. Thoreau is filled with aphorism, wit, and directive. "We cannot write well or truly but what we write with gusto." Indeed.

"He is an upright, conscientious, and courageous man, of whom it is impossible to conceive anything but the highest integrity," said Nathaniel Hawthorne, who for a time lived nearby Thoreau in Concord, Massachusetts, where Thoreau was born and raised, and where, as an adult and an antislavery advocate, he refused to pay the town poll tax to protest slavery. Arrested and later jailed until someone, probably an aunt, paid the tax (against

Thoreau's wishes), Thoreau wrote the essay "Resistance to Civil Government" (1849), now acclaimed as the influential "Civil Disobedience."

Thoreau also shares with Whitman the sense that to write is to be alive, and to be alive is to think and feel in the present: "Obey the spur of the moment," he says (January 26, 1852), and four years later (October 18, 1856), he reminds himself that "the theme is nothing, the life is everything." In 1856 Thoreau met Whitman, whose *Leaves of Grass* (1855) he had read with pleasure, insight, and profit, and he recounts to a friend the meeting, excerpted here.

Like Emerson, Thoreau kept voluminous journals, and like him, he mined his own journals as inspiration for his published work, transforming the notes he took while living in a cabin by Walden Pond, for instance, into such a tour de force as *Walden, or Life in the Woods* (1854), an American classic that, since Thoreau's untimely death from tuberculosis in 1862, has never gone out of print. There is an excerpt here of the book's conclusion and meditation on writing. But despite the originality and beauty of published work like *Walden*, Thoreau's journal entries themselves are masterly, touching, evocative, smart, and beautifully articulated. Several of them are excerpted here, as well as a selection from *A Week on the Concord and Merrimack Rivers* (1849), "A Plea for John Brown" (1859), and *Walking* (1862), for taken together they give us insight into the life of the imagination of one who lived primarily in thought and for expression.

FROM *EARLY SPRING IN MASSACHUSETTS*

March 24, 1842. Those authors are successful who do not write down to others, but make their own taste and judgment their audience. By some strange infatuation we forget that we do not approve what yet we recommend to others. It is enough if I please myself with writing; I am then sure of an audience.

FROM *SUMMER*

July 7, 1851. [. . .] Only thought which is expressed by the mind in repose, or, as it were, lying on its back and contemplating the heavens, is adequately and fully expressed. [. . .] I can express adequately only the thought which I love to express. All the faculties in repose but the one you are using, the whole energy concentrated in that. Be so little distracted, your thoughts so little confused, your engagements so few, your attention so free, your existence so mundane that in all places and in all hours you can hear the sound of crickets in those seasons when they are to be heard. It is a mark of serenity and health of mind when a person hears this sound much in streets of cities as well as in fields. Some ears can never hear this sound; are called deaf. Is it not because they have so long attended to other sounds?

FROM *AUTUMN*

Nov. 12, 1851. Write often, write upon a thousand themes, rather than long at a time, not trying to turn too many feeble summersets in the air, and so come down upon your head at last. Antaeus-like, be not long absent from the ground. Those sentences are good and well discharged which are like so many little resiliencies from the spring-floor of our life, each a distinct fruit and kernel springing from terra firma. Let there be as many distinct plants as the soil and the light can maintain. Take as many bounds in a day as possible, sentences uttered with your back to the wall. Those are the admirable bounds when the performer has lately touched the spring-board. A good bound into the air from the air is a good and wholesome experience, but what shall we say to a man's leaping off precipices in the attempt to fly? He comes down like lead. But let your feet be planted upon the rock, with the rock also at your back, and as in the case of King James and Roderick Dhu, you can say—

"Come one, come all, this rock shall fly
From its firm base, as soon as I."

[. . .] Methinks the hawk that soars so loftily and circles so steadily and apparently without effort has earned this power by faithfully creeping on the ground as a reptile in a former state of existence. You must creep before you can run; you must run before you can fly. Better one effective bound upward with elastic limbs from the valley than a jumping from the mountain-tops in the attempt to fly. The observatories are not built high but deep; the foundation is equal to the superstructure. It is more important to a distinct vision that it be steady than it be from an elevated point of view.

FROM *THE WRITINGS OF HENRY DAVID THOREAU*

Nov. 16, 1851. Thinkers and writers are in foolish haste to come before the world with crude works. Young men are persuaded by their friends, or by their own restless ambition, to write a course of lectures in a summer against the ensuing winter; and what it took the lecture a summer to write, it will take his audience but an hour to forget. If time is short, you have no time to waste.

FROM *WINTER*

Dec. 17, 1851. Improve every opportunity to express yourself in writing, as if it were your last.

FROM *AUTUMN*

Dec. 25, 1851. Do not seek expressions, seek thoughts to be expressed.

FROM *THE WRITINGS OF HENRY DAVID THOREAU*

Jan. 22, 1852. [. . .] Perhaps this is the main value of a habit of writing, of keeping a journal, that so we remember our best hours, and stimulate ourselves. My thoughts are my company. They have a certain individuality and separate existence, aye, personality. Having by chance recorded a few disconnected thoughts, and then brought them into juxtaposition, they suggest a whole new field in which it was possible to labor and think. Thought begat thought. [. . .]

FROM *WINTER*

Jan. 24, 1856. A journal is a record of experiences and growth, not a preserve
of things well done or said. I am occasionally reminded of a statement which
I have made in conversation and immediately forgotten, which would read
much better than what I put in my journal. It is a ripe, dry fruit of long past
experience which falls from me easily without giving pain or pleasure. The
charm of the journal must consist in a certain greenness, though freshness,
and not in maturity. Here I cannot afford to be remembering what I said or
did, my scurf cast off, but what I am and aspire to become.

FROM *THE WRITINGS OF HENRY DAVID THOREAU*

Oct. 18, 1856. My work is writing, and I do not hesitate, though I know that
no subject is too trivial for me, tried by ordinary standards; for, ye fools, the
theme is nothing, the life is everything. All that interests the reader is the
depth and intensity of the life excited.

FROM *THE WRITINGS OF HENRY DAVID THOREAU*

To Harrison Blake

DECEMBER 7, 1856

That Walt Whitman, of whom I wrote to you, is the most interesting fact
to me at present. I have just read his second edition (which he gave me),
and it has done me more good than any reading for a long time. Perhaps
I remember best the poem of Walt Whitman, an American, and the Sun-
Down Poem. There are two or three pieces in the book which are disagreeable, to say the least; simply sensual. He does not celebrate love at
all. It is as if the beasts spoke. I think that men have not been ashamed of
themselves without reason. No doubt there have always been dens where
such deeds were unblushingly recited, and it is no merit to compete with
their inhabitants. But even on this side he has spoken more truth than any
American or modern that I know. I have found his poem exhilarating,
encouraging. As for its sensuality,—and it may turn out to be less sensual

than it appears,—I do not so much wish that those parts were not written, as that men and women were so pure that they could read them without harm, that is, without understanding them. One woman told me that no woman could read it,—as if a man could read what a woman could not. Of course Walt Whitman can communicate to us no experience, and if we are shocked, whose experience is that that we are reminded of?

On the whole, it sounds to me very brave and American, after whatever deductions. I do not believe that all the sermons, so called, that have been preached in this land put together are equal to it for preaching.

We ought to rejoice greatly in him. He occasionally suggests something a little more than human. You can't confound him with the other inhabitants of Brooklyn or New York. How they must shudder when they read him! He is awfully good.

To be sure I sometimes feel a little imposed on. By his heartiness and broad generalities he puts me into a liberal frame of mind prepared to see wonders,—as it were, sets me upon a hill or in the midst of a plain,—stirs me well up, and then—throws in a thousand of brick. Though rude, and sometimes ineffectual, it is a great primitive poem,—an alarum or trumpet-note ringing through the American camp. Wonderfully like the Orientals too, considering when I asked him if he had read them, he answered, "No: tell me about them."

I did not get far in conversation with him,—two more being present,— and among the few things which I chanced to say, I remember that one was, in answer to him as representing America, that I did not think much of America or of politics, and so on, which may have been somewhat of a damper to him.

Since I have seen him, I find that I am not disturbed by any brag or egoism in his book. He may turn out the least of a braggart of all, having a better right to be confident.

He is a great fellow.

FROM *THE WRITINGS OF HENRY DAVID THOREAU*

Jan. 2, 1859. [. . .] The first requisite and rule is that expression shall be vital and natural, as much as the voice of a brute or an interjection: first of all, mother tongue; and last of all, artificial or father tongue. Essentially your truest poetic sentence is as free and lawless as a lamb's bleat. The grammarian is often one who can neither cry nor laugh, yet thinks that he can express human emotions. So the posture-masters tell you how you shall walk,—turning your toes out, perhaps, excessively,—but so the beautiful walkers are not made.

Feb. 3, 1859. The writer must, to some extent, inspire himself. Most of the sentences may at first be dead in his essay, but when all are arranged, some life and color will be reflected on them from the mature and successful lines. They will appear to pulsate with past life, and he will be enabled to eke out their slumbering sense, and make them worthy of their neighborhood. In his first essay on a given theme, he produces scarcely more than a frame and ground-work for his sentiment and poetry. Each clear thought that he attains to, draws in its train many kindred thoughts or perceptions. The writer has much to do even to create a theme for himself. Most that is first written on any subject is a mere groping after it, mere rubble-stone and foundation. It is only when many observations of different periods have been brought together that he begins to grasp his subject, and can make one pertinent and just observation.

Feb. 20, 1859. How much the writer lives and endures in coming before the public so often! A few years or books are with him equal to a long life of experience, suffering, etc. It is well if he does not become hardened. He learns how to bear contempt and to despise himself. He makes, as it were, post-mortem examinations of himself before he is dead. Such is art.

from *A Week on the Concord and Merrimack Rivers*

A perfectly healthy sentence, it is true, is extremely rare. For the most part we miss the hue and fragrance of the thought; as if we could be satisfied with the dews of the morning or evening without their colors, or the heavens without their azure. The most attractive sentences are, perhaps, not the wisest, but the surest and roundest. They are spoken firmly and conclusively, as if the speaker had a right to know what he says, and if not wise, they have at least been well learned. Sir Walter Raleigh might well be studied if only for the excellence of his style, for he is remarkable in the midst of so many masters. There is a natural emphasis in his style, like a man's tread, and a breathing space between the sentences, which the best of modern writing does not furnish. His chapters are like English parks, or say rather like a Western forest, where the larger growth keeps down the underwood, and one may ride on horseback through the openings. All the distinguished writers of that period possess a greater vigor and naturalness than the more modern,—for it is allowed to slander our own time,—and when we read a quotation from one of them in the midst of a modern author, we seem to have come suddenly upon a greener ground, a greater depth and strength of soil. It is as if a green bough were laid across the page, and we are refreshed as by the sight of fresh grass in midwinter or early spring.

You have constantly the warrant of life and experience in what you read. The little that is said is eked out by implication of the much that was done. The sentences are verdurous and blooming as evergreen and flowers, because they are rooted in fact and experience, but our false and florid sentences have only the tints of flowers without their sap or roots. All men are really most attracted by the beauty of plain speech, and they even write in a florid style in imitation of this. They prefer to be misunderstood rather than to come short of its exuberance. . . .

The true poet will write for his peers alone. He will remember only that he saw truth and beauty from his position, and expect the time when a vision as broad shall overlook the same field as freely.

FROM *WALDEN*

I learned this, at least, by my experiment: that if one advances confidently in the direction of his dreams, and endeavors to live the life which he has imagined, he will meet with a success unexpected in common hours. He will put some things behind, will pass an invisible boundary; new, universal, and more liberal laws will begin to establish themselves around and within him; or the old laws be expanded, and interpreted in his favor in a more liberal sense, and he will live with the license of a higher order of beings. In proportion as he simplifies his life, the laws of the universe will appear less complex, and solitude will not be solitude, nor poverty poverty, nor weakness weakness. If you have built castles in the air, your work need not be lost; that is where they should be. Now put the foundations under them.

It is a ridiculous demand which England and America make, that you shall speak so that they can understand you. Neither men nor toadstools grow so. As if that were important, and there were not enough to understand you without them. As if Nature could support but one order of understandings, could not sustain birds as well as quadrupeds, flying as well as creeping things, and hush and whoa, which Bright can understand, were the best English. As if there were safety in stupidity alone. I fear chiefly lest my expression may not be *extra-vagrant* enough, may not wander far enough beyond the narrow limits of my daily experience, so as to be adequate to the truth of which I have been convinced. *Extra vagrance!* it depends on how you are yarded. The migrating buffalo, which seeks new pastures in another latitude, is not extravagant like the cow which kicks over the pail, leaps the cowyard fence, and runs after her calf, in milking time. I desire to speak somewhere without bounds; like a man in a waking moment, to men in their waking moments; for I am convinced that I cannot exaggerate enough even to lay the foundation of a true expression. Who that has heard a strain of music feared then lest he should speak extravagantly any more forever? In view of the future or possible, we should live quite laxly and undefined in front, our outlines dim and misty on that side; as our shadows reveal an insensible perspiration toward the sun. The volatile truth of our words should continually betray the inadequacy of the residual statement. Their truth is instantly translated; its literal monument alone remains. The words which express our faith and piety are not definite; yet they are significant and fragrant like frankincense to superior natures.

FROM "A PLEA FOR CAPTAIN JOHN BROWN"

A man of rare common sense and directness of speech, as of action; a transcendentalist above all, a man of ideas and principles, that was what distinguished him. Not yielding to a whim or transient impulse, but carrying out the purpose of a life. I noticed that he did not overstate anything, but spoke within bounds. I remember, particularly, how, in his speech here, he referred to what his family had suffered in Kansas, without ever giving the least vent to his pent-up fire. It was a volcano with an ordinary chimney-flue. Also referring to the deeds of certain Border Ruffians, he said, rapidly paring away his speech, like an experienced soldier, keeping a reserve of force and meaning, "They had a perfect right to be hung." He was not in the least a rhetorician, was not talking to Buncombe or his constituents anywhere, had no need to invent anything, but to tell the simple truth, and communicate his own resolution; therefore he appeared incomparably strong, and eloquence in Congress and elsewhere seemed to me at a discount. It was like the speeches of Cromwell compared with those of an ordinary king.

[. . .] If you read his words understandingly you will find out. In his case there is no idle eloquence, no made, nor maiden speech, no compliments to the oppressor. Truth is his inspirer, and earnestness the polisher of his sentences. He could afford to lose his Sharps rifles, while he retained his faculty of speech,—a Sharps rifle of infinitely surer and longer range.

FROM *WALKING*

In literature it is only the wild that attracts us. . . .

Frederick Douglass

(ca. 1818–1895)

Born into slavery, escaped out of bondage, and one of the most eloquent persons of his or any generation, Frederick Douglass was an orator, a journalist, a freedom-fighter, a politician, a diplomat, a revolutionary, and an indefatigable champion of civil rights who, in 1845, while "abolition" was a hated word even in the North, published his memoir of captivity—and of the brutal dehumanization known as the institution of slavery. Not just a slave narrative, not just a paean to freedom, not just an autobiography, not just a historical document, even though it is all of these, his *Narrative of the Life of Frederick Douglass, an American Slave* (1845) was and remains a beautifully constructed depiction of selfhood, self-making, freedom, oratory, and memory. And at its heart is the question of literacy and language, for to keep them enslaved and ignorant, slaves were in the main not allowed to learn to read and write. But Douglass's ability to master language so evocatively, his passion for words and the way he linked words to meaning and meaning to hope, offer us one of the most moving meditations on writers and writing of the nineteenth century.

In the pages below, taken from Douglass's *Narrative*, is the now-famous story of his education.

FROM *NARRATIVE OF THE LIFE OF FREDERICK DOUGLASS*

Very soon after I went to live with Mr. and Mrs. Auld, she very kindly commenced to teach me the A, B, C. After I had learned this, she assisted me in learning to spell words of three or four letters. Just at this point of my progress, Mr. Auld found out what was going on, and at once forbade Mrs. Auld to instruct me further, telling her, among other things, that it was unlawful, as well as unsafe, to teach a slave to read. To use his own words, further, he said, "If you give a nigger an inch, he will take an ell. A nigger should know nothing but to obey his master—to do as he is told to do. Learning would spoil the best nigger in the world. Now," said he, "if you teach that nigger (speaking of myself) how to read, there would be no keeping him. It would forever unfit him to be a slave. He would at once become unmanageable, and of no value to his master. As to himself, it could do him no good, but a great deal of harm. It would make him discontented and unhappy." These words sank deep into my heart, stirred up sentiments within that lay slumbering, and called into existence an entirely new train of thought. It was a new and special revelation, explaining dark and mysterious things, with which my youthful understanding had struggled, but struggled in vain. I now understood what had been to me a most perplexing difficulty—to wit, the white man's power to enslave the black man. It was a grand achievement, and I prized it highly. From that moment, I understood the pathway from slavery to freedom. It was just what I wanted, and I got it at a time when I the least expected it. Whilst I was saddened by the thought of losing the aid of my kind mistress, I was gladdened by the invaluable instruction which, by the merest accident, I had gained from my master. Though conscious of the difficulty of learning without a teacher, I set out with high hope, and a fixed purpose, at whatever cost of trouble, to learn how to read. The very decided manner with which he spoke, and strove to impress his wife with the evil consequences of giving me instruction, served to convince me that he was deeply sensible of the truths he was uttering. It gave me the best assurance that I might rely with the utmost confidence on the results which, he said, would flow from teaching me to read. What he most dreaded, that I most desired. What he most loved, that

I most hated. That which to him was a great evil, to be carefully shunned, was to me a great good, to be diligently sought; and the argument which he so warmly urged, against my learning to read, only served to inspire me with a desire and determination to learn. In learning to read, I owe almost as much to the bitter opposition of my master, as to the kindly aid of my mistress. I acknowledge the benefit of both. [. . .]

I lived in Master Hugh's family about seven years. During this time, I succeeded in learning to read and write. In accomplishing this, I was compelled to resort to various stratagems. I had no regular teacher. My mistress, who had kindly commenced to instruct me, had, in compliance with the advice and direction of her husband, not only ceased to instruct, but had set her face against my being instructed by any one else. It is due, however, to my mistress to say of her, that she did not adopt this course of treatment immediately. She at first lacked the depravity indispensable to shutting me up in mental darkness. It was at least necessary for her to have some training in the exercise of irresponsible power, to make her equal to the task of treating me as though I were a brute.

My mistress was, as I have said, a kind and tenderhearted woman; and in the simplicity of her soul she commenced, when I first went to live with her, to treat me as she supposed one human being ought to treat another. In entering upon the duties of a slaveholder, she did not seem to perceive that I sustained to her the relation of a mere chattel, and that for her to treat me as a human being was not only wrong, but dangerously so. Slavery proved as injurious to her as it did to me. When I went there, she was a pious, warm, and tender-hearted woman. There was no sorrow or suffering for which she had not a tear. She had bread for the hungry, clothes for the naked, and comfort for every mourner that came within her reach. Slavery soon proved its ability to divest her of these heavenly qualities. Under its influence, the tender heart became stone, and the lamblike disposition gave way to one of tiger-like fierceness. The first step in her downward course was in her ceasing to instruct me. She now commenced to practise her husband's precepts. She finally became even more violent in her opposition than her husband himself. She was not satisfied with simply doing as well as he had commanded; she seemed anxious to do better. Nothing seemed to make her more angry than to see me with a newspaper. She seemed to think that here lay the danger. I have had her rush at me with a face made all up of fury, and snatch from me a newspaper, in a manner that fully revealed her apprehension. She was an apt woman; and a little experience soon demonstrated, to her satisfaction, that education and slavery were incompatible with each other.

From this time I was most narrowly watched. If I was in a separate room any considerable length of time, I was sure to be suspected of having a book, and was at once called to give an account of myself. All this, however, was too late. The first step had been taken. Mistress, in teaching me the alphabet, had given me the inch, and no precaution could prevent me from taking the ell.

The plan which I adopted, and the one by which I was most successful, was that of making friends of all the little white boys whom I met in the street. As many of these as I could, I converted into teachers. With their kindly aid, obtained at different times and in different places, I finally succeeded in learning to read. When I was sent of errands, I always took my book with me, and by going one part of my errand quickly, I found time to get a lesson before my return. I used also to carry bread with me, enough of which was always in the house, and to which I was always welcome; for I was much better off in this regard than many of the poor white children in our neighborhood. This bread I used to bestow upon the hungry little urchins, who, in return, would give me that more valuable bread of knowledge. I am strongly tempted to give the names of two or three of those little boys, as a testimonial of the gratitude and affection I bear them; but prudence forbids;—not that it would injure me, but it might embarrass them; for it is almost an unpardonable offence to teach slaves to read in this Christian country. It is enough to say of the dear little fellows, that they lived on Philpot Street, very near Durgin and Bailey's ship-yard. I used to talk this matter of slavery over with them. I would sometimes say to them, I wished I could be as free as they would be when they got to be men. "You will be free as soon as you are twenty-one, but I am a slave for life! Have not I as good a right to be free as you have?" These words used to trouble them; they would express for me the liveliest sympathy, and console me with the hope that something would occur by which I might be free.

I was now about twelve years old, and the thought of being a slave for life began to bear heavily upon my heart. Just about this time, I got hold of a book entitled "The Columbian Orator." Every opportunity I got, I used to read this book. Among much of other interesting matter, I found in it a dialogue between a master and his slave. The slave was represented as having run away from his master three times. The dialogue represented the conversation which took place between them, when the slave was retaken the third time. In this dialogue, the whole argument in behalf of slavery was brought forward by the master, all of which was disposed of by the slave. The slave was made to say some very smart as well as impressive things in reply to his master—things which had the desired though unex-, pected effect; for the conversation resulted in the voluntary emancipation of the slave on the part of the master.

In the same book, I met with one of Sheridan's mighty speeches on and in behalf of Catholic emancipation. These were choice documents to me. I read them over and over again with unabated interest. They gave tongue to interesting thoughts of my own soul, which had frequently flashed through my mind, and died away for want of utterance. The moral which I gained from the dialogue was the power of truth over the conscience of even a slaveholder. What I got from Sheridan was a bold denunciation of slavery, and a powerful vindication of human rights. The reading of these documents enabled me to utter my thoughts, and to meet the arguments brought forward to sustain slavery; but while they relieved me of one difficulty, they brought on another even more painful than the one of which I was relieved. The more I read, the more I was led to abhor and detest my enslavers. I could regard them in no other light than a band of successful robbers, who had left their homes, and gone to Africa, and stolen us from our homes, and in a strange land reduced us to slavery. I loathed them as being the meanest as well as the most wicked of men. As I read and contemplated the subject, behold! that very discontentment which Master Hugh had predicted would follow my learning to read had already come, to torment and sting my soul to unutterable anguish. As I writhed under it, I would at times feel that learning to read had been a curse rather than a blessing. It had given me a view of my wretched condition, without the remedy. It opened my eyes to the horrible pit, but to no ladder upon which to get out. In moments of agony, I envied my fellow-slaves for their stupidity. I have often wished myself a beast. I preferred the condition of the meanest reptile to my own. Any thing, no matter what, to get rid of thinking! It was this everlasting thinking of my condition that tormented me. There was no getting rid of it. It was pressed upon me by every object within sight or hearing, animate or inanimate. The silver trump of freedom had roused my soul to eternal wakefulness. Freedom now appeared, to disappear no more forever. It was heard in every sound, and seen in every thing. It was ever present to torment me with a sense of my wretched condition. I saw nothing without seeing it, I heard nothing without hearing it, and felt nothing without feeling it. It looked from every star, it smiled in every calm, breathed in every wind, and moved in every storm.

I often found myself regretting my own existence, and wishing myself dead; and but for the hope of being free, I have no doubt but that I should have killed myself, or done something for which I should have been killed. While in this state of mind, I was eager to hear any one speak of slavery. I was a ready listener. Every little while, I could hear something about the abolitionists. It was some time before I found what the word meant. It was always used in such connections as to make it an interesting word to me. If a slave ran away and succeeded in getting clear, or if a slave killed his master, set fire to a barn, or did any thing very wrong in the mind of a slaveholder, it was spoken of as the fruit of abolition. Hearing the word in this connection very often, I set about learning what it meant. The dictionary afforded me little or no help. I found it was "the act of abolishing"; but then I did not know what was to be abolished. Here I was perplexed. I did not dare to ask any one about its meaning, for I was satisfied that it was something they wanted me to know very little about. After a patient waiting, I got one of our city papers, containing an account of the number of petitions from the north, praying for the abolition of slavery in the District of Columbia, and of the slave trade between the States. From this time I understood the words abolition and abolitionist, and always drew near when that word was spoken, expecting to hear something of importance to myself and fellow-slaves. The light broke in upon me by degrees. I went one day down on the wharf of Mr. Waters; and seeing two Irishmen unloading a scow of stone, I went, unasked, and helped them. When we had finished, one of them came to me and asked me if I were a slave. I told him I was. He asked, "Are ye a slave for life?" I told him that I was. The good Irishman seemed to be deeply affected by the statement. He said to the other that it was a pity so fine a little fellow as myself should be a slave for life. He said it was a shame to hold me. They both advised me to run away to the north; that I should find friends there, and that I should be free. I pretended not to be interested in what they said, and treated them as if I did not understand them; for I feared they might be treacherous. White men have been known to encourage slaves to escape, and then, to get the reward, catch them and return them to their masters. I was afraid that these seemingly good men might use me so; but I nevertheless remembered their advice, and from that time I resolved to run away. I looked forward to a time at which it would be safe for me to escape. I was too young to think of doing so immediately; besides, I wished to learn how to write, as I might have occasion to write my own pass. I consoled myself with the hope that I should one day find a good chance. Meanwhile, I would learn to write.

The idea as to how I might learn to write was suggested to me by being in Durgin and Bailey's ship-yard, and frequently seeing the ship carpenters, after hewing, and getting a piece of timber ready for use, write on the timber the name of that part of the ship for which it was intended. When a piece of timber was intended for the larboard side, it would be marked thus—"L." When a piece was for the starboard side, it would be marked thus—"S." A piece for the larboard side forward, would be marked thus—"L. F." When a piece was for starboard side forward, it would be marked thus—"S. F." For larboard aft, it would be marked thus—"L. A." For starboard aft, it would be marked thus—"S. A." I soon learned the names of these letters, and for what they were intended when placed upon a piece of timber in the ship-yard. I immediately commenced copying them, and in a short time was able to make the four letters named. After that, when I met with any boy who I knew could write, I would tell him I could write as well as he. The next word would be, "I don't believe you. Let me see you try it." I would then make the letters which I had been so fortunate as to learn, and ask him to beat that. In this way I got a good many lessons in writing, which it is quite possible I should never have gotten in any other way. During this time, my copy-book was the board fence, brick wall, and pavement; my pen and ink was a lump of chalk. With these, I learned mainly how to write. I then commenced and continued copying the Italics in Webster's Spelling Book, until I could make them all without looking on the book. By this time, my little Master Thomas had gone to school, and learned how to write, and had written over a number of copy-books. These had been brought home, and shown to some of our near neighbors, and then laid aside. My mistress used to go to class meeting at the Wilk Street meetinghouse every Monday afternoon, and leave me to take care of the house. When left thus, I used to spend the time in writing in the spaces left in Master Thomas's copy-book, copying what he had written. I continued to do this until I could write a hand very similar to that of Master Thomas. Thus, after a long, tedious effort for years, I finally succeeded in learning how to write.

Julia Ward Howe

(1819–1910)

Best known as author of the poem "The Battle Hymn of the Republic," soon set to music, Howe was also the author of the volume of verse *Passion-flowers* (1854), one that prompted Hawthorne to say expressed "a whole history of domestic unhappiness" and then to purposefully wonder, "What does her husband think of it?" (Howe had married the dashing Doctor Samuel Gridley Howe, who had served in the Greek war for independence before returning to Boston and becoming director of the Perkins Institute for the Blind.) Howe was not pleased; it was not a good marriage.

Despite her husband's disapprobrium, she kept writing, and was later a well-known social activist as well as first president of the New England Woman Suffrage Association. And through all this, she cleaved to a Romantic view of writing and inspiration, as the excerpt from a poem from *Passion-flowers* suggests; in fact, it's not very different from her explanation of how, in a single night, she came to write "The Battle Hymn." She and her husband, as members of the Sanitary Commission, had been touring a battlefield in Virginia with their friend the Reverend John Freeman Clarke, who suggested she write a song as memorable as "John Brown's Body." This excerpt tells the story of what presumably happened next—and what can actually happen, sometimes, in the midst of sleep.

FROM "MOTHER MIND"

I never *made* a poem, dear friend—
I never sat me down, and said,
This cunning brain and patient hand
Shall fashion something to be read. [. . .]

Yet all my thoughts to rhythms run,
To rhyme, my wisdom and my wit?
True, I consume my life in verse,
But wouldst thou know how that is writ?

'Tis thus—through weary length of days,
I bear a thought within my breast
That greatens from my growth of soul,
And waits, and will not be expressed.

It greatens, till its hour has come,
Not without pain, it sees the light;
'Twixt smiles and tears I view it o'er,
And dare not deem it perfect, quite.

These children of my soul I keep
Where scarce a mortal man may see,
Yet not unconsecrate, dear friend,
Baptismal rites they claim of thee.

FROM *THE STORY OF*
THE BATTLE HYMN OF THE REPUBLIC

I went to bed and slept as usual, but awoke the next morning in the gray
of the early dawn, and to my astonishment found that the wished-for lines
were arranging themselves in my brain. I lay quite still until the last verse
had completed itself in my thoughts, then hastily arose, saying to myself,
I shall lose this if I don't write it down immediately. I searched for an old

sheet of paper and an old stub of a pen which I had had the night before, and began to scrawl the lines almost without looking, as I learned to do by often scratching down verses in the darkened room when my little children were sleeping. Having completed this, I lay down again and fell asleep, but not before feeling that something of importance had happened to me.

James Russell Lowell

(1819–1891)

In his hugely popular masterpiece, *The Biglow Papers*, a series of poems
and prose pieces, Lowell developed a vernacular style to launch an acute,
well-aimed political satire in the Yankee, cracker-barrel dialect of a so-called
Hosea Biglow. It was so successful that Edgar Allan Poe called Lowell a rant-
ing abolitionist who should not write verse (although for a time the two men
were cordial) and similarly regarded Lowell's *Fable for Critics* (1848) a form
of retaliation against those, like Margaret Fuller, who dared criticize Lowell's
poetry. Maybe so, but *The Biglow Papers* (1848; 1867) are unique and rather
wonderful; and as for *A Fable for Critics*, though far less special, parts of it,
particularly Lowell's estimation of Emerson and, by implication, his definition
of poetry, deserve a look. After 1855, however, a few years after the death
of his beloved wife, Maria White, Lowell delivered a series of lectures on
the English poets and accepted the position as Smith Professor of the French
and Spanish Languages and Literatures at Harvard, succeeding Longfellow.
From then on, his own literary output diminished, for he also assumed the
editorship of the fledgling *Atlantic Monthly*, which he helped make one of
the best and most influential political and literary magazines of the day. He
continued to write, mostly prose essays on literary and political subjects and
occasionally satiric verse. He was a delegate to the Republican Convention in

Cincinnati and a presidential elector who helped Rutherford Hayes become president during a contested election. In 1877 President Hayes appointed Lowell minister to Spain, and three years later he was appointed minister to the court of St. James, in London. As unofficial ambassador of American letters, he met both Leslie Stephen and his young daughter Virginia, who later remembered him fondly—as a Victorian relic.

EMERSON

There comes Emerson first, whose rich words, every one,
Are like gold nails in temples to hang trophies on,
Whose prose is grand verse, while his verse, the Lord knows,
Is some of it pr— No, 'tis not even prose;
I'm speaking of metres; some poems have welled
From those rare depths of soul that have ne'er been excelled;
They're not epics, but that doesn't matter a pin,
In creating, the only hard thing's to begin;
A grass-blade's no easier to make than an oak,
If you've once found the way you've achieved the grand stroke;
In the worst of his poems are mines of rich matter,
But thrown in a heap with a crash and a clatter
Now it is not one thing nor another alone
Makes a poem, but rather the general tone,
The something pervading, uniting, the whole,
The before unconceived, unconceivable soul,
So that just in removing this trifle or that, you
Take away, as it were, a chief limb of the statue;
Roots, wood, bark, and leaves, singly perfect may be,
But, clapt hodge-podge together, they don't make a tree.
But, to come back to Emerson, (whom by the way,
I believe we left waiting,)—his is, we may say,
A Greek head on right Yankee shoulders, whose range

Has Olympus for one pole, for t'other the Exchange;
Life, nature, lore, God, and affairs of that sort,
He looks at as merely ideas; in short,
As if they were fossils stuck round in a cabinet,
Of such vast extent that our earth's a mere dab in it;
Composed just as he is inclined to conjecture her,
Namely, one part pure earth, ninety-nine parts pure lecturer;
You are filled with delight at his clear demonstration,
Each figure, word, gesture, just fits the occasion,
With the quiet precision of science he'll sort 'em,
But you can't help suspecting the whole a post mortem.

Herman Melville

(1819–1891)

One of the most original, searing, trenchant, tragic, and visionary writers of the nineteenth century—or any century—Herman Melville wore his writing heart on his sleeve, whether in his novels, autobiographies, or even in his last and highly cryptic poems, particularly *Clarel* (1876). He broke through the boundaries of all things, including the novel. In one sense, *Moby-Dick* (1851) is about the impossibility of capturing not just the whale but our vision of what it might represent in prose; for nothing, especially the way we feel, is final: "God keep me from ever completing anything. This whole book is but a draught—nay, but the draught of a draught. Oh, Time, Cash, Strength, and Patience."

Unique himself, Melville, like many of his contemporaries, believed that he stood at the birth of an American literature; that he in fact was a progenitor. And recognizing the same in Hawthorne, Melville boldly predicted that Hawthorne augured greatness for this new national literature. "Let him write like a man, for then he will be sure to write like an American," Melville boomed, sounding like Emerson and Thoreau and even Whitman, all of whom, on this subject, sounded like one another. "Let us away with this leaven of literary flunkeyism toward England." As for Hawthorne, "he is the flesh and blood of the land. The scent of beech and hemlock and tar is in his soul." Melville's paean to American writers, to himself, to Hawthorne, is the amazing review of Hawthorne's stories, "Hawthorne and His Mosses" (1850), for it extends the call for a new national literature and yet, at the same time, suggests that Melville already acknowledged how few would understand Hawthorne—or himself.

Hawthorne once wrote that any author addresses "not the many who will fling aside his volume, or never take it up, but the few who will under-stand him, better than his schoolmates or lifemates." This is the reader of "perfect sympathy" imagined by all writers, and Melville, on completing *Moby-Dick*, felt he had for a time found just this reader in Hawthorne him-self. His letter to Hawthorne, then, records the exuberance of the writer who feels he or she has been grasped fully by a simpatico author who also seeks to capture the ineffable in words. Thus, Melville's famous letters to Haw-thorne, excerpted here, lets us peek into the friendship that writers can—and need to—form with one another.

After the publication of *Moby-Dick*, Melville's view of the literary marketplace turned more sour, more satiric, and in the infamous and weird pages of his next book, *Pierre; or, The Ambiguities* (1852), he boldly and self-destructively skewered the smug and conservative literary community that had withdrawn its support, if ever it existed, of ambiguity, experiment, and originality. And so Melville was alone, one who could "neither believe, nor be comfortable in his unbelief," said Hawthorne; "and he is too honest and courageous not to try to do one or the other." The harrowing statement of disbelief in *Pierre*—of one's achievement never fulfilling one's desires, and of truth forever elusive—is also excerpted here.

FROM *THE CORRESPONDENCE OF HERMAN MELVILLE*

To Nathaniel Hawthorne

JUNE [1?] 1851

My Dear Hawthorne, [. . .] I mean to continue visiting you until you tell
me that my visits are both supererogatory and superfluous. With no son
of man do I stand upon any etiquette or ceremony, except the Christian
ones of charity and honesty. I am told, my fellow-man, that there is an
aristocracy of the brain. Some men have boldly advocated and asserted it.
Schiller seems to have done so, though I don't know much about him. At
any rate, it is true that there have been those who, while earnest in behalf
of political equality, will accept the intellectual estates. And I can well
perceive, I think, how a man of superior mind can, by its intense cultivation, bring himself, as it were, into a certain spontaneous aristocracy of
feeling,—exceedingly nice and fastidious,—similar to that which, in an
English Howard, conveys a torpedo-fish thrill at the slightest contact with
a social plebian. So, when you see or hear of my ruthless democracy on all
sides, you may possibly feel a touch of a shrink, or something of that sort.
It is but nature to be shy of a mortal who boldly declares that a thief in jail
is as honorable a personage as Gen. George Washington. This is ludicrous.
But Truth is the silliest thing under the sun. Try to get a living by the
Truth—and go to the Soup Societies. Heavens! Let any clergyman try to
preach the Truth from its very stronghold, the pulpit, and they would ride
him out of his church on his own pulpit bannister. It can hardly be doubted
that all Reformers are bottomed upon the truth, more or less; and to the
world at large are not reformers almost universally laughingstocks? Why
so? Truth is ridiculous to men. Thus easily in my room here do I, conceited
and garrulous, reverse the test of my Lord Shaftesbury.

   [. . .] I began by saying that the reason I have not been to Lenox is this,—
in the evening I feel completely done up, as the phrase is, and incapable
of the long jolting to get to your house and back. In a week or so, I go to
New York, to bury myself in a third-story room, and work and slave on my
"Whale" while it is driving through the press. *That* is the only way I can
finish it now,—I am so pulled hither and thither by circumstances. The

calm, the coolness, the silent grass-growing mood in which a man *ought* always to compose,—that, I fear, can seldom be mine. Dollars damn me; and the malicious Devil is forever grinning in upon me, holding the door ajar. My dear Sir, a presentiment is on me,—I shall at last be worn out and perish, like an old nutmeg-grater, grated to pieces by the constant attrition of the wood, that is, the nutmeg. What I feel most moved to write, that is banned,—it will not pay. Yet, altogether, write the *other* way I cannot. So the product is a final hash, and all my books are botches. I'm rather sore, perhaps, in this letter, but see my hand!—four blisters on this palm, made by hoes and hammers within the last few days. It is a rainy morning; so I am indoors, and all work suspended. I feel cheerfully disposed, and therefore I write a little bluely. Would the Gin were here! If ever, my dear Hawthorne, in the eternal times that are to come, you and I shall sit down in Paradise, in some little shady corner by ourselves; and if we shall by any means be able to smuggle a basket of champagne there (I won't believe in a Temperance Heaven), and if we shall then cross our celestial legs in the celestial grass that is forever tropical, and strike our glasses and our heads together, till both musically ring in concert,—then, O my dear fellow-mortal, how shall we pleasantly discourse of all the things manifold which now so distress us,—when all the earth shall be but a reminiscence, yea, its final dissolution an antiquity. Then shall songs be composed as when wars are over; humorous, comic songs,—"Oh, when I lived in that queer little hole called the world," or, "Oh, when I toiled and sweated below," or, "Oh, when I knocked and was knocked in the fight"—yes, let us look forward to such things. Let us swear that, though now we sweat, yet it is because of the dry heat which is indispensable to the nourishment of the vine which is to bear the grapes that are to give us the champagne hereafter.

But I was talking about the "Whale." As the fishermen say, "he's in his flurry" when I left him some three weeks ago. I'm going to take him by his jaw, however, before long, and finish him up in some fashion or other. What's the use of elaborating what, in its very essence, is so short-lived as a modern book? Though I wrote the Gospels in this century, I should die in the gutter.—I talk all about myself, and this is selfishness and egotism. Granted. But how help it? I am writing to you; I know little about you, but something about myself so I write about myself,—at least, to you. Don't trouble yourself, though, about writing; and don't trouble yourself about visiting; and when you *do* visit, don't trouble yourself about talking. I will do all the writing and visiting and talking myself—By the way, in the last "Dollar Magazine" I read "The Unpardonable Sin." He was a sad fellow, that Ethan Brand. I have no doubt you are by this time responsible for many a shake and tremor of the tribe of "general readers." It is a frightful poetical creed that the cultivation of the brain eats out the heart. But it's my *prose* opinion that in most cases, in those men who have fine brains and work them well, the heart extends down to hams. And though you smoke them with the fire of tribulation, yet, like veritable hams, the head only gives the richer and the better flavor. I stand for the heart. To the dogs with the head! I had rather be a fool with a heart, than Jupiter Olympus with his head. The reason the mass of men fear God, and *at bottom dislike* Him, is because they rather distrust His heart, and fancy Him all brain like a watch. (You perceive I employ a capital initial in the pronoun referring to the Deity; don't you think there is a slight dash of flunkeyism in that usage?) Another thing. I was in New York for four-and-twenty hours the other day, and saw a portrait of N.H. And I have seen and heard many flattering (in a publisher's point of view) allusions to the "Seven Gables." And I have seen "Tales," and "A New Volume" announced, by N.H. So upon the whole, I say to myself, this N.H. is in the ascendant. My dear Sir, they begin to patronize. All Fame is patronage. Let me be infamous: there is no patronage in *that*. What "reputation" H.M. has is horrible. Think of it! To go down to posterity is bad enough, any way; but to go down as a "man who lived among the cannibals"! When I speak of posterity, in reference to myself, I only mean the babies who will probably be born in the moment immediately ensuing upon my giving up the ghost. I shall go down to some of them, in all likelihood. *Typee* will be given to them, perhaps, with their gingerbread. I have come to regard this matter of Fame as the most transparent of all vanities. I read Solomon more and more, and every time see deeper and deeper and unspeakable meanings in him. I did not think of Fame, a year ago, as I do now. My development has been all within a few years past. I am like one of those seeds taken out of the Egyptian Pyramids, which, after being three thousand years a seed and nothing but a seed, being planted in English soil, it developed itself, grew to greenness, and then fell to mould. So I. Until I was twenty-five, I had no development at all. From my twenty-fifth year I date my life. Three weeks have scarcely passed, at any time between then and now, that I have not unfolded within myself. But I feel that I am now come to the inmost leaf of the bulb, and that shortly the flower must fall to the mould. It seems to be now that Solomon was the truest man who ever spoke, and yet that he a little *managed* the truth with a view to popular conservatism; or else there have been many corruptions and interpolations of the text.—In reading some of Goethe's sayings, so worshipped by his votaries, I came across this, *"Live in the all."* That is to say, your separate identity is but a wretched one,—good; but get out of yourself, spread and expand yourself, and bring to yourself the tinglings of life that are felt in the flowers and the woods, that are felt in the planets Saturn and Venus, and the Fixed Stars. What nonsense! Here is a fellow with a raging toothache. "My dear boy," Goethe says to him, "you are sorely afflicted with that tooth; but you must *live in the all*, and then you will be happy!" As with all great genius, there is an immense deal of flummery in Goethe, and in proportion to my own contact with him, a monstrous deal of it in me.

H. Melville.

P.S. "Amen!" saith Hawthorne.

N.B. This "all" feeling, though, there is some truth in. You must often have felt it, lying on the grass on a warm summer's day. Your legs seem to send out shoots into the earth. Your hair feels like leaves upon your head. This is the *all* feeling. But what plays the mischief with the truth is that men will insist upon the universal application of a temporary feeling or opinion.

P.S. You must not fail to admire my discretion in paying the postage on this letter.

FROM *THE CORRESPONDENCE OF HERMAN MELVILLE*

Your letter was handed to me last night on the road going to Mr. Morewood's, and I read it there. Had I been at home, I would have sat down at once and answered it. In me divine magnanimities are spontaneous and instantaneous—catch them while you can. The world goes round, and the other side comes up. So now I can't write what I felt. But I felt pantheistic then—your heart beat in my ribs and mine in yours, and both in God's. A sense of unspeakable security is in me this moment, on account of your having understood the book. I have written a wicked book, and feel spotless as the lamb. Ineffable socialities are in me. I would sit down and dine with you and all the Gods in old Rome's Pantheon. It is a strange feel-ing—no hopelessness is in it, no despair. Content—that is it; and irrespon-sibility; but without licentious inclination. I speak now of my profoundest sense of being, not of an incidental feeling.

Whence came you, Hawthorne? By what right do you drink from my flagon of life? And when I put it to my lips—lo, they are yours and not mine. I feel that the Godhead is broken up like the bread at the Supper, and that we are the pieces. Hence this infinite fraternity of feeling. Now sympathising with the paper, my angel turns over another leaf. You did not care a penny for the book. But, now and then as you read, you understood the pervading thought that impelled the book—and that you praised. Was it not so? You were archangel enough to praise the imperfect body, and embrace the soul. Once you hugged the ugly Socrates because you saw the flame in the mouth, and heard the rushing of the demon,—the familiar,—and recognised the sound; for you have heard it in your own solitudes.

My dear Hawthorne, the atmospheric scepticisms steal over me now, and make me doubtful of my sanity in writing you thus. But, believe me, I am not mad, most noble Festus! But truth is ever incoherent, and when the big hearts strike together, the concussion is a little stunning. Farewell. Don't write me a word about the book. That would be robbing me of my miserable delight. I am heartily sorry I ever wrote anything about you—it was paltry. Lord, when shall we be done growing? As long as we have any-thing more to do, we have done nothing. So, now, let us add Moby-Dick to our blessing, and step from that. Leviathan is not the biggest fish;—I have heard of Krakens.

This is a long letter, but you are not at all bound to answer it. Possibly if you do answer it, and direct it to Herman Melville, you will missend it—for the very fingers that now guide this pen are not precisely the same that just took it up and put it to the paper. Lord, when shall we be done changing? Ah! it is a long stage, and no inn in sight, and night coming, and the body cold. But with you for a passenger, I am content and can be happy. I shall leave the world, I feel, with more satisfaction for having come to know you. Knowing you persuades me more than the Bible of our immortality.

What a pity that, for your plain, bluff letter, you should get such gibberish! Mention me to Mrs. Hawthorne and to the children, and so, good-bye to you, with my blessing.

HERMAN.

P.S.

I can't stop yet. If the world was entirely made up of Magicians, I'll tell you what I should do. I should have a paper-mill established at one end of the house, and so have an extra riband for foolscap rolling in upon my desk; and upon that endless riband I should write a thousand—a million—a billion thoughts, all under the form of a letter to you. The divine magnet is on you, and my magnet responds. Which is the bigger? A foolish question—they are one.

H.

P.P.S.

Don't think that by writing me a letter, you shall always be bored with an immediate reply to it—and so keep both of us delving over a writing-desk eternally. No such thing! I sha'n't always answer your letters and you may do just as you please.

FROM *PIERRE; OR, THE AMBIGUITIES*

For the more and the more that he wrote, and the deeper and the deeper that he dived, Pierre saw the everlasting elusiveness of Truth; the universal lurking insincerity of even the greatest and purest written thoughts. Like knavish cards, the leaves of all great books were covertly packed. He was but packing one set the more; and that a very poor jaded set and pack indeed. So that there was nothing he more spurned, than his own aspirations; nothing he more abhorred than the loftiest part of himself. The brightest success, now seemed intolerable to him, since he so plainly saw, that the brightest success could not be the sole offspring of Merit; but of Merit for the one thousandth part, and nine hundred and ninety-nine combining and dovetailing accidents for the rest. So beforehand he despised those laurels which in the very nature of things, can never be impartially bestowed. But while thus all the earth was depopulated of ambition for him; still circumstances had put him in the attitude of an eager contender for renown. So beforehand he felt the unrevealable sting of receiving either plaudits or censures, equally unsought for, and equally loathed ere given. So, beforehand he felt the pyramidical scorn of the genuine loftiness for the whole infinite company of infinitesimal critics. His was the scorn which thinks it not worth the while to be scornful. Those he most scorned, never knew it. In that lonely little closet of his, Pierre foretasted all that this world hath either of praise or dispraise; and thus foretasting both goblets, anticipatingly hurled them both in its teeth. All panegyric, all denunciation, all criticism of any sort, would come too late for Pierre.

Walt Whitman

(1819–1892)

Three men had interested Thoreau in the last years of his life, Emerson had
remarked in his eulogy of Thoreau: one was Joseph Polis, his Penobscot guide
in Maine; another was John Brown, whom he defended against Concord
neighbors horrified by Harper's Ferry; and the third, unnamed, was Walt
Whitman.

In 1856, the year of the expanded, second edition of *Leaves of Grass*
(1855), Thoreau called upon Whitman and recorded the meeting (excerpted
in the Thoreau section). Whitman, too, remembered the meeting and later
said Thoreau had asked, "What is there in the people? Pshaw! What do you
(a man who sees as well as anybody) see in all this cheating political corrup-
tion?" They were walking Brooklyn streets and, as Whitman recalled, "I did
not like my Brooklyn spoken of in this way."

Whitman was no Thoreau devotee; rather, for Whitman, it was Emerson
who saw the horizon whole. Later Whitman described the excitement with
which he first read the older writer: "I was simmering, simmering, simmering; Emerson brought me to a boil." For in "The Poet" (as excerpted earlier),
Emerson said he looked "in vain for the poet whom I describe." Here I
am, Whitman virtually answered by mailing him a copy of *Leaves of Grass*.
Emerson responded warmly, greeting Whitman, as he said, "at the beginning

of a great career." Whitman then permitted Emerson's letter to be published without permission and even went so far as to use a section of it on the cover of the next edition of *Leaves of Grass*, which included new poems that later Emerson, annoyed, called "priapic." Nonetheless, Emerson knew that a unique, new poetic voice had arrived.

If Thoreau instructs, Whitman declaims. He is the man, the seer; he was there. Writing to reflect the cadence of the people and using slang and the language of the street, he speaks for all Americans, or says he does, in a generous vision that encompasses all things. Such is the energy and force of *Leaves of Grass*. Originally published with a great, grand oratorical preface, crucial to understanding many of its poems and announcing what would become one of the most important directions in American writing, this book demonstrates—it proclaims—Whitman's sense of himself as an American poet. Here I am; there you are, he says; there we are, and there we shall go forward, as writers with a vision and vast as the country itself. And so even though it is often anthologized, sections of this preface are reproduced here. Later, in his autobiographical potpourri, *Specimen Days* (1882), a more subdued Whitman reflects on his life of writing, but still in his usual vatic fashion. Included here, then, are the final pages of *Specimen Days* and the conclusion written in 1887 for the English edition; later this conclusion was revised as the prose piece "A Backward Glance o'er Travel'd Roads," which was published in the last ("deathbed") edition of *Leaves of Grass* (1892), and in that form loses some of the heartfelt spontaneity of the earlier piece. Finally, we hear Whitman speak to us directly on writing in the transcriptions of his conversation made by his friend Horace Traubel in the last years of Whitman's life.

FROM PREFACE TO *LEAVES OF GRASS*

The American poets are to enclose old and new for America is the race of races. Of them a bard is to be commensurate with a people. To him the other continents arrive as contributions . . . he gives them reception for their sake and his own sake. His spirit responds to his country's spirit . . . he incarnates its geography and natural life and rivers and lakes. [. . .]

Of all nations the United States with veins full of poetical stuff most need poets and will doubtless have the greatest and use them the greatest. Their Presidents shall not be their common referee so much as their poets shall. Of all mankind the great poet is the equable man. Not in him but off from him things are grotesque or eccentric or fail of their sanity. Nothing out of its place is good and nothing in its place is bad. He bestows on every object or quality its fit proportions neither more nor less. He is the arbiter of the diverse and he is the key. He is the equalizer of his age and land . . . he supplies what wants supplying and checks what wants checking. If peace is the routine out of him speaks the spirit of peace, large, rich, thrifty, building vast and populous cities, encouraging agriculture and the arts and commerce—lighting the study of man, the soul, immortality—federal, state or municipal government, marriage, health, freetrade, intertravel by land and sea . . . nothing too close, nothing too far off . . . the stars not too far off. In war he is the most deadly force of the war. Who recruits him recruits horse and foot . . . he fetches parks of artillery the best that engineer ever knew. If the time becomes slothful and heavy he knows how to arouse it . . . he can make every word he speaks draw blood. Whatever stagnates in the flat of custom or obedience or legislation he never stagnates. Obedience does not master him, he masters it. High up out of reach he stands turning a concentrated light . . . he turns the pivot with his finger . . . he baffles the swiftest runners as he stands and easily overtakes and envelops them. The time straying toward infidelity and confections and persiflage he withholds by his steady faith . . . he spreads out his dishes . . . he offers the sweet firm-fibred meat that grows men and women. His brain is the ultimate brain. He is no arguer . . . he is judgment. He judges not as the judge judges but as the sun falling around a helpless thing. As he sees the farthest he has the most faith. His thoughts are the hymns of the praise of things. In the talk on the soul and eternity and God off of his equal plane he is silent. He sees eternity less like a play with a prologue and denouement . . . he sees eternity in men and women . . . he does not see men and women as dreams or dots. Faith is the antiseptic of the soul . . . it pervades the common people and preserves them . . . they never give up believing and expecting and trusting. There is that indescribable freshness and unconsciousness about an illiterate person that humbles and mocks the power of the noblest expressive genius. The poet sees for a certainty how one not a great artist may be just as sacred and perfect as the greatest artist. . . . The power to destroy or remould is freely used by him but never the power of attack. What is past is past. If he does not expose superior models and prove himself by every step he takes he is not what is wanted. The presence of the greatest poet conquers . . . not parleying or struggling or any prepared attempts. Now he has passed that way see after him! there is not left any vestige of despair or misanthropy or cunning or exclusiveness or the ignominy of a nativity or color or delusion of hell or the necessity of hell . . . and no man thenceforward shall be degraded for ignorance or weakness or sin.

The greatest poet hardly knows pettiness or triviality. If he breathes into any thing that was before thought small it dilates with the grandeur and life of the universe. He is a seer . . . he is individual . . . he is complete in himself . . . the others are as good as he, only he sees it and they do not. He is not one of the chorus . . . he does not stop for any regulation . . . he is the president of regulation. [. . .]

The messages of great poets to each man and woman are, Come to us on equal terms, Only then can you understand us, We are no better than you, What we enclose you enclose, What we enjoy you may enjoy. Did you suppose there could be only one Supreme? We affirm there can be unnumbered Supremes, and that one does not countervail another any more than one eyesight countervails another . . . and that men can be good or grand only of the consciousness of their supremacy within them. What do you think is the grandeur of storms and dismemberments and the deadliest battles and wrecks and the wildest fury of the elements and the power of the sea and the motion of nature and of the throes of human desires and dignity and hate and love? It is that something in the soul which says, Rage on, Whirl on, I tread master here and everywhere, Master of the spasms of the sky and of the shatter of the sea, Master of nature and passion and death, And of all terror and all pain.

The American bards shall be marked for generosity and affection and for encouraging competitors. . . . They shall be kosmos . . . without monopoly or secresy . . . glad to pass any thing to any one . . . hungry for equals night and day. They shall not be careful of riches and privilege . . . they shall be riches and privilege . . . they shall perceive who the most affluent man is. The most affluent man is he that confronts all the shows he sees by equivalents out of the stronger wealth of himself. The American bard shall delineate no class of persons nor one or two out of the strata of interests nor love most nor truth most nor the soul most nor the body most . . . and not be for the eastern states more than the western or the northern states more than the southern. [. . .]

As the attributes of the poets of the kosmos concentre in the real body and soul and in the pleasure of things they possess the superiority of genuineness over all fiction and romance. As they emit themselves facts are showered over with light . . . the daylight is lit with more volatile light . . . also the deep between the setting and rising sun goes deeper many fold. Each precise object or condition or combination or process exhibits a beauty . . . the multiplication table its—old age its—the carpenter's trade its—the grand opera its—the hugehulled cleanshaped New-York clipper at sea under steam or full sail gleams with unmatched beauty . . . the American circles and large harmonies of government gleam with theirs . . . and the commonest definite intentions and actions with theirs. The poets of the kosmos advance through all interpositions and coverings and turmoils and stratagems to first principles. They are of use . . . they dissolve poverty from its need and riches from its conceit. You large proprietor, they say, shall not realize or perceive more than any one else. The owner of the library is not he who holds a legal title to it having bought and paid for it. Any one and every one is owner of the library who can read the same through all the varieties of tongues and subjects and styles, and in whom they enter with ease and take residence and force toward paternity and maternity, and make supple and powerful and rich and large. [. . .]

The great poets are also to be known by the absence in them of tricks and by the justification of perfect personal candor. Then folks echo a new cheap joy and a divine voice leaping from their brains: How beautiful is candor! All faults may be forgiven of him who has perfect candor. Henceforth let no man of us lie, for we have seen that openness wins the inner and outer world and that there is no single exception, and that never since our earth gathered itself in a mass have deceit or subterfuge or prevarication attracted its smallest particle or the faintest tinge of a shade—and that through the enveloping wealth and rank of a state or the whole republic of states a sneak or sly person shall be discovered and despised . . . and that the soul has never once been fooled and never can be fooled . . . and thrift without the loving nod of the soul is only a fœtid puff . . . and there never grew up in any of the continents of the globe nor upon any planet or satellite or star, nor upon the asteroids, nor in any part of ethereal space, nor in the midst of density, nor under the fluid wet of the sea, nor in that condition which precedes the birth of babes, nor at any time during the changes of life, nor in that condition that follows what we term death, nor in any stretch of abeyance or action afterward of vitality, nor in any process of formation or reformation anywhere, a being whose instinct hated the truth.

Extreme caution or prudence, the soundest organic health, large hope and comparison and fondness for women and children, large alimentiveness and destructiveness and causality, with a perfect sense of the oneness of nature and the propriety of the same spirit applied to human affairs . . . these are called up of the float of the brain of the world to be parts of the greatest poet from his birth out of his mother's womb and from her birth out of her mother's. Caution seldom goes far enough. It has been thought that the prudent citizen was the citizen who applied himself to solid gains and did well for himself and for his family and completed a lawful life without debt or crime. The greatest poet sees and admits these economies as he sees the economies of food and sleep, but has higher notions of prudence than to think he gives much when he gives a few slight attentions at the latch of the gate. The premises of the prudence of life are not the hospitality of it or the ripeness and harvest of it. Beyond the independence of a little sum laid aside for burial-money, and of a few clapboards around and shingles overhead on a lot of American soil owned, and the easy dollars that supply the year's plain clothing and meals, the melancholy prudence of the abandonment of such a great being as a man is to the toss and pallor of years of money-making with all their scorching days and icy nights and all their

stifling deceits and underhanded dodgings, or infinitesimals of parlors, or
shameless stuffing while others starve . . . and all the loss of the bloom and
odor of the earth and of the flowers and atmosphere and of the sea, and of
the true taste of the women and men you pass or have to do with in youth
or middle age, and the issuing sickness and desperate revolt at the close
of a life without elevation or naivete, and the ghastly chatter of a death
without serenity or majesty, is the great fraud upon modern civilization and
forethought, blotching the surface and system which civilization undeni-
ably drafts, and moistening with tears the immense features it spreads and
spreads with such velocity before the reached kisses of the soul.

Still the right explanation remains to be made about prudence. The
prudence of the mere wealth and respectability of the most esteemed life
appears too faint for the eye to observe at all when little and large alike
drop quietly aside at the thought of the prudence suitable for immortality. What is wisdom that fills the thinness of a year or seventy or eighty
years to wisdom spaced out by ages and coming back at a certain time with
strong reinforcements and rich presents and the clear faces of wedding-
guests as far as you can look in every direction, running gaily toward you?
Only the soul is of itself . . . all else has reference to what ensues. All that a
person does or thinks is of consequence. Not a move can a man or woman
make that effects him or her in a day or a month or any part of the direct
lifetime or the hour of death but the same affects him or her onward
afterward through the indirect lifetime. The indirect is always as great
and real as the direct. The spirit receives from the body just as much as it
gives to the body. Not one name of word or deed . . . not of venereal sores
or discolorations . . . not the privacy of the onanist . . . not of the putrid
veins of gluttons or rumdrinkers . . . not peculation or cunning or betrayal
or murder . . . no serpentine poison of those that seduce women . . . not the
foolish yielding of women . . . not prostitution . . . not of any depravity of
young men . . . not of the attainment of gain by discreditable means . . . not
any nastiness of appetite . . . not any harshness of officers to men or judges
to prisoners or fathers to sons or sons to fathers or of husbands to wives or
bosses to their boys . . . not of greedy looks or malignant wishes . . . nor any
of the wiles practised by people upon themselves . . . ever is or ever can be
stamped on the programme but it is duly realized and returned, and that
returned in further performances . . . and they returned again. Nor can the

push of charity or personal force ever be anything else than the profoundest reason, whether it bring argument to hand or no. No specification is
necessary . . . to add or subtract or divide is in vain. Little or big, learned or
unlearned, white or black, legal or illegal, sick or well, from the first inspiration down the windpipe to the last expiration out of it, all that a male
or female does that is vigorous and benevolent and clean is so much sure
profit to him or her in the unshakable order of the universe and through
the whole scope of it for ever. If the savage or felon is wise it is well . . . if
the greatest poet or savan is wise it is simply the same . . . if the President
or chief justice is wise it is the same . . . if the young mechanic or farmer is
wise it is no more or less . . . if the prostitute is wise it is no more nor less.
The interest will come round . . . all will come round. All the best actions
of war and peace . . . all help given to relatives and strangers and the poor
and old and sorrowful and young children and widows and the sick, and
to all shunned persons . . . all furtherance of fugitives and of the escape
of slaves . . . all the self-denial that stood steady and aloof on wrecks and
saw others take the seats of the boats . . . all offering of substance or life
for the good old cause, or for a friend's sake or opinion's sake . . . all pains
of enthusiasts scoffed at by their neighbors . . . all the vast sweet love and
precious sufferings of mothers . . . all honest men baffled in strifes recorded
or unrecorded . . . all the grandeur and good of the few ancient nations
whose fragments of annals we inherit . . . and all the good of the hundreds
of far mightier and more ancient nations unknown to us by name or date
or location . . . all that was ever manfully begun, whether it succeeded or
no . . . all that has at any time been well suggested out of the divine heart of
man or by the divinity of his mouth or by the shaping of his great hands . . .
and all that is well thought or done this day on any part of the surface of
the globe . . . or on any of the wandering stars or fixed stars by those there
as we are here . . . or that is henceforth to be well thought or done by you
whoever you are, or by any one—these singly and wholly inured at their
time and inure now and will inure always to the identities from which they
sprung or shall spring. . . . Did you guess any of them lived only its moment?
The world does not so exist . . . no parts palpable or impalpable so exist . . .
no result exists now without being from its long antecedent result, and that
from its antecedent, and so backward without the farthest mentionable

spot coming a bit nearer the beginning than any other spot. . . . Whatever satisfies the soul is truth. The prudence of the greatest poet answers at last the craving and glut of the soul, is not contemptuous of less ways of prudence if they conform to its ways, puts off nothing, permits no let-up for its own case or any case, has no particular sabbath or judgment-day, divides not the living from the dead or the righteous from the unrighteous, is satisfied with the present, matches every thought or act by its correlative, knows no possible forgiveness or deputed atonement . . . knows that the young man who composedly perilled his life and lost it has done exceeding well for himself, while the man who has not perilled his life and retains to old age in riches and ease has perhaps achieved nothing for himself worth mentioning . . . and that only that person has no great prudence to learn who has learnt to prefer real longlived things, and favors body and soul the same, and perceives the indirect assuredly following the direct, and what evil or good he does leaping onward and waiting to meet him again—and who in his spirit in any emergency whatever neither hurries or avoids death.

The direct trial of him who would be the greatest poet is to-day. If he does not flood himself with the immediate age as with vast oceanic tides . . . and if he does not attract his own land body and soul to himself, and hang on its neck with incomparable love and plunge his semitic muscle into its merits and demerits . . . and if he be not himself the age transfigured . . . and if to him is not opened the eternity which gives similitude to all periods and locations and processes and animate and inanimate forms, and which is the bond of time, and rises up from its inconceivable vagueness and infiniteness in the swimming shape of to-day, and is held by the ductile anchors of life, and makes the present spot the passage from what was to what shall be, and commits itself to the representation of this wave of an hour and this one of the sixty beautiful children of the wave—let him merge in the general run and wait his development.

Still the final test of poems or any character or work remains. The prescient poet projects himself centuries ahead and judges performer or performance after the changes of time. Does it live through them? Does it still hold on untired? Will the same style and the direction of genius to similar points be satisfactory now? Has no new discovery in science or arrival at superior planes of thought and judgment and behavior fixed him or his so that either can be looked down upon? Have the marches of tens and hundreds and thousands of years made willing detours to the right hand and the left hand for his sake? Is he beloved long and long after he is buried? Does the young man think often of him? and the young woman think often of him? and do the middle aged and the old think of him?

A great poem is for ages and ages in common, and for all degrees and complexions, and all departments and sects, and for a woman as much as a man and a man as much as a woman. A great poem is no finish to a man or woman but rather a beginning. Has any one fancied he could sit at last under some due authority and rest satisfied with explanations and realize and be content and full? To no such terminus does the greatest poet bring . . . he brings neither cessation or sheltered fatness and ease. The touch of him tells in action. Whom he takes he takes with firm sure grasp into live regions previously unattained . . . thenceforward is no rest . . . they see the space and ineffable sheen that turn the old spots and lights into dead vacuums. The companion of him beholds the birth and progress of stars and learns one of the meanings. Now there shall be a man cohered out of tumult and chaos . . . the elder encourages the younger and shows him how . . . they too shall launch off fearlessly together till the new world fits an orbit for itself and looks unabashed on the lesser orbits of the stars and sweeps through the ceaseless rings and shall never be quiet again.

There will soon be no more priests. Their work is done. They may wait awhile . . . perhaps a generation or two . . . dropping off by degrees. A superior breed shall take their place . . . the gangs of kosmos and prophets en masse shall take their place. A new order shall arise and they shall be the priests of man, and every man shall be his own priest. The churches built under their umbrage shall be the churches of men and women. Through the divinity of themselves shall the kosmos and the new breed of poets be interpreters of men and women and of all events and things. They shall find their inspiration in real objects to-day, symptoms of the past and future . . . They shall not deign to defend immortality or God or the perfection of things or liberty or the exquisite beauty and reality of the soul. They shall arise in America and be responded to from the remainder of the earth.

The English language befriends the grand American expression . . . it is brawny enough and limber and full enough . . . on the tough stock of a race who through all change of circumstance was never without the idea of political liberty, which is the animus of all liberty, it has attracted the terms of daintier and gayer and subtler and more elegant tongues. It is the powerful language of resistance . . . it is the dialect of common sense. It is the speech of the proud and melancholy races and of all who aspire. It is the chosen tongue to express growth faith self-esteem freedom justice equality friendliness amplitude prudence decision and courage. It is the medium that shall well nigh express the inexpressible.

No great literature nor any like style of behavior or oratory or social intercourse or household arrangements or public institutions or the treatment of bosses of employed people, nor executive detail or detail of the army and navy, nor spirit of legislation or courts or police or tuition or architecture or songs or amusements or the costumes of young men, can long elude the jealous and passionate instinct of American standards. Whether or no the sign appears from the mouths of the people, it throbs a live interrogation in every freeman's and freewoman's heart after that which passes by or this built to remain. Is it uniform with my country? Are its disposals without ignominious distinctions? Is it for the ever growing communes of brothers and lovers, large, well-united, proud beyond the old models, generous beyond all models? Is it something grown fresh out of the fields or drawn from the sea for use to me today here? I know that what answers for me an American must answer for any individual or nation that serves for a part of my materials. Does this answer? or is it without reference to universal needs? or sprung of the needs of the less developed society of special ranks? or old needs of pleasure overlaid by modern science or forms? Does this acknowledge liberty with audible and absolute acknowledgment, and set slavery at nought for life and death? Will it help breed one goodshaped and wellhung man, and a woman to be his perfect and independent mate? Does it improve manners? Is it for the nursing of the young of the republic? Does it solve readily with the sweet milk of the nipples of the breasts of the mother of many children? Has it too the old ever-fresh forbearance and impartiality? Does it look for the same love on the last born and on those hardening toward stature, and on the errant, and on those who disdain all strength of assault outside their own?

The poems distilled from other poems will probably pass away. The coward will surely pass away. The expectation of the vital and great can only be satisfied by the demeanor of the vital and great. The swarms of the polished deprecating and reflectors and the polite float off and leave no remembrance. America prepares with composure and goodwill for the visitors that have sent word. It is not intellect that is to be their warrant and welcome. The talented, the artist, the ingenious, the editor, the statesman, the erudite . . . they are not unappreciated . . . they fall in their place and do their work. The soul of the nation also does its work. No disguise can pass on it . . . no disguise can conceal from it. It rejects none, it permits all. Only toward as good as itself and toward the like of itself will it advance half-way. An individual is as superb as a nation when he has the qualities which make a superb nation. The soul of the largest and wealthiest and proudest nation may well go half-way to meet that of its poets. The signs are effectual. There is no fear of mistake. If the one is true the other is true. The proof of a poet is that his country absorbs him as affectionately as he has absorbed it.

FROM *SPECIMEN DAYS*

In reflections of objects, scenes, Nature's outpourings, to my senses and receptivity, as they seem'd to me—in the work of giving those who care for it, some authentic glints, specimen-days of my life—and in the bona fide spirit and relations, from author to reader, on all the subjects design'd, and as far as they go, I feel to make unmitigated claims.

The synopsis of my early life, Long Island, New York city, and so forth, and the diary-jottings in the Secession war, tell their own story. My plan in starting what constitutes most of the middle of the book, was originally for hints and data of a Nature-poem that should carry one's experiences a few hours, commencing at noon-flush, and so through the after-part of the day—I suppose led to such idea by my own life-afternoon now arrived. But I soon found I could move at more ease, by giving the narrative at first hand. (Then there is a humiliating lesson one learns, in serene hours, of a fine day or night. Nature seems to look on all fixed-up poetry and art as something almost impertinent.)

Thus I went on, years following, various seasons and areas, spinning forth my thought beneath the night and stars, (or as I was confined to my room by half-sickness,) or at midday looking out upon the sea, or far north steaming over the Saguenay's black breast, jotting all down in the loosest sort of chronological order, and here printing from my impromptu notes, hardly even the seasons group'd together, or anything corrected—so afraid of dropping what smack of outdoors or sun or starlight might cling to the lines, I dared not try to meddle with or smooth them. Every now and then, (not often, but for a foil,) I carried a book in my pocket—or perhaps tore out from some broken or cheap edition a bunch of loose leaves; most always had something of the sort ready, but only took it out when the mood demanded. In that way, utterly out of reach of literary conventions, I re-read many authors.

I cannot divest my appetite of literature, yet I find myself eventually trying it all by Nature—*first premises* many call it, but really the crowning results of all, laws, tallies and proofs. (Has it never occur'd to any one how the last deciding tests applicable to a book are entirely outside of technical and grammatical ones, and that any truly first-class production has little or nothing to do with the rules and calibres of ordinary critics? or the blood-less chalk of Allibone's Dictionary? I have fancied the ocean and the day-light, the mountain and the forest, putting their spirit in a judgment on our books. I have fancied some disembodied human soul giving its verdict.) . . .

Thus the last 14 years have passed. At present (end-days of March 1887— I am nigh entering my 69th year) I find myself continuing on here, quite dilapidated and even wreck'd bodily from the paralysis, etc.—but in good heart (to use a Long Island country phrase,) and with about the same men-tality as ever. The worst of it is, I have been growing feebler quite rapidly for a year, and now can't walk around—hardly from one room to the next. I am forced to stay in-doors and in my big chair nearly all the time. We have had a sharp, dreary winter too,. and it has pinched me. I am alone most of the time; every week, indeed almost every day, write some—reminiscences, essays, sketches, for the magazines; and read, or rather I should say dawdle over books and papers a good deal—spend half the day at that.

Nor can I finish this note without putting on record—wafting over sea from hence—my deepest thanks to certain friends and helpers (I would specify them all and each by name, but imperative reasons, outside of my own wishes, forbid,) in the British Islands, as well as in America. Dear, even in the abstract, is such flattering unction always no doubt to the soul! Nigher still, if possible, I myself have been, and am to-day indebted to such help for my very sustenance, clothing, shelter, and continuity. And I would not go to the grave without briefly, but plainly, as I here do, acknowledging—may I not say even glorying in it?

Finally, dear reader, to end all gossip and egotism, let me give you one of my own cherish'd thoughts for a parting word. I wrote and published it anent of "Leaves of Grass," but it will do just as well for the preceding volume:—Ever since what might be called thought, or the budding of thought, fairly began in my youthful mind, I had a desire to attempt some worthy record of that entire faith and acceptance ("to justify the ways of God to man" is Milton's well-known and ambitious phrase) which is the foundation of moral America. I felt it all as positively then in my young days as I do now in my old ones. To formulate a poem whose every line should directly or indirectly be an implicit belief in the wisdom, health, mystery, beauty of every process, every concrete object, every human or other existence, not only considered from the point of all, but of each. While I can not understand it or argue it out, I fully believe in a clue and purpose in Nature, entire and several; and that invisible spiritual results, just as real and definite as the visible, eventuate all concrete life and all materialism, through Time. The book [*Leaves of Grass*] ought to emanate buoyancy and gladness, too, for it has grown out of those elements, and has been the comfort of my life since it was originally commenced. I should be willing to jaunt the whole life over again, with all its worldly failures and serious detriments, deficiencies and denials, to get the happiness of retraveling that part of the road.

In the free evening of my day I give to you, whoever you are perusing this work, the foregoing garrulous talk, thoughts, reminiscences,

> As idly drifting down the ebb
> Such ripples, half-caught glimpses, echoes from the shore.

FROM *WITH WALT WHITMAN IN CAMDEN*

MAY 22, 1888

I don't seem to have any advice to give, except perhaps this: Be natural, be natural, be natural! Be a damned fool, be wise if you must (can't help it), be anything—only be natural! Almost any writer who is willing to be himself will amount to something—because we all amount to something, to about the same thing, at the roots. The trouble mostly is that writers become writers and cease to be men; writers reflect writers, writers again reflect writers, until the man is worn thin—worn through.

FROM *WITH WALT WHITMAN IN CAMDEN*

JULY 22, 1888

The secret of it all, is to write in the gush, the throb, the flood, of the moment—to put things down without deliberation—without worrying about their style—without waiting for a fit time or place. I always worked that way. I took the first scrap of paper, the first doorstep, the first desk, and wrote—wrote, wrote. No prepared picture, no elaborated poem, no after-narrative could be what the thing itself is. You want to catch its first spirit—to tally its birth. By writing at the instant the very heart-beat of life is caught.

FROM *WITH WALT WHITMAN IN CAMDEN*

OCTOBER 16, 1888

My rule has been, so far as I could have any rule (I could have no cast-iron rule)—my rule has been, to write what I have to say the best way I can—then lay it aside—taking it up again after some time and reading it afresh—the mind new to it. If there's no jar in the new reading, well and good—that's sufficient for me.

FROM *WITH WALT WHITMAN IN CAMDEN*

JUNE 23, 1888

The best writing has no lace on its sleeves.

Ulysses S. Grant

(1822–1885)

Why is President Grant here? The man considered for many years one of America's worst presidents is considered, too, if not a strategic genius during the Civil War, then an unfeeling butcher. Yet Whitman, in his *Specimen Days*, said Grant was nothing heroic, "yet the greatest hero," and Mark Twain thought Grant's *Memoirs* (1885) "a model narrative that will last as long as the language lasts." (It was Twain who encouraged the former president, at the end of his life, to write his memoirs.) And in the next century, Gertrude Stein noted more than once that she considered Grant's *Memoirs* one of the greatest of all American books. "I cannot think of Ulysses Simpson Grant without tears," she once remarked. It is a great book. To the extent that the nineteenth century was the age of nonfiction narrative, Grant's *Memoirs* holds its own with such masterworks as Emerson's *Nature*, Thoreau's *Walden*, Douglass's *Narrative*, and Alice James's *Diary*, to name just a few. The excerpt, then, is taken from the preface to the *Memoirs*, where Grant tells us why he wrote it—and he implies what it means to him—in the terms of direct, unaffected, and pellucid style that characterized the entire volume as well as much of the man's career, which is constantly being reevaluated. Not, however, his *Memoirs*. They shine.

FROM *PERSONAL MEMOIRS OF U. S. GRANT*

MOUNT MACGREGOR, NEW YORK, JULY 1, 1885

"Man proposes and God disposes." There are but few important events in the affairs of men brought about by their own choice.

Although frequently urged by friends to write my memoirs I had determined never to do so, nor to write anything for publication. At the age of nearly sixty-two I received an injury from a fall, which confined me closely to the house while it did not apparently affect my general health. This made study a pleasant pastime. Shortly after, the rascality of a business partner developed itself by the announcement of a failure. This was followed soon after by universal depression of all securities, which seemed to threaten the extinction of a good part of the income still retained, and for which I am indebted to the kindly act of friends. At this juncture the editor of the *Century Magazine* asked me to write a few articles for him. I consented for the money it gave me; for at that moment I was living upon borrowed money. The work I found congenial, and I determined to continue it. The event is an important one for me, for good or evil; I hope for the former.

In preparing these volumes for the public, I have entered upon the task with the sincere desire to avoid doing injustice to any one, whether on the National or Confederate side, other than the unavoidable injustice of not making mention often where special mention is due. There must be many errors of omission in this work, because the subject is too large to be treated of in two volumes in such way as to do justice to all the officers and men engaged. There were thousands of instances, during the rebellion, of individual, company, regimental and brigade deeds of heroism which deserve special mention and are not here alluded to. The troops engaged in them will have to look to the detailed reports of their individual commanders for the full history of those deeds.

The first volume, as well as a portion of the second, was written before I had reason to suppose I was in a critical condition of health. Later I was reduced almost to the point of death, and it became impossible for me to attend to anything for weeks. I have, however, somewhat regained my strength, and am able, often, to devote as many hours a day as a person should devote to such work. I would have more hope of satisfying the expectation of the public if I could have allowed myself more time. I have used my best efforts, with the aid of my eldest son, F. D. Grant, assisted by his brothers, to verify from the records every statement of fact given. The comments are my own, and show how I saw the matters treated of whether others saw them in the same light or not.

With these remarks I present these volumes to the public, asking no favor but hoping they will meet the approval of the reader.

Mary Boykin Chesnut

(1823–1886)

Married to a secessionist member of the United States Senate, Mary Boykin
Miller Chesnut did not however support the institution of slavery, even
though she firmly believed in states' rights. A southerner (from South
Carolina), she was a celebrated, well-read, gracious, and brilliant hostess
before the war. During the war she frequently accompanied her husband,
then a Confederate brigadier general, from post to Confederate outpost:
Montgomery, Alabama; Charleston, South Carolina; Richmond, Virginia;
North Carolina. All the while, she kept a wartime diary—an extraordinary
document, as Edmund Wilson noted, a literary masterpiece of clarity, insight,
and acute novelistic detail mustered together in an increasingly desperate
situation.

She rewrote and expanded the diary, some of which was published in
1905, long after her death, and in 1981 the historian C. Vann Woodward produced the Pulitzer Prize–winning *Mary Chesnut's Civil War;* three years later,
he and Elisabeth Muhlenfeld published an edition of the original diaries as
The Private Mary Chesnut: The Unpublished Civil War Diaries.

The following excerpts reflect the diarist's inevitable self-consciousness,
her awareness of the volatility of so-called fact (what she calls "current

rumor"); her sense of mission, private and public; her need of narrative and of those writers—Horace, Shakespeare, Pascal, Sir Thomas Browne—who offer comfort where there is none. Such is the solace of the word, particularly in wartime.

FROM *MARY CHESNUT'S CIVIL WAR*

MARCH 1861

What nonsense I write here. However, this journal is intended to be entirely *objective*. My subjective days are over. No more *silent* seating into my own heart, making my own misery, when without these morbid fantasies I could be so happy. [. . .]

I think this journal will be disadvantageous for me, for I spend the time now like a spider, spinning my own entrails instead of reading, as my habit was at all spare moments.

AUGUST 1861

"The Terror" has full swing at the North now. All papers favorable to us have been suppressed.

How long would one mob stand a Yankee paper here? But newspapers against our government, such as the Examiner and the Mercury, flourish like green bay trees.

A man up to the elbows in finance said today: "Clayton's story is all nonsense. They did pay out two million that week, but they paid the soldiers. They don't pay the soldiers every week."

"Not by a long shot," cried a soldier laddie with a gun.

"Why do you write in your diary at all, if, as you say, you have to contradict every day what you wrote yesterday?"

"Because I tell the tale as it is told to me. I write current rumor. I do not vouch for anything."

NOVEMBER 12, 1861

. . . everybody reads my journal as it lies on the table in my room.

DECEMBER 13, 1861

Everybody reads my journal, but since I have been making sketches of character at Mulberry I keep it under lock and key. Yesterday I handed this book to my new little maid Ellen, who is a sort of apprentice under Betsey, trying to learn her trade. When I gave Ellen the book I pointed to an armoire. She mistook the direction of my finger and took it into Miss Sally Chesnut's room, where she laid it on the table.

Today I looked for it in the armoire. It was gone. "Ellen, where is the book I write in? I gave it to you." She flew into Miss S. C.'s room, which happened to be empty just then, and brought it. Words were useless. And in my plain speaking and candor, what I have not said—intending no eye save mine to rest upon this page.

The things I cannot tell exactly as they are I do not intend to tell at all.

MARCH 10, 1862

Congaree House. Second year. Confederate independence. I write daily for my own distractions. These memoirs pour servir may some future day afford dates, facts, and prove useful to more important people than I am. I do not wish to do any harm or to hurt anyone. If any scandalous stories creep in, they are easily burned. It is hard, in such a hurry as things are in, to separate wheat from chaff.

Now I have made my protest and written down my wishes. I can scribble on with a free will and free conscience.

I destroyed all my notes and journal—from the time I arrived at Flat Rock—during a raid upon Richmond in 1863. Afterward—I tried to fill up the gap from memory.

SEPTEMBER 23, 1863

Bloomsbury. So this is no longer a journal but a narrative of all I cannot bear in mind which has occurred since August 1862. So I will tell all I know of that brave spirit, George Cuthbert. During the winter of '63, while I was living at the corner of Clay and 12th St., he came to see me. Never did many enjoy life more. The Preston girls were staying at my house then, and it was very gay for the young soldiers who ran down from the army for a day or so. We had heard of him, as usual gallantly facing odds at Sharpsburg. And he asked, if he should chance to be wounded, would I have him brought to Clay St.

He was shot at Chancellorsville, leading his men. The surgeon did not think him mortally wounded. He sent me a message that he was coming at once to our house. He knew he would soon get well there. Also that I need not be alarmed; those Yankees could not kill him.

He asked one of his friends to write a letter to his mother. Afterward he said he had another letter to write but that he wished to sleep first—he felt so exhausted. At his request they then turned his face away from the light and left him. When they came again to look after him, they found him dead. He had been dead for a long time. It was so bitter cold—and the wounded who had lost so much blood weakened in that way. Lacking warm blankets and all comforts, many died who might have been saved by one good hot drink or a few mouthfuls of nourishing food.

One of his generals said to me: "Fire and reckless courage like Captain Cuthbert's were contagious. Such men in an army were invaluable. Such losses weakened us indeed."

But I must go back to Flat Rock and not linger longer around the memory of the bravest of the brave—a true specimen of our old regime—gallant, gay, unfortunate.

NOVEMBER 25, 1864

Things are growing hopelessly mixed up.

My journal—a quire of Confederate paper—lies wide open on my desk in the corner of my drawing room. Everybody reads it who chooses. Buck came regularly to see what I had written last and made faces when it did not suit her. Isabella calls me Cassandra and puts her hands to her ears when I begin to wail. Well, Cassandra only records what she hears—she does not vouch for it. For really, one never nowadays feels certain of anything.

FEBRUARY 1865

My days are past—my purposes broken off—even the thoughts of my heart (Job).

Be fair or foul—or rain, or shine,
The joys I have possessed in spite of fate are mine,

Not Jove himself upon the past has power,
What has been—has been—and I have had my hour.

"Time and the hour run through the roughest day."

Mrs. Glover gave us Dr. Palmer's last sermon. "We are on a lone rock—Atlantic and Pacific Ocean surging around—every point of land submerged—we alone—the waters closing over us—slowly but surely."

MARCH 12, 1865

Then they overhauled my library, which was on the floor because the only table in the room they had used for a tea table.

Shakespeare—Molière—Sir Thomas Browne—*Arabian Nights* in French—Pascal's letters—folk songs.

"*Lear* I read last. The tragedy of the world—it entered into my heart to understand it first—now."

"Spare us Regan and Goneril and the storm and eyeballs rolling around."

"And an old king, and I am every inch a king."

That is not it. It is the laying bare the seamy side—going behind the pretty curtain of propriety we hold up. Poor humanity morally stripped makes us shiver. Look at that judge—look at that thief. Preston—change sides—which is the judge, which is the thief? And more unmentionable horrors.

Thomas Wentworth Higginson

(1823–1911)

Said Thoreau of Thomas Higginson: he was "the only Harvard Phi Beta Kappa, Unitarian minister, and master of seven languages who has led a storming party against a federal bastion with a battering ram in his hands." True enough—in 1854 Thomas Wentworth Higginson attempted to free the fugitive slave Anthony Burns; this was just one of his many exploits as a longtime abolitionist. During the Civil War he became leader of the first federally authorized regiment of black troops; his book about this experience, *Army Life in a Black Regiment* (1869), remains astonishing. At this time, he also became the friend and confidant of none other than Emily Dickinson, whom he visited twice. Contacting him in 1862 to ask whether he was "too deeply occupied to say if my Verse is alive?," Dickinson had just read his *Atlantic Monthly* article "Letter to a Young Contributor," though later she admitted to reading everything he ever wrote, no mean feat; for this was a man who wrote easily, fluidly, elegantly, and prolifically about all manner of subjects: slave uprisings, physical fitness, equal rights, and civil rights as well as the subjects fascinating to her: writing, nature, and the relation between them.

She quoted, for instance, his sentence from "Letter to a Young Contributor" that "such being the majesty of the art you seek to practise, you can at least take time and deliberation before dishonoring it." Since Higginson's commonsensical, supportive, and amusing essay, often anthologized, does not give one the full range of what Dickinson so deeply admired in this radical agitator and prose stylist, only a section of it is included; also excerpted are passages from two of Higginson's nature essays published before "Letter"; the subsequent passages also exemplify what early drew the reclusive Dickinson to a man seemingly unlike her but who also questioned convention, propriety, and the status quo.

FROM "WATER-LILIES"

1858

The fair vision will not fade from us, though the paddle has dipped its last crystal drop from the waves, and the boat is drawn upon the shore. We may yet visit many lovely and lonely places,—meadows thick with violet, or the homes of the shy Rhodora, or those sloping forest-haunts where the slight Linnina hangs its twin-born heads,—but no scene will linger on our vision like this annual Feast of the Lilies. On scorching mountains, amid raw prairie-winds, or upon the regal ocean, the white pageant shall come back to us again, with all the luxury of summer heats, and all the fragrant coolness that can relieve them. We shall fancy ourselves again among these fleets of anchored lilies,—again, like Urvasi, sporting amid the Lake of Lotuses.

For that which is remembered is often more vivid than that which is seen. The eye paints better in the presence, the heart in the absence, of the object most dear. "He who longs after beautiful Nature can best describe her," said Bettine; "he who is in the midst of her loveliness can only lie down and enjoy." It enhances the truth of the poet's verses, that he writes them in his study. Absence is the very air of passion, and all the best description is in memoriam. As with our human beloved, when the graceful presence is with us, we cannot analyze or describe, but merely possess, and only after its departure can it be portrayed by our yearning desires; so is it with Nature: only in losing her do we gain the power to describe her, and we are introduced to Art, as we are to Eternity, by the dropping away of our companions.

FROM "MY OUT-DOOR STUDY"

1861

What has been done by all the art and literature of the world towards describing one summer day? The most exhausting effort brings us no nearer to it than to the blue sky which is its dome; our words are shot up against it like arrows, and fall back helpless. Literary amateurs go the tour of the globe to renew their stock of materials, when they do not yet know a bird or a bee or a blossom beside their homestead-door; and in the hour of their greatest success they have not an horizon to their life so large as that of yonder boy in his punt. All that is purchasable in the capitals of the world is not to be weighed in comparison with the simple enjoyment that may be crowded into one hour of sunshine. [. . .]

For literary training, especially, the influence of natural beauty is simply priceless. Under the present educational systems, we need grammars and languages far less than a more thorough out-door experience. On this flowery bank, on this ripple-marked shore, are the true literary models. How many living authors have ever attained to writing a single page which could be for one moment compared, for the simplicity and grace of its structure, with this green spray of wild woodbine or yonder white wreath of blossoming clematis? A finely organized sentence should throb and palpitate like the most delicate vibrations of the summer air. We talk of literature as if it were a mere matter of rule and measurement, a series of processes long since brought to mechanical perfection: but it would be less incorrect to say that it all lies in the future; tried by the outdoor standard, there is as yet no literature, but only glimpses and guideboards; no writer has yet succeeded in sustaining, through more than some single occasional sentence, that fresh and perfect charm. If by the training of a lifetime one could succeed in producing one continuous page of perfect cadence, it would be a life well spent, and such a literary artist would fall short of Nature's standard in quantity only, not in quality.

It is one sign of our weakness, also, that we commonly assume Nature to be a rather fragile and merely ornamental thing, and suited for a model of the graces only. But her seductive softness is the last climax of magnificent strength. The same mathematical law winds the leaves around the stem and the planets round the sun. The same law of crystallization rules the slight-knit snow-flake and the hard foundations of the earth. The thistle-down floats secure upon the same summer zephyrs that are woven into the tornado. The dew-drop holds within its transparent cell the same electric fire which charges the thunder-cloud. In the softest tree or the airiest water-fall, the fundamental lines are as lithe and muscular as the crouching haunches of a leopard; and without a pencil vigorous enough to render these, no mere mass of foam or foliage, however exquisitely finished, can tell the story. Lightness of touch is the crowning test of power.

Yet Nature does not work by single spasms only. That chestnut spray is not an isolated and exhaustive effort of creative beauty: look upward and see its sisters rise with pile above pile of fresh and stately verdure, till tree meets sky in a dome of glorious blossom, the whole as perfect as the parts, the least part as perfect as the whole. Studying the details, it seems as if Nature were a series of costly fragments with no coherency,—as if she would never encourage us to do anything systematically,—would tolerate no method but her own, and yet had none of her own,—were as abrupt in her transitions from oak to maple as the heroine who went into the garden to cut a cabbage-leaf to make an apple-pie; while yet there is no conceivable human logic so close and inexorable as her connections. How rigid, how flexible are, for instance, the laws of perspective! If one could learn to make his statements as firm and unswerving as the horizon-line,—his continuity of thought as marked, yet as unbroken, as yonder soft gradations by which the eye is lured upward from lake to wood, from wood to hill, from hill to heavens,—what more bracing tonic could literary culture demand? As it is, Art misses the parts, yet does not grasp the whole.

Literature also learns from Nature the use of materials: either to select only the choicest and rarest, or to transmute coarse to fine by skill in using. How perfect is the delicacy with which the woods and fields are kept, throughout the year! All these millions of living creatures born every season, and born to die; yet where are the dead bodies? We never see them.

Buried beneath the earth by tiny nightly sextons, sunk beneath the waters, dissolved into the air, or distilled again and again as food for other organizations,—all have had their swift resurrection. Their existence blooms again in these violet-petals, glitters in the burnished beauty of these golden beetles, or enriches the veery's song. It is only out of doors that even death and decay become beautiful. The model farm, the most luxurious house, have their regions of unsightliness; but the fine chemistry of Nature is constantly clearing away all its impurities before our eyes, and yet so delicately that we never suspect the process. The most exquisite work of literary art exhibits a certain crudeness and coarseness, when we turn to it from Nature,—as the smallest cambric needle appears rough and jagged, when compared through the magnifier with the tapering fineness of the insect's sting.

Once separated from Nature, literature recedes into metaphysics. [. . .]

On this continent, especially, people fancied that all must be tame and second-hand, everything long since duly analyzed and distributed and put up in appropriate quotations, and nothing left for us poor American children but a preoccupied universe. And yet Thoreau camps down by Walden Pond and shows us that absolutely nothing in Nature has ever yet been described,—not a bird nor a berry of the woods, nor a drop of water, nor a spicula of ice, nor summer, nor winter, nor sun, nor star.

FROM "LETTER TO A YOUNG CONTRIBUTOR"

1862

Do not despise any honest propitiation, however small, in dealing with your editor. Look to the physical aspect of your manuscript, and prepare your page so neatly that it shall allure instead of repelling. Use good pens, black ink, nice white paper and plenty of it. Do not emulate "paper-sparing Pope," whose chaotic manuscript of the "Iliad," written chiefly on the backs of old letters, still remains in the British Museum. If your document be slovenly, the presumption is that its literary execution is the same, Pope to the contrary notwithstanding. An editor's eye becomes carnal, and is easily attracted by a comely outside. If you really wish to obtain his good-will for your production, do not first tax his time for deciphering it, any more than in visiting a millionaire to solicit a loan you would begin by asking him to pay for the hire of the carriage which takes you to his door.

On the same principle, send your composition in such a shape that it shall not need the slightest literary revision before printing. Many a bright production dies discarded which might have been made thoroughly presentable by a single day's labor of a competent scholar, in shaping, smoothing, dovetailing, and retrenching. The revision seems so slight an affair that the aspirant cannot conceive why there should be so much fuss about it. [. . .]

Rules for style, as for manners, must be chiefly negative: a positively good style indicates certain natural powers in the individual, but an unexceptionable style is merely a matter of culture and good models. Dr. Channing established in New England a standard of style which really attained almost the perfection of the pure and the colorless, and the disciplinary value of such a literary influence, in a raw and crude nation, has been very great; but the defect of this standard is that it ends in utterly renouncing all the great traditions of literature, and ignoring the magnificent mystery of words. Human language may be polite and powerless in itself, uplifted with difficulty into expression by the high thoughts it utters, or it may in itself become so saturated with warm life and delicious association that every sentence shall palpitate and thrill with the mere fascination of the syllables. The statue is not more surely included in the block of marble than is all conceivable splendor of utterance in "Worcester's Unabridged." And as Ruskin says of painting that it is in the perfection and precision of the instantaneous line that the claim to immortality is made, so it is easy to see that a phrase may outweigh a library. Keats heads the catalogue of things real with "sun, moon, and passages of Shakespeare"; and Keats himself has left behind him winged wonders of expression which are not surpassed by Shakespeare, or by any one else who ever dared touch the English tongue. There may be phrases which shall be palaces to dwell in, treasure-houses to explore; a single word may be a window from which one may perceive all the kingdoms of the earth and the glory of them. Oftentimes a word shall speak what accumulated volumes have labored in vain to utter: there may be years of crowded passion in a word, and half a life in a sentence.

Such being the majesty of the art you seek to practise, you can at least take time and deliberation before dishonoring it. [. . .]

So few men in any age are born with a marked gift for literary expression, so few of this number have access to high culture, so few even of these have the personal nobleness to use their powers well, and this small band is finally so decimated by disease and manifold disaster, that it makes one shudder to observe how little of the embodied intellect of any age is left behind. Literature is attar of roses, one distilled drop from a million blossoms. [. . .]

Yet, if our life be immortal, this temporary distinction is of little moment, and we may learn humility, without learning despair, from earth's evanescent glories. Who cannot bear a few disappointments, if the vista be so wide that the mute inglorious Miltons of this sphere may in some other sing their Paradise as Found? War or peace, fame or forgetfulness, can bring no real injury to one who has formed the fixed purpose to live nobly day by day. I fancy that in some other realm of existence we may look back with a kindly interest on this scene of our earlier life, and say to one another, "Do you remember yonder planet, where once we went to school?" And whether our elective study here lay chiefly in the fields of action or of thought will matter little to us then, when other schools shall have led us through other disciplines.

FROM "THE PROCESSION OF THE FLOWERS"

1862

We strive to picture heaven, when we are barely at the threshold of the inconceivable beauty of earth. Perhaps the truant boy who simply bathes himself in the lake and then basks in the sunshine, dimly conscious of the exquisite loveliness around him, is wiser, because humbler, than is he who with presumptuous phrases tries to utter it. There are multitudes of moments when the atmosphere is so surcharged with luxury that every pore of the body becomes an ample gate for sensation to flow in, and one has simply to sit still and be filled. In after-years the memory of books seems barren or vanishing, compared with the immortal bequest of hours like these.

[. . .] No man can measure what a single hour with Nature may have contributed to the moulding of his mind. The influence is self-renewing, and if for a long time it baffles expression by reason of its fineness, so much the better in the end. [. . .]

If, in the simple process of writing, one could physically impart to this page the fragrance of this spray of azalea beside me, what a wonder would it seem and yet one ought to be able, by the mere use of language, to supply to every reader the total of that white, honeyed, trailing sweetness, which summer insects haunt and the Spirit of the Universe loves. The defect is not in language, but in men. There is no conceivable beauty of blossom so beautiful as words, none so graceful, none so perfumed. It is possible to dream of combinations of syllables so delicious that all the dawning and decay of summer cannot rival their perfection, nor winters stainless white and azure match their purity and their charm. To write them, were it possible, would be to take rank with Nature; nor is there any other method, even by music, for human art to reach so high.

FROM "LITERATURE AS AN ART"

1867

Probably the truth is, that art precedes criticism, and that every great writer creates or revives the taste by which he is appreciated.

Francis Parkman

(1823–1893)

The Oregon Trail, Francis Parkman's masterpiece, grew out of a trip that the
Boston Brahmin had taken with a cousin to the Wyoming Territory, California, St. Louis, Fort Laramie, and other frontier sites where he studied Native
Americans and tried, as Theodore Roosevelt later would, to compensate for
his frail, sickly constitution. ("Pluck is a good thing," he told a friend, "but so
is a good carcass.") Beset for a lifetime by depression, insomnia, headaches,
rheumatism, and indigestion as well as such weak eyesight that he often
wrote in the dark, Parkman was an estimable historian nonetheless, one
of the very best. With quick, narrative style, he chronicled the presence of
the French in Canada until they surrendered it to the British (the subject of
his wonderful volume *Montcalm and Wolfe*, 1884). And as a crack writer of
narrative nonfiction—a forte of the nineteenth century—Parkman is rightly
considered in the same breath as Thoreau, Richard Henry Dana, Grant, and,
later, even Hemingway.

In this excerpt, Parkman's preface to the 1851 edition of *The Conspiracy
of Pontiac*, the historian tells us how he did his research, what primary
materials he had to gather, what travel he undertook, and then compares his
writing up his findings with struggling in the wilderness—before confessing
he was blind for the three years it took him to do it. It's a kind of writer's pity

party, said a friend of mine, but poignant in its direct confrontation of the writer with his odd materials—and his equally odd foibles.

FROM *THE CONSPIRACY OF PONTIAC*

BOSTON, AUGUST 1, 1851

The conquest of Canada was an event of momentous consequence in American history. It changed the political aspect of the continent, prepared a way for the independence of the British colonies, rescued the vast tracts of the interior from the rule of military despotism, and gave them, eventually, to the keeping of an ordered democracy. Yet to the red natives of the soil its results were wholly disastrous. Could the French have maintained their ground, the ruin of the Indian tribes might long have been postponed; but the victory of Quebec was the signal of their swift decline. Thenceforth they were destined to melt and vanish before the advancing waves of Anglo-American power, which now rolled westward unchecked and unopposed. They saw the danger, and, led by a great and daring champion, struggled fiercely to avert it. The history of that epoch, crowded as it is with scenes of tragic interest, with marvels of suffering and vicissitude, of heroism and endurance, has been, as yet, unwritten buried in the archives of governments, or among the obscurer records of private adventure. To rescue it from oblivion is the object of the following work. It aims to portray the American forest and the American Indian at the period when both received their final doom.

It is evident that other study than that of the closet is indispensable to success in such an attempt. Habits of early reading had greatly aided to prepare me for the task; but necessary knowledge of a more practical kind has been supplied by the indulgence of a strong natural taste, which, at various intervals, led me to the wild regions of the north and west. Here, by the camp-fire, or in the canoe, I gained familiar acquaintance with the men and scenery of the wilderness. In 1846, I visited various primitive tribes of the Rocky Mountains, and was, for a time, domesticated in a village of the western Dahcotah, on the high plains between Mount Laramie and the range of the Medicine Bow.

The most troublesome part of the task was the collection of the necessary documents. These consisted of letters, journals, reports, and despatches, scattered among numerous public offices, and private families, in Europe and America. When brought together, they amounted to about three thousand four hundred manuscript pages. Contemporary newspapers, magazines, and pamphlets have also been examined, and careful search made for every book which, directly or indirectly, might throw light upon the subject. I have visited the sites of all the principal events recorded in the narrative, and gathered such local traditions as seemed worthy of confidence.

I am indebted to the liberality of Hon. Lewis Cass for a curious collection of papers relating to the siege of Detroit by the Indians. Other important contributions have been obtained from the state paper offices of London and Paris, from the archives of New York, Pennsylvania, and other states, and from the manuscript collections of several historical societies. [. . .] The crude and promiscuous mass of materials presented an aspect by no means inviting. The field of the history was uncultured and unreclaimed, and the labor that awaited me was like that of the border settler, who, before he builds his rugged dwelling, must fell the forest-trees, burn the undergrowth, clear the ground, and hew the fallen trunks to due proportion.

Several obstacles have retarded the progress of the work. Of these, one of the most considerable was the condition of my sight. For about three years, the light of day was insupportable, and every attempt at reading or writing completely debarred. Under these circumstances, the task of sifting the materials and composing the work was begun and finished. The papers were repeatedly read aloud by an amanuensis, copious notes and extracts were made, and the narrative written down from my dictation. This process, though extremely slow and laborious, was not without its advantages; and I am well convinced that the authorities have been even more minutely examined, more scrupulously collated, and more thoroughly digested, than they would have been under ordinary circumstances.

In order to escape the tedious circumlocution, which, from the nature of the subject, could not otherwise have been avoided, the name English is applied, throughout the volume, to the British American colonists, as well as to the people of the mother country. The necessity is somewhat to be regretted, since, even at an early period, clear distinctions were visible between the offshoot and the parent stock.

Frances Ellen Watkins Harper

(1825–1911)

Feminist, abolitionist, essayist, and well-known lecturer, the freeborn Frances
Ellen Watkins Harper was also an enormously popular poet known as the
"Bronze Muse" of the nineteenth century; her first book, *Forest Leaves*
(1845), went into at least twenty editions. Before and after the Civil War, her
verse included such subjects such as slavery, women's suffrage, and racism, all
presented accessibly in conventional forms although Harper did, long before
Paul Laurence Dunbar, pioneer the use of dialect in verse. In 1892, when she
was sixty-seven, she published *Iola Leroy; or, Shadows Uplifted*, a novel later
dismissed as a book of sentimental uplift (as the title indicates)—and even
later, rediscovered as a complex (and the first) novel about Reconstruction.
For her, civil rights were a matter of race and of gender, always, and as she
autobiographically wrote in the final paragraph of the short story "The Two
Offers" (1859), "she had a higher and better object in all her writings than
the mere acquisition of gold, or acquirement of fame." Literature needed to
be purposeful and didactic, as she explained, almost three decades later at
the end of *Iola Leroy:* "The race has not had very long to straighten its hands
from the hoe, to grasp the pen and wield it as a power for good, and to erect
above the ruined auction-block and slave-pen institutions of learning." But
as her poem "Learning to Read" makes clear, literature to her represents the
ageless assertion of freedom and power.

"Learning to Read"

Very soon the Yankee teachers
Came down and set up school;
But, oh! how the Rebs did hate it,—
It was agin' their rule.

Our masters always tried to hide
Book learning from our eyes;
Knowledge didn't agree with slavery—
'Twould make us all too wise.

But some of us would try to steal
A little from the book,
And put the words together,
And learn by hook or crook.

I remember Uncle Caldwell,
Who took pot liquor fat
And greased the pages of his book,
And hid it in his hat.

And had his master ever seen
The leaves upon his head,
He'd have thought them greasy papers,
But nothing to be read.

And there was Mr. Turner's Ben,
Who heard the children spell,
And picked the words right up by heart,
And learned to read 'em well.

Well, the Northern folks kept sending
The Yankee teachers down;
And they stood right up and helped us,
Though Rebs did sneer and frown.

And, I longed to read my Bible,
For precious words it said;
But when I begun to learn it,
Folks just shook their heads,

And said there is no use trying,
Oh! Chloe, you're too late;
But as I was rising sixty,
I had no time to wait.

So I got a pair of glasses,
And straight to work I went,
And never stopped till I could read
The hymns and Testament.

Then I got a little cabin
A place to call my own—
And I felt as independent
As the queen upon her throne.

John De Forest

(1826–1906)

As a young man supported by a small inheritance, the Connecticut-born John De Forest traveled to Europe, lived in Syria for two years, and by 1859 had published five books, including two rather Romantic novels. But in 1862 he was commissioned as a captain in the Union army and served in the occupation of New Orleans, the siege of Port Hudson, Louisiana, and in the battles of Winchester, Fisher's Hill, and Cedar Creek, Virginia.

After the war, as brevet major, he joined the Freedmen's Bureau in Greenville, South Carolina, and in 1867 published *Miss Ravenel's Conversion from Secession to Loyalty* (1867), a novel of "advanced realism," said William Dean Howells, "before realism was known by that name." Howells later urged De Forest to read Tolstoy's *War and Peace*, and when he did, he said, "nobody but he has written the whole truth about war and battle. I tried, and I told all I dared, or perhaps all I could. But there was one thing I did not dare tell [. . .], the extreme horror of battle and the anguish with which the bravest soldiers struggle through it."

A prolific writer, De Forest recounted his experiences after the war in a series of articles much later collected as *A Union Officer in the Reconstruction* (1948), and he also continued to publish novels and essays. One of these, "The Great American Novel" (1868), from which this excerpt is taken, is the first use of the term that would later haunt and taunt writers in the twentieth century.

FROM "THE GREAT AMERICAN NOVEL"

We may be confident that the Great American Poem will not be written, no matter what genius attempts it, until democracy, the idea of our day and nation and race, has agonized and conquered through centuries, and made its work secure. [. . .]

But the Great American Novel—the picture of the ordinary emotions and manners of American existence—the American "Newcomes" or "Miserables" will, we suppose, be possible earlier. "Is it time?" the benighted people in the earthen jars or commonplace life are asking. And with no intention of being disagreeable, but rather with sympathetic sorrow, we answer, "Wait." At least we fear that such ought to be our answer. This task of painting the American soul within the framework of a novel has seldom been attempted, and has never been accomplished further than very partially—in the production of a few outlines. Washington Irving was too cautious to make the trial; he went back to fictions of Knickerbockers and Rip Van Winkles and Ichabod Cranes; these he did well, and we may thank him for not attempting more and failing in the attempt. With the same consciousness of incapacity Cooper shirked the experiment; he devoted himself to Indians, of whom he knew next to nothing, and to backwoodsmen and sailors, whom he idealized; or where he attempted civilized groups, he produced something less natural than the wax figures of Barnum's old museum. If all Americans were like the heroes and heroines of Cooper, Carlyle might well enough call us "eighteen millions of bores." As for a tableau of American society, as for anything resembling the tableaux of English society by Thackeray and Trollope, or the tableaux of French society by Balzac and George Sand, we had better not trouble ourselves with looking for it in Cooper. [. . .]

The nearest approach to the desired phenomenon is "Uncle Tom's Cabin." There were very noticeable faults in that story; there was a very faulty plot; there was (if idealism be a fault) a black man painted whiter than the angels, and a girl such as girls are to be, perhaps, but are not yet; there was a little village twaddle. But there was also a national breadth to the picture, truthful outlining of character, natural speaking, and plenty of strong feeling. Though comeliness of form was lacking, the material of the work was in many respects admirable. Such Northerners as Mrs. Stowe painted we have seen; and we have seen such Southerners, no matter what the people south of Mason and Dixon's line may protest; we have seen such negroes, barring, of course, the impeccable Uncle Tom—uncle of no extant nephews, so far as we know. It was a picture of American life, drawn with a few strong and passionate strokes, not filled in thoroughly, but still a portrait. It seemed, then, when that book was published, easy to have more American novels. But in "Dred" it became clear that the soul which a throb of emotion had enabled to grasp this whole people was losing its hold on the vast subject which had not stirred us. Then, stricken with timidity, the author shrank into her native shell of New England. Only certain recluse spirits, who dwell between the Dan and Beersheba of Yankeedom, can care much for Doctor Hopkins as he goes through his exercises in "The Minister's Wooing," while the attempt to sketch Aaron Burr as a contrast to the clerical hero shows most conclusively happy ignorance of the style of heartless men of the world. "The Pearl of Orr's Island" is far better. It is an exquisite little story, a thoroughly finished bit of work, but · how small! There, microscope in hand over the niceties of Orr's Island, we wait for another cameo of New England life. But what special interest have Southerners and Westerners and even New Yorkers in Yankee cameos? [. . .]

So much for the artist; now for the sitter. Ask a portrait-painter if he can make a good likeness of a baby, and he will tell you that the features are not sufficiently marked nor the expression sufficiently personal. Is there not the same difficulty in limning this continental infant of American society, who is changing every year not only in physical attributes but in the characteristics of his soul? Fifteen years ago it was morality to return fugitive slaves to their owners—and now? Our aristocracy flies through the phases of Knickerbocker, codfish, shoddy and petroleum. Where are the "high-toned gentlemen" whom North and South gloried in a quarter of a century since? Where are the Congressmen who could write "The Federalist"? Where is everything that was? Can a society which is changing so rapidly be painted except in the daily newspaper? Has anyone photographed fireworks of the shooting-stars? And then there is such variety and even such antagonism in the component parts of this cataract. When you have made your picture of petrified New England village life, left around like a boulder near the banks of the Merrimac, does the Mississippian or the Minnesotian or the Pennsylvanian recognize it as American society? We are a nation of provinces, and each province claims to the court. [. . .]

Well, what are our immediate chances for a "great American novel"? We fear that the wonder will not soon be wrought unless more talent can be enlisted in the work, and we are sure that this sufficient talent can hardly be obtained without the encouragement of an international copyright. And, even then, is it time?

Henry Timrod

(1828–1867)

Frequently called the "laureate of the Confederacy," Henry Timrod was one of the Charleston, South Carolina, poets who gathered at a bookstore in that city for mutual support and emotional sustenance. In his antebellum prose pieces, he deplored the fact that Southern writers went unappreciated at home by an audience mainly interested in chivalry or amusement (see the first excerpt); he also thought the vogue for an Americanism in literature silly if it meant local color, not style. Admired by Whittier and Longfellow, Timrod's *Poems* were published by the distinguished northern firm Ticknor and Fields in 1860.

During the war, though, he served as a war correspondent for the *Charleston Mercury* and subsequently took part in the retreat from Shiloh, although he was discharged because of his tenaciously poor health; he later moved to Columbia, where he became associate editor for the *South Carolinian*. In 1865, after Sherman's army burned the city, Timrod's only child died; the impoverished and disheartened poet, himself ill with tuberculosis, died two years later—on the anniversary of Poe's death.

Not a fire-eating secessionist—even though his ode "Ethnogenesis" (1861) responded with full southern loyalty to Howe's "Battle Hymn of the Republic"—he intended to vitiate the aestheticism of Poe's "Poetic Principle."

Timrod, still himself something of a romantic, argued in his Emersonian and Wordsworthian "A Theory of Poetry" (1864), from which an excerpt is taken here, that true poetry contains a moral power; his own poetry, affecting that moral power, visibly darkened as the war pressed desperately on, but he never relinquished his belief in emotion as the wellspring of poetry, even though he would insist on the poet as a maker more than emoter.

Though largely forgotten for much of the twentieth century, Timrod was rediscovered by the singer/songwriter Bob Dylan, whose voracious interest in the Civil War drew him to the Charleston poet.

FROM "LITERATURE OF THE SOUTH"

We think that at no time, and in no country, has the position of an author been beset with such peculiar difficulties as the Southern writer is compelled to struggle with from the beginning to the end of his career. In no country in which literature has ever flourished has an author obtained so limited an audience. In no country, and at no period that we can recall, has an author been constrained by the indifference of the public amid which he lived, to publish with a people who were prejudiced against him. It would scarcely be too extravagant to entitle the Southern author the Pariah of modern literature.

FROM "DREAMS"

[. . .] dreams in sooth,
Come they in shape of demons, gods, or elves,
Are allegories with deep hearts of truth
That tell us solemn secrets of ourselves.

FROM "A THEORY OF POETRY"

I look upon every poem as strictly a work of art, and on the Poet, in the act of putting poetry into verse, simply as an artist. If the Poet have his hour of inspiration (though I am so sick of the cant of which this word has been the fruitful source, that I dislike to use it) it is not during the work of composition. A distinction must be made between the moment when the great thought strikes for the first time along the brain, and flushes the cheek with the sudden revelation of beauty, or grandeur,—and the hour of patient and elaborate execution. The soul of the Poet, though constrained to utter itself at some time or other, does not burst into song as readily as a maiden of sixteen bursts into musical laughter. Many poets have written of grief, but no poet with the first agony of his heart, ever sat down to strain that grief through iambics. Many poets have given expression to the first raptures of successful love, but no poet, in the delirium of the joy, has ever babbled it in anapests. Could this have been possible, the poet would be the most wonderful of improvisers, and perhaps a poem would be no better than what improvisations always are.

Emily Dickinson

(1830–1886)

Born in 1830 in Amherst, Massachusetts, this amazingly original American voice came of age during the waning of the transcendental movement— never strong among the Congregationalists of Amherst—as well as the antislavery and women's rights movements that rocked New England (in particular) during the middle and end of the century. But to the poet Emily Dickinson, who after her year at Mt. Holyoke increasingly did not leave home, these transitory upheavals, however important in the body politic, affected her far less than the life of the mind to which she had thoroughly and unswervingly committed herself. "Is it Intellect that the Patriot means when he speaks of his 'Native Land'?" she slyly asked Thomas Wentworth Higginson, one of her few friends outside her Amherst orbit and the man largely responsible for her posthumous publication—even though, for many years, he has been pilloried for making these strange poems more acceptable to the public. And yet he compared them to Blake's, rightly so. Intellectual and often gnomic, their rhythms reproducing and then mimicking Protestant hymns, their images wondrous, Dickinson's poems reach into the heart of darkness, bringing light; as Henry James once said of Hawthorne, she had catlike eyes that saw in the dark. (She adored Hawthorne's work but was noncommittal about James.) Her flinty sense of our inner life—unassailable and often lacerating—and her unswerving loyalty to her art did not exclude

the world as much as focus it more finely: "The missing all—prevented me /
From missing minor things—"

   But Dickinson herself was loath to publish in her lifetime, refusing many
offers to do so. In fact, she worked and reworked her poems almost in Whit-
manian fashion, changing, revising, reconsidering, and after her death, when
her sister discovered hundreds and hundreds of poems, her first editors
(and editors today) had trouble choosing which variants to use. Moreover,
her wondrous letters, themselves lyric apothegms, are as stunning as her
poems—they themselves are a form of poem—and so excerpted here are her
poetic meditations, in prose and poetry, on the art of writing, which she had
made her lifework, "For Curiosity—."

from *Letters of Emily Dickinson*

To Thomas Wentworth Higginson
July 1862

When I state myself, as Representative of the Verse—it does not mean—
me—but a supposed person.

To Thomas Wentworth Higginson
[August 1862]

"When I try to organize—my little Force explodes," she told him, "and
leaves me bare and charred."

from *The Poems of Emily Dickinson*

[Franklin 278]

A word is dead, when it is said
Some say—
I say it just begins to live
That day

FROM *LETTERS OF EMILY DICKINSON*

To Thomas Wentworth Higginson

JUNE 1869

A letter always feels to me like immortality because it is the mind alone without corporeal friend. Indebted in our talk to attitude and accent, there seems a spectral power in thought that walks alone. I would like to thank you for your great kindness, but never try to lift the words which I cannot hold.

To Thomas Wentworth Higginson

NOVEMBER 1871

While Shakespeare remains Literature is firm—

To Elizabeth Holland

JUNE 1878

How lovely are the wiles of Words!

To Thomas Wentworth Higginson

1876

Nature is a Haunted House—but Art—a House that tries to be haunted.

To Thomas Wentworth Higginson

DECEMBER 1879

Hawthorne appalls, entices. . . .

FROM *THE POEMS OF EMILY DICKINSON*

[Franklin 512]

Unto my Books—so good to turn—
Far ends of tired Days—
It half endears the Abstinence—
And Pain—is missed—in Praise.

As Flavors—cheer Retarded Guests
With Banquettings to be—
So Spices—stimulate the time
Till my small Library—

It may be Wilderness—without—
Far feet of failing Men—
But Holiday—excludes the night—
And it is Bells—within—

I thank these Kinsmen of the Shelf—
Their Countenances Kid
Enamor—in Prospective—
And satisfy—obtained—

[Franklin 665]

The Martyr Poets—did not tell—
But wrought their Pang in syllable—
That when their mortal name be numb—
Their mortal fate—encourage Some—
[. .]

[Franklin 772]

Essential Oils—are wrung—
The Attar from the Rose
Be not expressed by Suns—alone—
It is the gift of Screws—

The General Rose—decay—
But this—in Lady's Drawer·
Make Summer—When the Lady lie
In Ceaseless Rosemary—

[Franklin 930]

The Poets light but Lamps—
Themselves—go out—
The Wicks they stimulate
If vital Light

Inhere as do the Suns—
Each Age a Lens
Disseminating their
Circumference—

[*Franklin 1491*]

To see the Summer Sky
Is Poetry, though never in a Book it lie—
True Poems flee—

Helen Hunt Jackson

(1830–1885)

Born the same year as Emily Dickinson and in the same town, Amherst, Massachusetts, and also acquainted with the Dickinson family, Helen Hunt Jackson could not have been more unlike the eremitic poet whom she unsuccessfully begged to publish. Twice married (her first husband died while testing a submarine battery) and the mother of two small sons who also died young, as a widow Hunt settled for a time in Newport, Rhode Island, where she met the literary booster Thomas Wentworth Higginson; he encouraged her to publish a book of poems in 1870 that even Emerson would praise.

A popular writer who appeared under the initials "H.H.," she was soon producing travel sketches, personal essays, children's stories, and short fiction. After settling in Colorado with her second husband, William Sharpless Jackson, she composed *A Century of Dishonor* (1881), her impassioned and well-researched investigation into the horrid treatment of Indian tribes by the United States government. Literature could now be, to her, a forum for social change, which was her intent in the didactic, popular novel *Ramona* (1884): "I am going to write a novel, in which will be set forth some Indian experiences in a way to move people's hearts," she said. "People will read a novel when they will not read serious books."

The first excerpt here is taken from Jackson's extraordinary letter to

Emily Dickinson encouraging her to publish and asking to be Dickinson's executrix (Dickinson outlived her). The second excerpt is from a letter to Thomas Wentworth Higginson written during her last illness and revealing Jackson to be a woman who believed that life is short, art long, and that the artist has, indeed, a mission.

FROM *LETTERS OF EMILY DICKINSON*

1884

My dear friend,

[. . .] I trust you are well—and that life is going pleasantly with you.—What portfolios of verses you must have.—

It is a cruel wrong to your "day and generation" that you will not give them light.—If such a thing should happen as that I should outlive you, I wish you would make me your literary legatee & executor. Surely, after you are what is called "dead," you will be willing that the poor ghosts you have left behind, should be cheered and pleased by your verse, will you not?—You ought to be.—I do not think we have a right to with hold from the world a word or a thought any more than a *deed*, which might help a single soul.

FROM *CONTEMPORARIES*, BY THOMAS WENTWORTH HIGGINSON

I feel that my work is done, and I am heartily, honestly, and cheerfully ready to go. In fact, I am glad to go. You have never fully realized how for the last four years my whole heart has been full of the Indian cause—how I felt, as the Quakers say, "a concern" to work for it. My "Century of Dishonor" and "Ramona" are the only things I have done of which I am glad now. The rest is of no moment. They will live and they will bear fruit. They already have. The change in public feeling on the Indian question in the last three years is marvelous; an Indian Rights' Association in every large city in the land.

[. . .] Every word of the Indian history in "Ramona" is literally true, and it is being reenacted here every day.

I did mean to write a child's story on the same theme as "Ramona," but I doubt if I could have made it so telling a stroke, so perhaps it is as well that I should not do it. And perhaps I shall do it after all, but I cannot conceive of getting well after such an illness as this.

Louisa May Alcott

(1832–1888)

Though born in Pennsylvania, Louisa May Alcott largely grew up in the hothouse atmosphere of Concord, Massachusetts, the transcendental stomping ground of the likes of Emerson and Thoreau and even the more skeptical Hawthorne. Concord was also the intellectual playroom of Alcott's good-hearted, brilliant, and feckless father, Bronson, who kept his family impoverished with his various schemes (vegetarian communes, for instance) and who believed in and supported his daughter's talent. During the Civil War, Alcott *jeune fille* volunteered as an army nurse and while in Washington, before she contracted typhoid fever, wrote the sketches she soon revised as her first major work, *Hospital Sketches* (1863). Scribbling sensational stories under a pseudonym, she supported her family with her income and in 1864, under her own name, published *Moods*, her first novel, which Henry James, fledgling author, condescendingly reviewed. James's sister Alice said the piece "reminded [me] of Father's having met Mr. Alcott in the street one day and saying to him: 'They are reading *Dumps* at home with great interest.'"

But with the publication in 1868 of the now-canonical *Little Women*, Louisa May Alcott could no longer be ridiculed. Never out of print, the story of the March sisters and their mother has been for generations of girls the charming and sometimes satiric female *ur*-text, combining love, creativity, suppressed anger, and vocation.

Alcott's later work includes *Little Men* (1871) and *Jo's Boys* (1886)—spin-offs of *Little Women*—as well as the more interesting novels *Work* (1873), *A Modern Mephistopheles* (1877), and the recently discovered *A Long Fatal Love Chase* (written in 1866, published in 1995).

The following excerpt comes from chapter 27, "Literary Lessons," of *Little Women*. It's an amusing account of how Jo March, the heroine (modeled on Alcott herself), retires to the attic to write in her special writing outfit and fantasizes about writing for publication and profit. No quixotic dreamer, Jo is hardworking, professional, ambitious, savvy, talented, and utterly realistic, and Alcott recounts her travails—the travails of one who writes for a popular audience—with brevity, humor, and a bit of refreshing satire.

FROM *LITTLE WOMEN*

Fortune suddenly smiled upon Jo, and dropped a good luck penny in her path. Not a golden penny, exactly, but I doubt if half a million would have given more real happiness than did the little sum that came to her in this wise.

Every few weeks she would shut herself up in her room, put on her scribbling suit, and "fall into a vortex," as she expressed it, writing away at her novel with all her heart and soul, for till that was finished she could find no peace. Her "scribbling suit" consisted of a black woolen pinafore on which she could wipe her pen at will, and a cap of the same material, adorned with a cheerful red bow, into which she bundled her hair when the decks were cleared for action. This cap was a beacon to the inquiring eyes of her family, who during these periods kept their distance, merely popping in their heads semi-occasionally to ask, with interest, "Does genius burn, Jo?" [. . .]

She did not think herself a genius by any means, but when the writing fit came on, she gave herself up to it with entire abandon, and led a blissful life, unconscious of want, care, or bad weather, while she sat safe and happy in an imaginary world, full of friends almost as real and dear to her as any in the flesh. Sleep forsook her eyes, meals stood untasted, day and night were all too short to enjoy the happiness which blessed her only at such times, and made these hours worth living, even if they bore no other fruit. The divine afflatus usually lasted a week or two, and then she emerged from her "vortex," hungry, sleepy, cross, or despondent.

She was just recovering from one of these attacks when she was prevailed upon to escort Miss Crocker to a lecture, and in return for her virtue was rewarded with a new idea. It was a People's Course, the lecture on the Pyramids, and Jo rather wondered at the choice of such a subject for such an audience, but took it for granted that some great social evil would be remedied or some great want supplied by unfolding the glories of the Pharaohs to an audience whose thoughts were busy with the price of coal and flour, and whose lives were spent in trying to solve harder riddles than that of the Sphinx.

They were early, and while Miss Crocker set the heel of her stocking, Jo amused herself by examining the faces of the people who occupied the seat with them. [. . .] On her right, her only neighbor was a studious looking lad absorbed in a newspaper. It was a pictorial sheet, and Jo examined the work of art nearest her, idly wondering what fortuitous concatenation of circumstances needed the melodramatic illustration of an Indian in full war costume, tumbling over a precipice with a wolf at his throat, while two infuriated young gentlemen, with unnaturally small feet and big eyes, were stabbing each other close by, and a disheveled female was flying away in the background with her mouth wide open. Pausing to turn a page, the lad saw her looking and, with boyish good nature offered half his paper, saying bluntly, "want to read it? That's a first-rate story."

Jo accepted it with a smile, for she had never outgrown her liking for lads, and soon found herself involved in the usual labyrinth of love, mystery, and murder, for the story belonged to that class of light literature in which the passions have a holiday, and when the author's invention fails, a grand catastrophe clears the stage of one half the dramatis personae, leaving the other half to exult over their downfall.

"Prime, isn't it?" asked the boy, as her eye went down the last paragraph of her portion.

"I think you and I could do as well as that if we tried," returned Jo, amused at his admiration of the trash.

"I should think I was a pretty lucky chap if I could. She makes a good living out of such stories, they say." And he pointed to the name of Mrs. S.L.A.N.G. Northbury, under the title of the tale.

"Do you know her?" asked Jo, with sudden interest.

"No, but I read all her pieces, and I know a fellow who works in the office where this paper is printed."

"Do you say she makes a good living out of stories like this?" and Jo looked more respectfully at the agitated group and thickly sprinkled exclamation points that adorned the page.

"Guess she does! She knows just what folks like, and gets paid well for writing it."

Here the lecture began, but Jo heard very little of it, for while Professor Sands was prosing away about Belzoni, Cheops, scarabei, and hieroglyphics, she was covertly taking down the address of the paper, and boldly resolving to try for the hundred-dollar prize offered in its columns for a sensational story. By the time the lecture ended and the audience awoke, she had built up a splendid fortune for herself (not the first founded on paper), and was already deep in the concoction of her story, being unable to decide whether the duel should come before the elopement or after the murder.

She said nothing of her plan at home, but fell to work next day, much to the disquiet of her mother, who always looked a little anxious when "genius took to burning." Jo had never tried this style before, contenting herself with very mild romances for *The Spread Eagle*. Her experience and miscellaneous reading were of service now, for they gave her some idea of dramatic effect, and supplied plot, language, and costumes. Her story was as full of desperation and despair as her limited acquaintance with those uncomfortable emotions enabled her to make it, and having located it in Lisbon, she wound up with an earthquake, as a striking and appropriate denouement. The manuscript was privately dispatched, accompanied by a note, modestly saying that if the tale didn't get the prize, which the writer hardly dared expect, she would be very glad to receive any sum it might be considered worth.

Six weeks is a long time to wait, and a still longer time for a girl to keep a secret, but Jo did both, and was just beginning to give up all hope of ever seeing her manuscript again, when a letter arrived which almost took her breath away, for on opening it, a check for a hundred dollars fell into her lap. For a minute she stared at it as if it had been a snake, then she read her letter and began to cry. If the amiable gentleman who wrote that kindly note could have known what intense happiness he was giving a fellow creature, I think he would devote his leisure hours, if he has any, to that amusement, for Jo valued the letter more than the money, because it was encouraging, and after years of effort it was so pleasant to find that she had learned to do something, though it was only to write a sensation story.

A prouder young woman was seldom seen than she, when, having composed herself, she electrified the family by appearing before them with the letter in one hand, the check in the other, announcing that she had won the prize. Of course there was a great jubilee, and when the story came everyone read and praised it, though after her father had told her that the language was good, the romance fresh and hearty, and the tragedy quite thrilling, he shook his head, and said in his unworldly way, "You can do better than this, Jo. Aim at the highest, and never mind the money."

"I think the money is the best part of it. What will you do with such a fortune?" asked Amy, regarding the magic slip of paper with a reverential eye.

"Send Beth and Mother to the seaside for a month or two," answered Jo promptly.

To the seaside they went, after much discussion, and though Beth didn't come home as plump and rosy as could be desired, she was much better, while Mrs. March declared she felt ten years younger. So Jo was satisfied with the investment of her prize money, and fell to work with a cheery spirit, bent on earning more of those delightful checks.

She did earn several that year, and began to feel herself a power in the house, for by the magic of a pen, her "rubbish" turned into comforts for them all. "The Duke's Daughter" paid the butcher's bill, "A Phantom Hand" put down a new carpet, and the "Curse of the Coventrys" proved the blessing of the Marches in the way of groceries and gowns. [. . .]

Little notice was taken of her stories, but they found a market, and encouraged by this fact, she resolved to make a bold stroke for fame and fortune. Having copied her novel for the fourth time, read it to all her confidential friends, and submitted it with fear and trembling to three publishers, she at last disposed of it, on condition that she would cut it down one third, and omit all the parts which she particularly admired.

"Now I must either bundle it back in to my tin kitchen to mold, pay for printing it myself, or chop it up to suit purchasers and get what I can for it. Fame is a very good thing to have in the house, but cash is more convenient, so I wish to take the sense of the meeting on this important subject," said Jo, calling a family council.

"Don't spoil your book, my girl, for there is more in it than you know, and the idea is well worked out. Let it wait and ripen," was her father's advice, and he practiced what he preached, having waited patiently thirty years for fruit of his own to ripen, and being in no haste to gather it even now when it was sweet and mellow.

"It seems to me that Jo will profit more by taking the trial than by waiting," said Mrs. March. "Criticism is the best test of such work, for it will show her both unsuspected merits and faults, and help her to do better next time. We are too partial, but the praise and blame of outsiders will prove useful, even if she gets but little money."

"Yes," said Jo, knitting her brows, "that's just it. I've been fussing over the thing so long, I really don't know whether it's good, bad, or indifferent. It will be a great help to have cool, impartial persons take a look at it, and tell me what they think of it."

"I wouldn't leave a word out of it. You'll spoil it if you do, for the interest of the story is more in the minds than in the actions of the people, and it will be all a muddle if you don't explain as you go on," said Meg, who firmly believed that this book was the most remarkable novel ever written.

"But Mr. Allen says, 'Leave out the explanations, make it brief and dramatic, and let the characters tell the story,'" interrupted Jo, turning to the publisher's note.

"Do as he tells you. He knows what will sell, and we don't. Make a good, popular book, and get as much money as you can. By-and-by, when you've got a name, you can afford to digress, and have philosophical and metaphysical people in your novels," said Amy, who took a strictly practical view of the subject. [. . .]

So, with Spartan firmness, the young authoress laid her first-born on her table, and chopped it up as ruthlessly as any ogre. In the hope of pleasing everyone, she took everyone's advice, and like the old man and his donkey in the fable suited nobody. Her father liked the metaphysical streak which had unconsciously got into it, so that was allowed to remain though she had her doubts about it. Her mother thought that there was a trifle too much description. Out, therefore it came, and with it many necessary links in the story. Meg admired the tragedy, so Jo piled up the agony to suit her, while Amy objected to the fun, and, with the best intentions in life, Jo quenched the spritely scenes which relieved the somber character of the story. Then, to complicate the ruin, she cut it down one third, and confidingly sent the poor little romance, like a picked robin, out into the big, busy world to try its fate.

Well, it was printed, and she got three hundred dollars for it, likewise plenty of praise and blame, both so much greater than she expected that she was thrown into a state of bewilderment from which it took her some time to recover.

"You said, Mother, that criticism would help me. But how can it, when it's so contradictory that I don't know whether I've written a promising book or broken all the ten commandments?" cried poor Jo, turning over a heap of notices, the perusal of which filled her with pride and joy one minute, wrath and dismay the next. "This man says, 'An exquisite book, full of truth, beauty, and earnestness.' 'All is sweet, pure, and healthy,'" continued the perplexed authoress. "The next, 'The theory of the book is bad, full of morbid fancies, spiritualistic ideas, and unnatural characters.' Now, as I had no theory of any kind, don't believe in Spiritualism, and copied my characters from life, I don't see how this critic can be right. Another says, 'It's one of the best American novels which has appeared for years' (I know better than that); and the next asserts that 'Though it is original, and written with great force and feeling, it is a dangerous book.' 'Tisn't! Some make fun of it, some overpraise, and nearly all insist that I had a deep theory to expound, when I only wrote it for the pleasure and the money. I wish I'd printed the whole or not at all, for I do hate to be so misjudged."

Her family and friends administered comfort and commendation liberally. Yet it was a hard time for sensitive, high-spirited Jo, who meant so well and had apparently done so ill. But it did her good, for those whose opinion had real value gave her the criticism which is an author's best education, and when the first soreness was over, she could laugh at her poor little book, yet believe in it still, and feel herself the wiser and stronger for the buffeting she had received.

"Not being a genius, like Keats, it won't kill me," she said stoutly, "and I've got the joke on my side, after all, for the parts that were taken straight out of real life are denounced as impossible and absurd, and the scenes that I made up out of my own silly head are pronounced 'charmingly natural, tender, and true.' So I'll comfort myself with that, and when I'm ready, I'll up again and take another."

Celia Thaxter

(1835–1894)

The daughter of a lighthouse keeper in southern New Hampshire who ran a hotel that catered to the literary and political figures of the day, Celia Laighton at sixteen married Levi Thaxter, her tutor, her father's business partner, and a man eleven years her senior. A poetry enthusiast later known for his readings of Robert Browning, Thaxter's husband was instrumental in snagging the attention of editors James Russell Lowell and James Fields, who first published her poems in the *Atlantic Monthly* in 1861. But though the couple never divorced, it was an unstable marriage, and legend says that Thaxter's career (she became a beloved and popular poet of the nineteenth century) helped destroy it. Perhaps. But Thaxter did crave the sea and the isolation of the Isles of Shoals, which she also beautifully described in prose; and a somewhat reclusive person devoted to her brother and her parents, she took refuge—or solace—in nature, in words, and later in painting.

In friendship as well. Close to John Greenleaf Whittier, Thaxter was also the friend of Annie Fields, wife of the publisher, and Sarah Orne Jewett, another writer who understood the New England landscape both as refuge and scourge. The letters excerpted here, to James Fields, Annie Fields, and Sarah Orne Jewett, reveal the voice of a woman poet sure of herself and given to depression, a woman beset by the family she adores and a writer intent on getting it right.

FROM *The Letters of Celia Thaxter*

To James T. Fields

NEWTONVILLE, OCTOBER 25 [1862]

My dear friend: I'm sorry I've as yet no prosaic manuscripts for you, but I pray you patience for a little longer. Meanwhile here are some verses which have been evolved among the pots and kettles, to which you're welcome, if they're good enough for you. Verses can grow when prose can't,
    "While greasy Joan doth keel the pot"!
    The rhymes in my head are all that keep me alive, I do believe, lifting me in a half unconscious condition over the ashes heap, so that I don't half realize how dry and dusty it is!

To Annie Fields

SHOALS, MARCH 22, 1876

Mr. Howells has returned my MS., and wants me to make it more imaginative,—set my "constructive faculty" to work upon it, for it is full of fine material. He is right, but supposing one hasn't any constructive faculty? Du Lieber Gott! then one must live without any gowns. Plain facts won't earn them. If one could only be as economical as Mr. Emerson's aunt, who wore her shroud alike for life and death!
    I am so blue (let me whisper in your kind ear!) that I feel as if I bore the car of Juggernaut upon my back day after day. I totally disbelieve in any sunrise to follow this pitch-black night. I believe I am going to see everything of a funereal purple color from this time forth and forever! But nobody guesses it.

To Annie Fields

1877

I am up at six o'clock every morning, often before, laying my plans for dinner for the family of eleven (for since mother has been ill, six weeks now, I have attended to the housekeeping), getting ready the dessert, and laying everything in train for the noonday meal, that I may paint every minute of daylight that I can steal. I take a cup of coffee, then arrange my cooking, and then sit down at my desk and write till the sun rises, by my student lamp, as fast as I can, so not to take my time of sunshine for it. We have breakfast at eight, when my brothers come down.

To Sarah Orne Jewett

PORTSMOUTH [1893]

Thank you for your sweet letter and all your kind suggestions. I had already begun to "reef" my MS., and perceived at once, when I read it aloud, that it must be cut ever so much in places. Dear, you have given me a real helpful lift, because I have been doing this work without a particle of enthusiasm, in a most perfunctory manner, from the bits of notes I had made; and my mind has been so saddened by deep shadows for many months, somehow I had no heart in it at all. I am hoping, when I go to the Shoals presently, to get some of the real flavor of the place and the work into it. It doesn't satisfy me one bit. I began to write the introductory chapter right off, and shall I send it to you as you said? I am so glad for every bit of criticism. I was so happy when I wrote the Shoals book—it wrote itself. I seemed to have very little to do with it anyway. But now the shadows are so long, and it grows so lonesome on this earth, and there is such a chill where there used to be such warmth and bliss.

Mark Twain

(1835–1910)

"Writing is easy. All you have to do is cross out the wrong words," said Mark Twain, né Samuel Clemens, a man of inimitable wit. A self-educated printer-journalist (like Bret Harte and Lafcadio Hearn) born in Missouri, Twain paddled the Mississippi until the Civil War, when for two weeks he served as a Confederate soldier; he then moved to Nevada and San Francisco, first to work as a prospector and then as a newspaperman. In San Francisco it was Harte, Twain later recollected, who "trimmed and trained and schooled me patiently until he changed me from an awkward utterer of coarse grotesque-ness to a writer of paragraphs and chapters." Later, Twain settled in Hart-ford, Connecticut, and then New York City. No one part of the United States could contain him.

If Whitman became Emerson's poet, then Mark Twain became Emerson's man of letters in common form, or so Twain's friend William Dean Howells virtually canonized him, dubbing Twain the "Lincoln of our literature." A man of a thousand parts—atheist, humorist, satirist, novelist, travel writer, lecturer, celebrity, inventor, part-time capitalist, and social critic—Twain as writer lived inside and on the outside of mainstream literature, both at the same time, distrusting everything that was bogus, inflated, predictable, or empty (particularly verbiage). Instrumental in persuading Ulysses S. Grant to write his memoirs, which Twain published, Twain was a speculator and

enthusiast as well as pessimist and iconoclast; he is Tom Sawyer and especially Huck Finn, the rugged boy-individualist of sound heart and, as Twain
later said, deformed conscience. One can see this in part in his 1885 letter
to Howells, in which Twain delivers sly literary criticism and at the same
time a sense of what he considers good narrative—or in his famous send-up
of James Fenimore Cooper (both excerpted below). And as a diligent and
dedicated writer, Twain is a serious craftsperson who does not suffer fools
gladly, though he may skewer them comically. Such is the content of his
marvelous letters and his varied and considered comments on the nitty-gritty
of creative writing.

To his brother Orion

MARCH 23, 1878

My dear Bro.,

—Every man must learn his trade—not pick it up. God requires that
he learn it by slow and painful processes. The apprentice-hand, in black-
smithing, in medicine, in literature, in everything, is a thing that can't be
hidden. It always shows.

But happily there is a market for apprentice work, else the "Innocents
Abroad" would have had no sale. Happily, too, there's a wider market for
some sorts of apprentice literature than there is for the very best of the
journey-work. This work of yours is exceedingly crude, but I am free to say
it is less crude than I expected it to be, and considerably better work than I
believed you could do, it is too crude to offer to any prominent periodical,
so I shall speak to the N.Y. Weekly people. To publish it there will be to
bury it. Why could not some good genius have sent me to the N.Y. with my
apprentice sketches?

You should not publish it in book form at all—for this reason: it is only an imitation of Verne—it is not a burlesque. But I think it may be regarded as proof that Verne cannot be burlesqued.

In accompanying notes I have suggested that you vastly modify the first visit to hell, and leave out the second visit altogether. Nobody would, or ought to print those things. You are not advanced enough in literature to venture upon a matter requiring so much practice. Let me show what a man has got to go through:

Nine years ago I mapped my "Journey in Heaven." I discussed it with literary friends whom I could trust to keep it to themselves.

I gave it a deal of thought, from time to time. After a year or more I wrote it up. It was not a success. Five years ago I wrote it again, altering the plan. That MS is at my elbow now. It was a considerable improvement on the first attempt, but still it wouldn't do—last year and year before I talked frequently with Howells about the subject, and he kept urging me to do it again.

So I thought and thought, at odd moments and at last I struck what I considered to be the right plan! Mind I have never altered the ideas, from the first—the plan was the difficulty. When Howells was here at last, I laid before him the whole story without referring to my MS and he said: "You have got it sure this time. But drop the idea of making mere magazine stuff of it. Don't waste it. Print it by itself—publish it first in England—ask Dean Stanley to endorse it, which will draw some of the teeth of the religious press, and then reprint it in America." I doubt my ability to get Dean Stanley to do anything of the sort, but I shall do the rest—and this is all a secret which you must not divulge.

Now look here—I have tried, all these years, to think of some way of "doing" hell too—and have always had to give it up. Hell, in my book, will not occupy five pages of MS I judge—it will be only covert hints, I suppose, and quickly dropped, I may end by not even referring to it.

And mind you, in my opinion you will find that you can't write up hell so it will stand printing. Neither Howells nor I believe in hell or the divinity of the Savior, but no matter, the Savior is none the less a sacred Personage and a man should have no desire or disposition to refer to him lightly, profanely, or otherwise than with the profoundest reverence.

The only safe thing is not to introduce him, or refer to him at all, I suspect. I have entirely rewritten one book 3 (perhaps 4) times, changing the plan every time—1200 pages of MS. wasted and burned—and shall tackle it again, one of these years and maybe succeed at last. Therefore you need not expect to get your book right the first time. Go to work and revamp or rewrite it. God only exhibits his thunder and lightning at intervals, and so they always command attention. These are God's adjectives. You thunder and lightning too much; the reader ceases to get under the bed, by and by.

FROM *MARK TWAIN–HOWELLS LETTERS*

To William Dean Howells
NOVEMBER 23, 1875

My dear Howells,

—Herewith is the proof. In spite of myself, how awkwardly I do jumble words together; and how often I do use three words where one would answer—a thing I am always trying to guard against. I shall become as slovenly a writer as Charles Francis Adams, if I don't look out. (That is said in jest; because of course I do not seriously fear getting so bad as that. I never shall drop so far toward his and Bret Harte's level as to catch myself saying "It must have been wiser to have believed that he might have accomplished it if he could have felt that he would have been supported by those who should have &c. &c. &c.") The reference to Bret Harte reminds me that I often accuse him of being a deliberate imitator of Dickens; and this in turn reminds me that I have charged unconscious plagiarism upon Charley Warner; and this in turn reminds me that I have been delighting my soul for two weeks over a brand new and ingenious way of beginning a novel—and behold, all at once it flashes upon me that Charley Warner originated the idea 3 years ago and told me about it! Aha! So much for self-righteousness! I am well repaid. Here are 108 pages of MS, new and clean, lying disgraced in the waste paper basket, and I am beginning the novel over again in an unstolen way. I would not wonder if I am the worst literary thief in the world, without knowing it.

July 21, 1885

My dear Howells,

—You are really my only author; I am restricted to you, I wouldn't give a damn for the rest.

I bored through *Middlemarch* during the past week, with its labored and tedious analyses of feelings and motives, its paltry and tiresome people, its unexciting and uninteresting story, and its frequent blinding flashes of single-sentence poetry, philosophy, wit, and what not, and nearly died from the overwork. I wouldn't read another of those books for a farm. I did try to read one other—*Daniel Deronda*. I dragged through three chapters, losing flesh all the time, and then was honest enough to quit, and confess to myself that I haven't any romance literature appetite, as far as I can see, except for your books.

But what I started to say, was, that I have just read Part II of *Indian Summer*, and to my mind there isn't a waste line in it, or one that could be improved. I read it yesterday, ending with that opinion; and read it again to-day, ending with the same opinion emphasized. I haven't read Part I yet, because that number must have reached Hartford after we left; but we are going to send down town for a copy, and when it comes I am to read both parts aloud to the family. It is a beautiful story, and makes a body laugh all the time, and cry inside, and feel so old and so forlorn; and gives him gracious glimpses of his lost youth that fill him with a measureless regret, and build up in him a cloudy sense of his having been a prince, once, in some enchanted far-off land, and of being an exile now, and desolate—and Lord, no chance ever to get back there again! That is the thing that hurts. Well, you have done it with marvelous facility and you make all the motives and feelings perfectly clear without analyzing the guts out of them, the way George Eliot does. I can't stand George Eliot and Hawthorne and those people; I see what they are at a hundred years before they get to it and they just tire me to death. And as for "The Bostonians," I would rather be damned to John Bunyan's heaven than read that.

Yrs Ever

Mark

FROM *MARK TWAIN: THE COMPLETE INTERVIEWS*

A man cannot tell the whole truth about himself, even if convinced that what he wrote would never be seen by others. I have personally satisfied myself of that and have got others to test it also. You cannot lay bare your private soul and look at it. You are too much ashamed of yourself. It is too disgusting. For that reason I confine myself to drawing the portraits of others.

FROM *MARK TWAIN–HOWELLS LETTERS*

To William Dean Howells

MARCH 14, 1904

An Autobiography is the truest of all books; for while it inevitably consists mainly of extinctions of the truth, shirkings of the truth, partial reveal-ments of the truth, with hardly an instance of plain straight truth, the remorseless truth is there, between the lines, where the author-cat is rak-ing dust upon it which hides from the disinterested spectator neither it nor its smell . . . the result being that the reader knows the author in spite of his wily diligences. [. . .]

Some authors overdo the stage directions, they elaborate them quite beyond necessity; they spend so much time and take up so much room in telling us how a person said a thing and how he looked and acted when he said it that we get tired and vexed and wish he hadn't said it at all. Other authors' directions are brief enough, but it is seldom that the brevity con-tains either wit or information. Writers of this school go in rags, in the matter of stage directions; the majority of them have nothing in stock but a cigar, a laugh, a blush, and a bursting into tears. In their poverty they work these sorry things to the bone. They say:

". . . replied Alfred, flipping the ash from his cigar." (This explains noth-ing; it only wastes space.)

". . . responded Richard, with a laugh." (There was nothing to laugh about; there never is. The writer puts it in from habit—automatically; he is paying no attention to his work, or he would see that there is nothing to laugh at; often, when a remark is unusually and poignantly flat and silly, he tries to deceive the reader by enlarging the stage direction and making

Richard break into "frenzies of uncontrollable laughter." This makes the reader sad.)

"... murmured Gladys, blushing." (This poor old shop-worn blush is a tiresome thing. We get so we would rather Gladys would fall out of the book and break her neck than do it again. She is always doing it, and usually irrelevantly. Whenever it is her turn to murmur she hangs out her blush; it is the only thing she's got. In a little while we hate her, just as we do Richard.)

"... repeated Evelyn, bursting into tears." (This kind keep a book damp all the time. They can't say a thing without crying. They cry so much about nothing that by and by when they have something to cry about they have gone dry; they sob, and fetch nothing; we are not moved. We are only glad.)

They gravel me, these stale and overworked stage directions, these carbon films that got burnt out long ago and cannot now carry any faintest thread of light. It would be well if they could be relieved from duty and flung out in the literary back yard to rot and disappear along with the discarded and forgotten "steeds" and "halidomes" and similar stage-properties once so dear to our grandfathers.

FROM "IS SHAKESPEARE DEAD?"

Experience is an author's most valuable asset; experience is the thing that puts the muscle and the breath and warm blood into the book he writes.

FROM "FENIMORE COOPER'S LITERARY OFFENSES"

The Pathfinder and *The Deerslayer* stand at the head of Cooper's novels as artistic creations. There are others of his works which contain parts as perfect as are to be found in these, and scenes even more thrilling. Not one can be compared with either of them as a finished whole.

The defects in both of these tales are comparatively slight. They were pure works of art. — *Prof. Lounsbury.*

The five tales reveal an extraordinary fulness of invention.

... One of the very greatest characters in fiction, Natty Bumppo. ...

The craft of the woodsman, the tricks of the trapper, all the delicate art of the forest, were familiar to Cooper from his youth up. — *Prof. Brander Matthews.*

Cooper is the greatest artist in the domain of romantic fiction yet produced by America. — *Wilkie Collins.*

It seems to me that it was far from right for the Professor of English Literature in Yale, the Professor of English Literature in Columbia, and Wilkie Collins to deliver opinions on Cooper's literature without having read some of it. It would have been much more decorous to keep silent and let persons talk who have read Cooper.

Cooper's art has some defects. In one place in "Deerslayer," and in the restricted space of two-thirds of a page, Cooper has scored 114 offences against literary art out of a possible 115. It breaks the record.

There are nineteen rules governing literary art in the domain of romantic fiction—some say twenty-two. In "Deerslayer" Cooper violated eighteen of them. These eighteen require:

1. That a tale shall accomplish something and arrive somewhere. But the Deerslayer tale accomplishes nothing and arrives in the air.

2. They require that the episodes of a tale shall be necessary parts of the tale, and shall help to develop it. But as the Deerslayer tale is not a tale, and accomplishes nothing and arrives nowhere, the episodes have no rightful place in the work, since there was nothing for them to develop.

3. They require that the personages in a tale shall be alive, except in the case of corpses, and that always the reader shall be able to tell the corpses from the others. But this detail has often been overlooked in the Deerslayer tale.

4. They require that the personages in a tale, both dead and alive, shall exhibit a sufficient excuse for being there. But this detail also has been overlooked in the Deerslayer tale.

5. They require that when the personages of a tale deal in conversation, the talk shall sound like human talk, and be talk such as human beings would be likely to talk in the given circumstances, and have a discoverable meaning, also a discoverable purpose, and a show of relevancy, and remain in the neighborhood of the subject in hand, and be interesting to the reader, and help out the tale, and stop when the people cannot think of anything more to say. But this requirement has been ignored from the beginning of the Deerslayer tale to the end of it.

6. They require that when the author describes the character of a personage in his tale, the conduct and conversation of that personage shall justify said description. But this law gets little or no attention in the Deerslayer tale, as Natty Bumppo's case will amply prove.

7. They require that when a personage talks like an illustrated, gilt-edged, tree-calf, hand-tooled, seven-dollar Friendship's Offering in the beginning of a paragraph, he shall not talk like a negro minstrel in the end of it. But this rule is flung down and danced upon in the Deerslayer tale.

8. They require that crass stupidities shall not be played upon the reader as "the craft of the woodsman, the delicate art of the forest," by either the author or the people in the tale. But this rule is persistently violated in the Deerslayer tale.

9. They require that the personages of a tale shall confine themselves to possibilities and let miracles alone; or, if they venture a miracle, the author must so plausibly set it forth as to make it look possible and reasonable. But these rules are not respected in the Deerslayer tale.

10. They require that the author shall make the reader feel a deep interest in the personages of his tale and in their fate; and that he shall make the reader love the good people in the tale and hate the bad ones. But the reader of the Deerslayer tale dislikes the good people in it, is indifferent to the others, and wishes they would all get drowned together.

11. They require that the characters in a tale shall be so clearly defined that the reader can tell beforehand what each will do in a given emergency. But in the Deerslayer tale this rule is vacated.

In addition to these large rules there are some little ones. These require that the author shall:

12. Say what he is proposing to say, not merely come near it.

13. Use the right word, not its second cousin.

14. Eschew surplusage.

15. Not omit necessary details.
16. Avoid slovenliness of form.
17. Use good grammar.
18. Employ a simple and straightforward style. [. . .]

I may be mistaken, but it does seem to me that Deerslayer is not a work of art in any sense; it does seem to me that it is destitute of every detail that goes to the making of a work of art; in truth, it seems to me that Deerslayer is just simply a literary delirium tremens.

A work of art? It has no invention; it has no order, system, sequence, or result; it has no lifelikeness, no thrill, no stir, no seeming of reality; its characters are confusedly drawn, and by their acts and words they prove that they are not the sort of people the author claims that they are; its humor is pathetic; its pathos is funny; its conversations are—oh! indescribable; its love-scenes odious; its English a crime against the language.

Counting these out, what is left is Art. I think we must all admit that.

Francis (Bret) Harte

(1836–1902)

After the earthquake of 1906, when Alice Toklas woke her father, so the story goes, to tell him San Francisco was now on fire, he replied, "That will give us a black eye in the East," and immediately fell back to sleep. The situation wasn't much different in Bret Harte's day: after the Civil War, the West was coming into its own in literary terms—but insecurely. As Bret Harte himself recounts in the excerpt below, the San Francisco literary establishment considered his famous story "The Luck of Roaring Camp" morally offensive until it received an eastern stamp of approval.

Though born in Albany, New York, and for the last twenty-five years of his life an expatriate, Bret Harte is associated forevermore with California, about which he wrote extensively and well. As newspaperman (who lost his job when he excoriated the perpetrators of the Mad River Indian massacre), as editor of California's fine literary magazine the *Overland Monthly*, as poet and crack short-story writer, as the man who urged Mark Twain to write out the tale that became "The Jumping Frog of Calaveras County," and as literary celebrity after the 1868 publication of "The Luck of Roaring Camp" and the poem "Plain Language from Truthful James," Bret Harte may have suffered from too much early success. In 1871 the *Atlantic Monthly* offered him the unheard-of sum of $10,000 to write for a year, but Harte, once in the East, couldn't deliver and eventually sank into debt, depression, and the horror of unfulfilled promise. Yet, as the second excerpt below implies, to him, as a writer, the American short story that appeared after the Civil War was an avatar of a new realism, a refreshed vernacular, and the indigenous humor that would characterize American fiction henceforth.

FROM "A MORNING WITH BRET HARTE"

I was eventually offered the editorship of a new magazine, the "Overland Monthly," which was about to make its first issue, and it was through the acceptance of this post that my career, generally speaking, began. As the editor of this magazine, I received for its initial number many contributions in the way of stories. After looking these over, it impressed me as a strange thing that not one of the writers had felt inspired to treat the fresh subjects which lay ready to his hand in California. All the stories were conventional, the kind of thing that would have been offered to an editor in the Atlantic States, stories of those localities and of Europe, in the customary form. I talked the matter over with Mr. Roman, the proprietor, and then wrote a story whose sole object was to give the first number a certain amount of local coloring. It was called "The Luck of Roaring Camp." It was a single picture out of the panorama which had impressed me years before. It was put into type. The proof-reader and printer declared it was immoral and indecent. I read it over again in proof, at the request of the publisher, and was touched, I am afraid, only with my own pathos. I read it to my wife—I had married in the meantime—and it made her cry also. I am told that Mr. Roman also read it to his wife, with the same diabolically illogical result. Nevertheless, the opposition was unshaken.

I had a serious talk with an intimate friend of mine, then the editor of the "Alta California." He was not personally opposed to the story, but felt that that sort of thing might be injudicious and unfavorably affect immigration. I was without a sympathizer or defender. Even Mr. Roman felt that it might imperil the prospects of the magazine. I read the story again, thought the matter over, and told Mr. Roman that if "The Luck of Roaring Camp" was not a good and suitable story I was not a good and suitable editor for his magazine. I said that the chief value of an editor lay in the correctness of his judgment, and if his view was the true one, my judgment was clearly at fault. I am quite sure that if the decision had been left to San Francisco, the series of mining pictures that followed the first would not have been written—at least, not in that city. But the editor remained, and the story appeared. It was received harshly. The religious papers were unanimous in declaring it immoral, and they published columns in its disfavor. The local press, reflecting the pride of a young and new community, could not see why stories should be printed by their representative magazine which put the community into such unfavorable contrast with the effete civilization of the East. They would have none of it!

A month later, however, by return of mail from Boston, there came an important letter. It was from Fields & Osgood, the publishers, and was addressed to me as editor. It requested me to hand the enclosed note to the author of "The Luck of Roaring Camp." The note was their offer to publish anything he chose to write, upon his own terms. This became known, and it turned the tide of criticism. Since Boston indorsed the story, San Francisco was properly proud of it. Thenceforth I had my own way without interruption. Other stories, the mining tales with which you are familiar, followed in quick succession. The numberless impressions of the earlier days were all vividly fixed in my mind, waiting to be worked up, and their success was made apparent to me in very substantial ways, though the religious press continued to suffer from the most painful doubts, and certain local critics who had torn my first story to pieces, fell into a quiet routine of stating that each succeeding story was the worst thing that had yet appeared from my pen.

Local color having been placed, through the dictum of the Atlantic States, at a premium, "The Overland" became what it should have been from the start, truly Californian in tone. [. . .]

In America, the great field is the late war. The dramatists have found and utilized it, but the novelists, the romance writers, have in it the richest possible field for works of serious import, and yet, outside of short stories, they seem to have passed it by. If I had time, nothing would please me better than to go over the ground, or portions of it, and make use of it for future work. Our war of the Revolution is not good material for cosmopolitan purposes. This country has never quite forgotten the way in which it ended. But the war of the Rebellion was our own and is our own; its dramatic and emotional aspects are infinite; and while American writers are coming abroad for scenes to picture, I am in constant fear that some Englishman or Frenchman will go to America and reap the field in romance which we should now, all local feeling having passed away, be utilizing to our own fame and profit.

FROM "THE RISE OF THE SHORT STORY"

While the American literary imagination was still under the influence of English tradition, an unexpected factor was developing to diminish its power. It was Humour—of a quality as distinct and original as the country and civilisation in which it was developed. It was at first noticeable in the anecdote or "story," and, after the fashion of such beginnings, was orally transmitted. It was common in the bar-rooms, the gatherings in "country stores," and finally at public meetings in the mouths of "stump orators." Arguments were clinched and political principles illustrated by "a funny story." It invaded even the camp meetings and pulpit. It at last received the currency of the public Press. But wherever met it was so distinctly original and novel, so individual and characteristic, that it was at once known and appreciated abroad as "an American story."

Crude at first, it received a literary polish in the Press, but its dominant quality remained. It was concise and condensed, yet suggestive. It was delightfully extravagant—or a miracle of understatement.—It voiced not only the dialect, but the habits of thought of a people or locality. It gave a new interest to slang. From a paragraph of a dozen lines it grew into half a column, but always retaining its conciseness and felicity of statement. It was a foe to prolixity of any kind. It admitted no fine writing nor affectation or style. It went directly to the point. It was burdened by no conscientiousness; it was often irreverent; it was devoid of all moral responsibility—but it was original! By degrees it developed character with its incident, often, in a few lines, gave a striking photograph of a community or a section, but always reached its conclusion without an unnecessary word. It became—and still exists as—an essential-feature of newspaper literature. It was the parent of the American "short story." [. . .]

The secret of the American short story is the treatment of characteristic American life, with absolute knowledge of its peculiarities and sympathy with its methods; with no fastidious ignoring of its habitual expression, or the inchoate poetry that may be found even hidden in its slang; with no moral determination except that which may be the legitimate outcome of the story itself; with no more elimination than may be necessary for the artistic conception, and never from the fear of the "fetich" of conventionalism. Of such is the American short story of to-day—the germ of American literature to come.

John Burroughs

(1837–1921)

The most popular writer of his period in a field he virtually made his own, Burroughs was a pioneer in the (new) school of nature writing. As he tells it, he wrote his first nature book, *Wake-Robin* (1871), while a clerk in the Department of the Treasury in Washington, D.C., as he sat at a high mahogany desk and guarded a vault from which money was taken and replaced. "The vault gave me a good surface to rebound from," he later said, "and my fancy bounded back to green things." Influenced by Emerson and later Whitman, whom he knew, adored, and championed, and also a good friend of Theodore Roosevelt, Burroughs wrote some twenty-five volumes; more than a million and a half copies were sold during his lifetime. How we see and appreciate nature are his constant theme; a "poet-naturalist," as he called himself, committed to seeing nature in specifics and whole, Burroughs also wrote philosophical essays and literary criticism in which he talked about style and of which he was a master; his prose is graceful, clear, and unassuming. Without the terse wit of Thoreau—Burroughs was more influenced by Thomas Higginson—he nonetheless shares Whitman's sheer exuberance in closely observing the things of this earth and writing of them, as he says in "The Vital Touch in Literature" (1899), in a new, vivid, personal light. "Thoreau does not interpret nature," Burroughs notes, "but nature interprets him."

Largely forgotten for much of the twentieth century—perhaps because unlike the canonical John Muir he was not an activist—Burroughs has been recently reappraised and appreciated as a latter-day transcendentalist who possessed Whitman's commitment to the secular, the humanistic, and the small. One can hear this as Burroughs explains how he writes and for whom (himself and strangers, as Gertrude Stein would say).

FROM "THE VITAL TOUCH IN LITERATURE"

It is not what the writer tells us that makes literature; it is the way he tells it; or rather, it is the degree in which he imparts to it some rare personal quality or charm that is the gift of his own spirit, something which cannot be detached from the work itself, and which is as vital as the sheen of a bird's plumage, as the texture of a flower's petal. In other words, that which makes literature in all its forms—poetry, fiction, history, oratory—is personal and subjective, in a sense and to a degree that that which makes science, erudition, and the like is not. There is this analogy in nature. The hive bee does not get honey from the flowers; honey is a product of the bee. What she gets from the flowers is mainly sweet water or nectar; this she puts through a process of her own, and to it adds a minute drop of her own secretion, formic acid. It is her special personal contribution that converts the nectar into honey.

In the work of the literary artist, common facts and experiences are changed and heightened in the same way. Sainte-Beuve, speaking of certain parts of Rousseau's *Confessions*, says, "Such pages were, in French literature, the discovery of a new world, a world of sunshine and of freshness, which men had near them without having perceived it." They had not perceived it because they had not had Rousseau's mind to mirror it for them. The sunshine and the freshness were a gift of his spirit. The new world was the old world in a new light. What charmed them was a quality personal to Rousseau. Nature they had always had, but not the Rousseau sensibility to nature.

The same may be said of more recent writers upon outdoor themes.

Readers fancy that in the works of Thoreau or Jefferies some new charm
or quality of nature is disclosed, that something hidden in field or wood
is brought to light. They do not see that what they are in love with is the
mind or spirit of the writer himself. Thoreau does not interpret nature, but
nature interprets him. The new thing disclosed in bird and flower is simply
a new sensibility to these objects in the beholder. In morals and ethics the
same thing is true. Let an essayist like John Foster or Dr. Johnson state a
principle or an idea, and it has a certain value; let an essayist like Ruskin or
Emerson or Carlyle state the same principle, and it has an entirely different
value, makes an entirely different impression, the qualities of mind and
character of these writers are so different. The reader's relation with them
is much more intimate and personal.

   This intimate personal quality is no doubt one of the secrets of what is
called style, perhaps the most important one. If the essay, poem, novel, has
not this personal quality or flavor, it falls short of being good literature.
If it has this, and has not common sense, it still has a good lease of life. It
is quality of mind which makes the writings of Burke rank above those
of Gladstone, Ruskin's criticism rank above that of Hamerton, Froude's
histories above Freeman's, Renan's *Life of Jesus* above that of Strauss; which
makes the pages of Goethe, Coleridge, Lamb, literature in a sense that the
works of many able minds are not. These men impart something personal
and distinctive to the language they use. They make the words their own.
The literary quality is not something put on or superadded. It is not of the
hand, it is of the mind; it is not of the mind, but of the soul; it is of whatever
is most vital and characteristic in the writer. It is confined to no particular
manner and to no particular matter. It may be the gift of writers of widely
different manners, of Carlyle as well as of Arnold; and in men of similar
manners, one may have it, and the other may not. It is as subtle as the tone
of the voice or the glance of the eye. Quality is the one thing in life that
cannot be analyzed, and it is the one thing in art that cannot be imitated.
A man's manner may be copied, but his style, his charm, his real value, can
only be parodied. In the conscious or unconscious imitations of the major
poets by the minor, we get only a suggestion of the manner of the former;
their essential quality cannot be reproduced.

William Dean Howells

(1837–1920)

Born in Ohio, Howells worked in his father's print shops before becoming a
newspaperman and, like his father, connected to the newly formed Republican Party, he wrote a campaign biography for Abraham Lincoln in 1860 that
earned him the post of United States consul in Venice. He was twenty-three.
That same year, the *Atlantic Monthly* published one of his poems, and Howells went to Boston where he met Lowell, Hawthorne, Emerson, Longfellow,
Holmes, and Whittier, all the aging literati associated with the magazine. In
1866 he became its assistant editor, and in 1871 its editor—and kept publishing his own reviews, essays, travel books (three volumes' worth), and then
novels, all while supporting the new tendency in American writing toward
native realism, which he influentially championed while occupying "The Editor's Study" and then "The Easy Chair" at *Harper's Magazine*. Prolific, widely
read, powerful, and enormously supportive of other writers such as Mark
Twain, Henry James, Turgenev, Tolstoy, and Paul Laurence Dunbar, whom he
boosted with unfettered passion, Howells and his novels were unfortunately
ignored by the next generation; Sinclair Lewis called him dead wood, and
the modernists generally decried his saying that "whatever their desserts,
very few American novelists have been led out to be shot, or finally exiled to
the rigors of a winter at Duluth; and in a land where journeymen carpenters

and plumbers strike for four dollars a day the sum of hunger and cold is comparatively small, and the wrong from class to class has been almost inappreciable, though all this is changing for the worse. Our novelists, therefore, concern themselves with the more smiling aspects of life, which are the more American." Yet Howells, of all novelists, was the social activist who, for instance, defended in 1886 the eight Haymarket anarchists hurriedly arrested for allegedly throwing a bomb that killed a policeman. Howells was also the man who ruefully told Edith Wharton that "Americans only want tragedies with happy endings."

Yet today there is no Howells vogue despite wonderful novels like *Indian Summer* (1886), a superbly ironic and compassionate book about aging. Thoroughly committed to writing as a democratic art—that is the nub of his belief in realism—and to writers themselves, Howells was also passionate about the art and craft of writing, about style itself. Style and democracy: such were his life's work, both in practice and preachment, and the following excerpts have been selected to suggest just that.

FROM "CRITICISM AND FICTION"

1893

If I were authorized to address any word directly to our novelists I should say, Do not trouble yourselves about the standards or ideals; but try to be faithful and natural: remember that there is no greatness, no beauty, which does not come from truth to your own knowledge of things; and keep on working, even if your work is not long remembered.

At least three-fifths of the literature called classic, in all languages, no more lives than the poems and stories that perish monthly in our magazines. It is all printed and reprinted, generation after generation, century after century; but it is not alive; it is as dead as the people who wrote it and read it, and to whom it meant something, perhaps; with whom it was a fashion, a caprice, a passing taste. A superstitious piety preserves it, and pretends that it has aesthetic qualities which can delight or edify; but nobody really enjoys it, except as a reflection of the past moods and humors of the race, or a revelation of the author's character; otherwise it is trash, and often very filthy trash, which the present trash generally is not. [. . .]

Sometimes it has seemed to me that the crudest expression of any creative art is better than the finest comment upon it.

FROM "NOVEL-WRITING AND NOVEL-READING"

1899

Each novel has a law of its own, which it seems to create for itself. Almost from the beginning it has its peculiar temperament and quality, and if you happen to be writing that novel you feel that you must respect its law. You, who are master of the whole affair, cannot violate its law without taking its life. It may grow again, but it will be of another generation and another allegiance. No more can you change the nature of a character without spoiling it. You cannot even change the name of a character without running great risk of affecting its vital principle.

FROM *THE RISE OF SILAS LAPHAM*

1884

Miss Kingsbury leaned forward and asked Charles Bellingham if he had read *Tears, Idle Tears,* the novel that was making such a sensation; and when he said no, she said she wondered at him. "It's perfectly heart-breaking, as you'll imagine from the name; but there's such a dear old-fashioned hero and heroine in it, who keep dying for each other all the way through, and making the most wildly satisfactory and unnecessary sacrifices for each other. You feel as if you'd done them yourself."

"Ah, that's the secret of its success," said Bromfield Corey. "It flatters the reader by painting the characters colossal, but with his limp and stoop, so that he feels himself of their supernatural proportions. You've read it, Nanny?"

"Yes," said his daughter. "It ought to have been called *Slop, Silly Slop*."
[. . .]

"Yes," said Mr. Sewell, the minister. [. . .] "The novelists might be the greatest possible help to us if they painted life as it is, and human feelings in their true proportion and relation, but for the most part they have been and are altogether noxious."

This seemed like sense to Lapham; but Bromfield Corey asked: "But what if life as it is isn't amusing? Aren't we to be amused?"

"Not to our hurt," sturdily answered the minister. "And the self-sacrifice painted in most novels like this—"

"*Slop, Silly Slop*?" suggested the proud father of the inventor of the phrase.

"Yes—is nothing but psychical suicide, and is as wholly immoral as the spectacle of a man falling upon his sword." [. . .]

"Right? To be sure I am right. The whole business of love, and love-making and marrying, is painted by the novelists in a monstrous disproportion to the other relations of life. Love is very sweet, very pretty— [. . .] But it's the affair, commonly, of very young people, who have not yet character and experience enough to make them interesting. In novels it's treated, not only as if it were the chief interest of life, but the sole interest of the lives of two ridiculous young persons; and it is taught that love is perpetual, that the glow of a true passion lasts forever; and that it is sacrilege to think or act otherwise." [. . .]

"Commonplace? The commonplace is just that light, impalpable aerial essence which they've never got into their confounded books yet. The novelist who could interpret the common feelings of commonplace people would have the answer to 'the riddle of the painful earth' on his tongue."

FROM "THE EDITOR'S RELATION WITH THE YOUNG CONTRIBUTOR"

Style is only a man's way of saying a thing.

FROM *SELECTED LETTERS*

To James Parton

MARCH 27, 1885

I put all my sense into my novels—I keep none for myself.

FROM AN INTERVIEW WITH STEPHEN CRANE

"I believe that every novel should have an intention. A man should mean something when he writes. [. . .] But, on the other hand, a novel should never preach and berate and storm. [. . .]

"You have often said that the novel is a perspective." [. . .]

"A perspective, certainly."

FROM *SELECTED LETTERS*

To Hugo Erichsen

JUNE 20, 1884

Questionnaire:

1. Do you write during the day or at night? "Daytime; forenoon."
2. Do you make an outline first? "Generally not—almost never."
3. Do you use stimulants such as wine, coffee, or tobacco? "No."
4. Do you have any particular habits at work? "None."
5. How many hours do you work at a time? "Two or three; sometimes four."
6. Do you ever force yourself to work? "I am lazy, and always force myself more or less to work, keeping from it as long as I can invent any excuse. I often work when dull or heavy from a bad night, and find that the indisposition wears off. I rarely miss a day from any cause. After my early dinner I read, correct proof, walk about and pay visits. For a lazy man I am extremely industrious."

FROM *SELECTED LETTERS*

To Charles Eliot Norton

APRIL 23, 1905

I have often thought my intellectual raiment was more than my intellectual body, and that I might finally be convicted, not of having nothing *on*, but that worse nakedness of having nothing *in*. He [James] speaks of me with my style, and such mean application as I was making of it, as seeming to him like a poor man with a diamond which he does not know what to do with; and mostly I suppose I *have* cut rather inferior window glass with it. But I am not sorry for having wrought in common, crude material so much; that is the right American stuff; and perhaps hereafter, when my din is done, if any one is curious to know what that noise was it will be found to have proceeded from a small insect which was scraping about on the surface of our life and trying to get into its meaning for the sake of the other insects larger or smaller. That is, such has been my unconscious work; consciously, I was always, as I still am, trying to fashion a piece of literature out of the life next at hand.

FROM *SELECTED LETTERS*

To Henry James

MAY 19, 1911

I write, and find greater happiness in writing than I ever did.

Henry Adams

(1838–1918)

If there's a first family in nineteenth-century America, the Adams family is it, and Henry Adams its beneficiary. But the legacy is a mixed blessing, as Adams made clear later in life in his tour de force, *The Education of Henry Adams.* For as a direct descendant of two presidents (John Adams and John Quincy Adams), this preeminent historian, political journalist, novelist, editor, and all-around man of letters, Henry Adams, was borne back ceaselessly into the past—in particular, to the medieval past. That made him a skeptical modern with an ironic eye, even though as a private secretary to his father, Charles Francis Adams, the United States minister to Great Britain during the Civil War, he learned quite a bit about the present. Freelance journalist and then professor of history at Harvard for seven years, he wrote that "on the whole, he was content neither with what he had taught nor with the way he had taught it," and he resigned and subsequently wrote a nine-volume history of the United States covering the years 1801 to 1817, biographies of Albert Gallatin and John Randolph, and two novels after moving to Washington, D.C., with his wife, Marion (Clover) Hooper Adams, a photographer who killed herself in 1885 by drinking potassium cyanide (developing fluid). The horrific event sent Adams to Japan and later Tahiti and Samoa to recover; subsequently, he returned to the United States and also lived in Paris, and in

1905 privately published his marvelous meditation, *Mont-Saint-Michel and Chartres;* to the dry-eyed Adams, the Golden Age had ended circa 1066.

Adams relished privacy; he was a snob and a social historian of great insight and perspicacity; he was a prose stylist of rare gift, sort of a politically centered Thoreau (Adams had no use for the transcendentalists). Between 1904 and 1906, he began to circulate his peerless autobiography, *The Education of Henry Adams,* among friends. Written in the third person, the millennial *Education* asserts with typical mordancy that education, and even nature, have taught the narrator nothing; only the laws of force had anything to say to the coming century.

The first excerpt here, from a letter to a friend about the recent biography of Richard Monckton Milnes (Lord Houghton) reveals why Adams would try to prevent anyone from writing a biography of him. In fact, his *Education,* from which the second excerpt, about apprenticeship, was taken, is an attempt, among other things, to fend off future chroniclers. The third excerpt comes from sections of Frederic Bancroft's published diary and tells of conversations with Adams in which the latter uncharacteristically talks about his writing process.

FROM *Selected Letters*

To Charles Milnes Gaskell
August 17, 1891

In fact, unless one or two biographers are assassinated, no considerable man can hope for peace in Heaven—or, for that matter, in Hell. Self-defense is a natural right, and what should be done with a wretch who kills your soul forever, and piles feather-bolsters on it till eternity becomes immortal struggling for breath and air. [. . .] What annoys me is the want of art; the lack of a sharp outline, of moving figures and defined character; the washed-out feeling as though the author sponged every one's face; the

slovenly way in which good material is handled; above all, the constant attitude of defense, almost apology, and the complaints of non-appreciation
which are worse than stupid. If Houghton never understood himself, this
is no excuse for his biographer's not understanding him. The greatest men
generally pride themselves on qualities which the world denies them; but
their biographers do not accent the weakness. Houghton as a statesman
was a failure; as a poet, he was not in the first rank; as a social centre for the
intelligent world he was an unrivaled and unapproachable success; but the
biography proves only the two introductory axioms.

The moral seems to be that every man should write his own life, to
prevent some other fellow from taking it. The moral is almost worse than
the vicious alternative, and, after all, the sacrifice would not ensure safety.
I know no other escape except to be so obscure as not to need gibbeting at
all; but who is safe even then? [. . .]

The world wants so much to be amused, or thinks it does, that, if every
known figure in the Men and Women of the Time is to be made to dance
and grimace and grin and blubber to entertain it, at least the utmost possible entertainment ought to be got out of the unlucky actor. I hate botched
work.

FROM *THE AUTOBIOGRAPHY OF HENRY ADAMS*

So Henry Adams, well aware that he could not succeed as a scholar, and
finding his social position beyond improvement or need of effort, betook
himself to the single ambition which otherwise would scarcely have seemed
a true outcome of the college, though it was the last remnant of the old
Unitarian supremacy. He took to the pen. He wrote. [. . .]

One profession alone seemed possible—the press. In 1860 he would have
said that he was born to be an editor, like at least a thousand other young
graduates from American colleges who entered the world every year enjoy-
ing the same conviction; but in 1866 the situation was altered; the possession of money had become doubly needful for success, and double energy
was essential to get money. America had more than doubled her scale. Yet
the press was still the last resource of the educated poor who could not
be artists and would not be tutors. Any man who was fit for nothing else

could write an editorial or a criticism. The enormous mass of misinforma-
tion accumulated in ten years of nomad life could always be worked off
on a helpless public, in diluted doses, if one could but secure a table in the
corner of a newspaper office. The press was an inferior pulpit; an anony-
mous schoolmaster; a cheap boarding-school; but it was still the nearest
approach to a career for the literary survivor of a wrecked education.

FROM "CHATS WITH HENRY ADAMS"

1910

I was surprised and pleased when I learned that Henry Adams was to be
of the party. He is always quaint, to me at least, and altogether interesting.
His humor is always that of reticence almost to the point of bashfulness,
except that he has no hesitancy in saying whatever he wishes to. Probably
as a result of talk about archaeology, Henry Adams observed in his odd
quiet way, "I am 2550 years old." This caused some of us to smile and object
that we felt pretty old ourselves. Looking at me he said, "You are only half
as old."

Just what he meant in either case was not quite apparent. Probably it was
merely a humorous way of saying that he at seventy-two felt that he was
very old in comparison with the others. At another time he said that he had
found Paris is the only place to live in; the only place where one could find
and do everything that one wished.

We walked away together from the luncheon and as we neared his house
he asked me to come in and sit awhile. To my suggestion that probably
he wished to work, he answered that he never did any work, so I gladly
stopped for half an hour.

I had often wished that I could get him to tell me about his own literary methods and points of view. Now I found it not at all difficult to draw
him out. He said that he had found that what would make thirty or forty
printed pages was about all his mind could turn over and put into proper
shape at one time. As to whether he revised much, he answered: "I doubt
if there is a chapter in my history that I have written less than four or five
times." [. . .]

1911

I have long been waiting for a good opportunity to ask him to let me read his autobiography, which he calls *The Education of Henry Adams*. It is two or three years since I first heard of printed copies being in the hands of some of his friends. He does not give away the copies but lends them with the request that they be returned with criticisms. He exclaimed, "I supposed that I had given you a copy." Then he looked about in the drawers of his writing desk and drew out a large quarto volume with the remark that this was the only one he had at hand, and it was his own copy in which he had made some notes, but I was very welcome to take it; and he put it down on the table before me. [. . .] He stated that his condition in lending a copy was that each reader should contribute at least one marginal criticism. As a rule he had found it difficult to get criticisms. . . .

As we were coming down the stairs I made some remark about the luxury of being able to have one's book printed privately. He said that he had made up his mind never to give another dollar to publishers; that having his books printed this way was a form of indulgence which he could afford because he had no other expensive vices to spend his surplus on—not caring for drinking or cards or women. Then his few words about publishers indicated clearly that he had anything but a high opinion of them. "I will have nothing to do with them or their ways; I have resolved never to give them another dollar because I think they are a bad lot; all except one—and I always decline to name that one," he added with a slight chuckle.

Constance Fenimore Woolson

(1840–1894)

The grandniece of James Fenimore Cooper, Constance Fenimore Woolson
was raised in Cleveland, Ohio, where she attended the Cleveland Female
Seminary and later Madame Chegaray's School in New York City. In 1872,
under the pseudonym Anne March, she published *The Old Stone House;*
three years after that, the publisher James Osgood brought out a collection
of her early stories, *Castle Nowhere*, and in 1880 her popular novel *Anne*
appeared in *Harper's New Monthly Magazine*.

By then Woolson had settled in Europe, residing in Italy, Switzerland,
and England, and there she met Henry James, her great friend. Though belit-
tled by Henry James's biographer Leon Edel as "a somewhat deaf spinster,
trim, compulsive, and meticulous, who wrote popular fiction for the women's
magazines," and though she retains a firm place in the James legend—after
her untimely death, perhaps a suicide, in Venice, where she fell from her
balcony, James famously tried to destroy her papers and drown her clothes—
Woolson is more and more considered a fine writer of books about women
artists. In this, her story "Miss Grief" (1880) reads like a parable of the
woman writer too gifted for the world of "literary men." And James himself admired her preference for "the private side of that somewhat evasive
and exceedingly shifting line which divides human affairs into the profane
and the sacred." This is what she called "suppressed passion" in one of the

excerpts from her notebooks; other comments suggest her abiding concern with matters of style, character, and plot.

FROM *CONSTANCE FENIMORE WOOLSON*

To Arabella Carter Washburn

I have such a horror of "pretty," "sweet" writing that I should almost prefer a style that was ugly and bitter, provided it was *strong*.

To Harriet Benedict Sherman

Anthony Trollope's *Autobiography*, yes. I have read it. It gave me such a feeling! Naturally I noticed more especially his way of working. What could he have been made of! What would I not give for the hundredth part of his robust vitality. I never can do anything by lamplight, nothing when I am tired, nothing—it almost seems sometimes—at any time! . . . And here was this great English Trollope hauled out of bed long before daylight every morning for years, writing by lamplight three hours before he began the "regular" work (post office and hunting!) of the day. Well, he was English and therefore had no nerves, fortunate man!

FROM "REFLECTIONS UPON ART, MUSIC, AND LITERATURE"

Story writers who have eyes and ears (occasionally noses—for scents); but no imagination, or soul; or else, while possessing these last, they rigidly keep them down, not allowing them to enter at all into their literary work. Such writers produce a photographic and phonographic copy of real life as it is on the surface. But is this correct? Is such a copy accurate? Do we interpret our mother, our child, our husband, our wife, by simply what each actually does or says? Have we not, under each act, a thousand intuitions that modify it, or even falsify it? Don't we know that they do not mean this or that because of our under-knowledge of their character? . . .

The plot must be a riddle, so as to excite curiosity.

Ambrose Bierce

(1842–1914?)

Ambrose Bierce disappeared in Mexico in 1914, his end unknown although
it has been speculated that he either killed himself, joined Pancho Villa's
revolution, or never even crossed the border. Maybe all three. If the fate of
humor is despair, as it's been said of Mark Twain, then the fate of Bierce's
gallows humor, his darkly brilliant knowledge of humankind, and his compassionate commitment to the terrible truths we'd rather evade add up to
mystery. Bierce had served in the bloody killing fields of the Civil War; he was
wounded three times and captured once. These experiences clearly shaped
his subsequent fiction into lean, eerie, unsentimental accounts of the worst
people can do. (His most frequently anthologized stories are "Occurrence at
Owl's Creek Bridge" and the fiercely macabre "Chickamauga," a combination
of O. Henry and Kafka and first collected in *Tales of Soldiers and Civilians*
[1892].) Influenced by Poe, disdainful of the "realism" preached by Howells,
and bristling with corrosive wit, as a prolific and pre-muckraking journalist
Bierce also for many years wrote for William Randolph Hearst's *San Francisco
Examiner,* where, he said, he persuaded himself "I could do more good by
addressing those who had the greatest need of me—the millions of readers to whom Mr. Hearst is a misleading light." But he was also an estimable
poet, who wrote against the grain of Whitman's optimism and ego. Typically,

he said, "Great poets fire the world with fagots big / That make a crackling racket, / But I'm content with but a whispering twig / To warm some single jacket."

Excerpts from his wickedly amusing *The Devil's Dictionary* (1906; 1911), which was written in desultory fashion over two decades, show Bierce at his satiric best; from another perspective, his letters reveal an almost idealistic commitment to literature as distinct from moralization, journalism, propaganda, and the cry for reform, which was a mantra of the end of the century.

FROM *THE DEVIL'S DICTIONARY*

EDITOR, n. [. . .] Master of mysteries and lord of law, high-pinnacled upon the throne of thought, his face suffused with the dim splendors of the Transfiguration, his legs intertwisted and his tongue a-cheek, the editor spills his will along the paper and cuts it off in lengths to suit. And at intervals from behind the veil of the temple is heard the voice of the foreman demanding three inches of wit and six lines of religious meditation, or bidding him turn off the wisdom and whack up some pathos. [. . .]

ELEGY, n. A composition in verse, in which, without employing any of the methods of humor, the writer aims to produce in the reader's mind the dampest kind of dejection. [. . .]

EPIGRAM, n. A short, sharp saying in prose or verse, frequently characterized by acidity or acerbity and sometimes by wisdom. Following are some of the more notable epigrams of the learned and ingenious Dr. Jamrach Holobom:

> We know better the needs of ourselves than of others. To serve oneself is economy of administration.

> In each human heart are a tiger, a pig, an ass and a nightingale. Diversity of character is due to their unequal activity. [. . .]

NOVEL, n. A short story padded. A species of composition bearing the same relation to literature that the panorama bears to art. As it is too long to be

read at a sitting the impressions made by its successive parts are successively effaced, as in the panorama. Unity, totality of effect, is impossible;
for besides the few pages last read all that is carried in mind is the mere plot
of what has gone before. To the romance the novel is what photography is
to painting. Its distinguishing principle, probability, corresponds to the
literal actuality of the photograph and puts it distinctly into the category of
reporting; whereas the free wing of the romancer enables him to mount to
such altitudes of imagination as he may be fitted to attain; and the first three
essentials of the literary art are imagination, imagination and imagination.
The art of writing novels, such as it was, is long dead everywhere except in
Russia, where it is new. Peace to its ashes—some of which have a large sale.

ROMANCE, n. Fiction that owes no allegiance to the God of Things as They
Are. In the novel the writer's thought is tethered to probability, as a domestic
horse to the hitching-post, but in romance it ranges at will over the entire
region of the imagination—free, lawless, immune to bit and rein. Your novelist is a poor creature, as Carlyle might say—a mere reporter. He may invent
his characters and plot, but he must not imagine anything taking place that
might not occur, albeit his entire narrative is candidly a lie. Why he imposes
this hard condition on himself, and "drags at each remove a lengthening
chain" of his own forging he can explain in ten thick volumes without illumi-
nating by so much as a candle's ray the black profound of his own ignorance
of the matter. There are great novels, for great writers have "laid waste their
powers" to write them, but it remains true that far and away the most fascinating fiction that we have is "The Thousand and One Nights."

SCRIBBLER, n. A professional writer whose views are antagonistic to one's
own.

SERIAL, n. A literary work, usually a story that is not true, creeping through
several issues of a newspaper or magazine. Frequently appended to each
installment is a "synopsis of preceding chapters" for those who have not
read them, but a direr need is a synopsis of succeeding chapters for those
who do not intend to read them. A synopsis of the entire work would be
still better. [. . .]

SUCCESS, n. The one unpardonable sin against one's fellows.

FROM *THE LETTERS OF AMBROSE BIERCE*

To Blanche Partington

JULY 31, 1892

You receive my suggestion about trying your hand [. . .] at writing, with assent and apparently pleasure. But, alas, not for love of the art, but for the purpose of helping God re-pair his botchwork world. You want to "reform things," poor girl—to rise and lay about you, slaying monsters and liberating captive maids. You would "help to alter for the better the position of working-women." You would be a missionary—and the rest of it. Perhaps I shall not make myself understood when I say that this discourages me; that in such aims (worthy as they are) I would do nothing to assist you; that such ambitions are not only impracticable but incompatible with the spirit that gives success in art; that such ends are a prostitution of art; that "helpful" writing is dull reading. If you had had more experience of life I should regard what you say as entirely conclusive against your possession of any talent of a literary kind. But you are so young and untaught in that way—and I have the testimony of little felicities and purely literary touches (apparently unconscious) in your letters—perhaps your unschooled heart and hope should not be held as having spoken the conclusive word. But surely, my child—as surely as anything in mathematics—Art will laurel no brow having a divided allegiance. Love the world as much as you will, but serve it otherwise. The best service you can perform by writing is to write well with no care for anything but that. [. . .]

Literature (I don't mean journalism) is an art;—it is not a form of benevolence. It has nothing to do with "reform," and when used as a means of reform suffers accordingly and justly.

To Blanche Partington

AUGUST 17, 1892

It seems to me that men holding Tolstoi's view are not properly literary men (that is to say, artists) at all. They are "missionaries," who, in their zeal to lay about them, do not scruple to seize any weapon that they can lay their hands on; they would grab a crucifix to beat a dog. The dog is well beaten, no doubt (which makes him a worse dog than he was before) but note the condition of the crucifix!

To Robert H. Davis

OCTOBER 12, 1904

Read—but that will do at present. And as you read don't forget that the rules of the literary art are deduced from the work of the masters who wrote in ignorance of them or in unconsciousness of them. That fixes their value; it is secondary to that of natural qualifications. None the less, it is considerable.

If I have to write rot, I prefer to do it for the newspapers, which make no false pretences and are frankly rotten, and in which the badness of a bad thing escapes detection or is forgotten as soon as it is cold.

William James

(1842–1910)

"How you produce volume after volume the way you do is more than I can conceive," William James once wrote his novelist brother Henry. "But you haven't to forge every sentence in the teeth of irreducible and stubborn facts as I do. It is like walking through the densest brush wood." Henry may be the novelist—the *consummate* novelist—but the older William cared just as much about prose style. That William Dean Howells, reviewing his *Principles of Psychology* (1890), emphasized the book's literariness, and that he wrote in a vivid, accessible, and dynamic style, were great achievements to this consummate philosopher. Born the eldest of five strikingly talented children of a mercurial, brilliant father, William James suffered from a prolonged crisis in vocation until he at last developed a point of view indelibly his own and one that altered the course of American philosophy and psychology. But with his own emphasis on plain style, he often found the work of his brother Henry somewhat discomfiting; and though he eventually praised and supported him, as suggested by these excerpts from three letters, one written in 1872 and the others three decades later, William often took him to task for "freezing the genial current" in ways that afford us a peek through this nonfiction writer's window as he addresses himself to matters verbal and stylistic. They also afford some criticism of method that

Henry James would receive at the hands of less enthusiastic and intelligent readers than his dazzling brother.

FROM *THE SELECTED LETTERS OF WILLIAM JAMES*

To Henry James

NOVEMBER 24, 1872

I have said nothing to you about "Guest's Confession" which I read and enjoyed, admiring its cleverness though not loving it exactly. I noted at the time a couple of blemishes, one of the French phrase *les indifférents* at the end of one of her sentences which suddenly chills one's very marrow. The other expression: "to whom I had dedicated a sentiment," earlier in the story, — I cannot well look up the page, but you will doubtless identify it. Of the people who experience a personal dislike, so to speak, of your stories, the most I think will be repelled by the element which gets expression in these two phrases, something cold, thin-blooded and priggish suddenly popping in and freezing the genial current. And I think that is the principal defect you have now to guard against. In flexibility, ease, and light power of style you clearly continue to gain — "Guest's Confession" and this last letter [published in *The Nation*] are proofs of it; but I think you should fight shy of that note of literary reminiscence in the midst of what ought to be pure imagination absorbed in the object, which keeps every now and then betraying itself, as in these French phrases. I criticize you so much as perhaps to seem a mere caviler, but I think it ought to be of use to you to have any detailed criticism from even a wrong judge, and you don't get much from anyone else. I meanwhile say nothing of the great delight which all your pieces give me by their insight into the shades of being, and their exquisite diction and sense of beauty and expression in the sights of the world. I still believe in your greatness as a critic and hope you will send home something good of that kind. Alice said you were going to do *Middlemarch*.

FROM *WILLIAM AND HENRY JAMES,*
SELECTED LETTERS

To Henry James

NOVEMBER 24, 1872

You've reversed every traditional canon of story-telling (especially the fundamental one of *telling* the story, which you carefully avoid) and have created a new *genre littéraire* which I can't help thinking perverse, but in which you nevertheless *succeed*, for I read with interest to the end (many pages and innumerable sentences twice over to see what the dickens they could possibly mean) and all with unflagging curiosity to know what the upshot might become.

FROM *THE SELECTED LETTERS OF WILLIAM JAMES*

To Henry James

OCTOBER 1902

I've been so overwhelmed with work, and the mountain of the *Unread* has piled up so, that only in these days here have I really been able to settle down to your "American Scene," which in its peculiar way seems to me *supremely great*. You know how opposed your whole "third manner" of execution is to the literary ideals which animate my crude and Orson-like breast, mine being to say a thing in one sentence as straight and explicit as it can be made, and then to drop it forever; yours being to avoid naming it straight, but by dint of breathing and sighing all round and round it, to arouse in the reader who may have had a similar perception already (Heaven help him if he hasn't!) the illusion of a solid object, made (like the "ghost" at the Polytechnic) wholly out of impalpable materials, air, and the prismatic interferences of light, ingeniously focused by mirrors upon empty space. But you do it, that's the queerness! And the complication of innuendo and associative reference on the enormous scale to which you give way to it does so build out the matter for the reader that the result is to solidify, by the mere bulk of the process, the like perception from which he has to start. As air, by dint of its volume, will weigh like a corporeal body; so his own poor little initial perception, swathed in this gigantic envelopment of suggestive atmosphere, grows like a germ into something vastly bigger and more substantial. But it's the rummest method for one to employ systematically as you do nowadays; and you employ it at your peril. In this crowded and hurried reading age, pages that require such close attention remain unread and neglected. You can't skip a word if you are to get the effect, and 19 out of 20 worthy readers grow intolerant. The method seems perverse: "Say it out, for God's sake," they cry, "and have done with it." And so I say now, give us one thing in your older directer manner, just to show that, in spite of your paradoxical success in this unheard-of method, you can still write according to accepted canons. Give us that interlude; and then continue like the "curiosity of literature" which you have become. For gleams and innuendoes and felicitous verbal insinuations you are unapproachable, but the core of literature is solid. Give it to us once again! The bare perfume of things will not support existence, and the effect of solidity you reach is but perfume and simulacrum.

For God's sake don't answer these remarks, which [. . .] are but the peristaltic belchings of my own crabbed organism. For one thing, your account of America is largely one of its omissions, silences, vacancies. You work them up like solids, for those readers who already germinally perceive them (to others you are totally incomprehensible). I said to myself over and over in reading: "How much greater the triumph, if instead of dwelling thus only upon America's vacuities, he could make positive suggestion of what in 'Europe' or Asia may exist to fill them." That would be nutritious to so many American readers whose souls are only too ready to leap to suggestion, but who are now too inexperienced to know what is meant by the contrast-effect from which alone your book is written. If you could supply the background which is the foil, in terms more full and positive! At present it is supplied only by the abstract geographic term "Europe." But of course anything of that kind is excessively difficult; and you will probably say that you are supplying it all along by your novels. Well, the verve and animal spirits with which you can keep your method going, first on one place then on another, through all those tightly printed pages is something marvelous; and there are pages surely doomed to be immortal, those on the "drummers," e.g., at the beginning of "Florida." They are in the best sense Rabelaisian.

But a truce, a truce! I had no idea, when I sat down, of pouring such a bath of my own subjectivity over you. Forgive! forgive! and don't reply, don't at any rate in the sense of defending yourself, but only in that of attacking me, if you feel so minded. [. . .]

Sidney Lanier

(1842–1881)

Born in Macon, Georgia, the same year as Ambrose Bierce, Lanier's foreshort-
ened life resembles Henry Timrod's. A poet and amateur musician, Lanier
joined the Macon Volunteers in July 1861; captured and imprisoned in 1864,
he contracted the tuberculosis that would later kill him. Impoverished after
the war, he worked for a time as a hotel clerk and then as a law clerk in his
father's office, and, though admitted to the bar in 1869, he managed to
pursue his music. "An impulse, simply irresistible, drives me into the world
of poetry and music," he told his brother. Named first flutist of the Peabody
Conservatory's orchestra in Baltimore, Maryland, in 1873, he also published
his first poem, the popular "Corn," in *Lippincott's Magazine* in 1874; in the
excerpt below, Lanier talks about the initial rejection of this poem and how
that confirmed him, finally, in his vocation, and over time (which was short)
he bucked the trend of poetic convention with his passionate interest in and
gift for metrics, sound pattern, and rhythm. As he once told his wife, "The
forms of today require a certain trim smugness and clean-shaven propriety in
the face and dress of a poem." Only one volume of poems appeared during
his lifetime, though he lectured on poetry at Johns Hopkins University and
wrote what is considered an important critical work, *The Science of English
Verse* (1880), based on his knowledge both of music and of Elizabethan

verse. How he thinks about verse is evident from his letters—and from his poetry. As he famously wrote in "The Symphony," "Music is Love in search of a word."

FROM *The Centennial Edition of the Works of Sidney Lanier*

To Virginia Hankins
July 1870

Dear Friend, be not persuaded that the taste of the world is immoral. It is not so. The world bites at the high and the pure and the true, as a fish at its bait. It is only necessary that the writer should do one of two things: let him either promulgate his high, his pure, his true thought in the forms which his particular age demands, or, let him create NEW forms, and learn the age to appropriate and utilize and enjoy them. Either of these methods is open to the faithful and conscientious writer: Either is good.

Observe then that the Successful writer must look to his matter, and to his form. Each age has its particular forms, under which it can most easily recognize the noble thought of genius. Genius must consult these forms: or, if it think of better forms, it must learn the age (and this is a hard task) to use the new forms. [. . .]

To Bayard Taylor

Now it seems to me—as a mere extended formulation of the thoroughly unconscious action of the mind in this poem—that every poem, from a Sonnet to *Macbeth*, has substantially these elements,—(1) a Hero, (2) a Plot, and (3) a Crisis: and that its perfection as a work of art will consist in the simplicity and the completeness with which the first is involved in the second and illustrated in the third. In the case of a short poem the hero is the central Idea, whatever that may be: the plot is whatever is said about that idea, its details all converging, both in tone and in general direction, thereupon: and the crisis is the unity of impression sealed or confirmed or climax'd by the last connected sentence, or sentiment, or verse, of the poem. Of course I mean that this is the most general expression of the artistic plan of a poem: it is the system of verses, which may be infinitely varied, but to which all variations may be finally referred. I do not think that there is, as you feared, any necessary reason why a poem so constructed should present "a too-conscious air of design": that is a matter which will depend solely upon the genuineness of the inspiration and the consummate command of his resources by the artist.

Is not this frame-work essentially that of every work of any art? Does not every painting, every statue, every architectural design owe whatever it has of artistic perfection to the nearness with which it may approach the fundamental scheme of a Ruling Idea (or Hero), a Plot (or involution of the Ruling Idea in complexities related to or clustering about it), and a Dénouement, or Impression-as-a-whole?

I don't mean this for a theory: I hate theories, I intend it only to be a convenient synthesis of a great number of small facts: and therefore I don't stickle at all for calling the elements of a work of art "Heroes," or "Plots," or "Crises," and the like—, only using those terms as the shortest way of expressing my meaning.

In looking around at the publications of the younger American poets I am struck with the circumstance that none of them even attempt anything great. The morbid fear of doing something wrong or unpolished appears to have influenced their choice of subjects. Hence the endless multiplication of those little feeble magazine-lyrics which we all know; consisting of one minute idea, each, which is put in the last line of the fourth verse, the other three verses and three lines being mere sawdust and surplusage.

FROM "MARSH SONG — AT SUNSET"

Over the monstrous shambling sea,
    Over the Caliban sea,
Bright Ariel-cloud, though lingerest:
Oh wait, oh wait, in the warm red West,—
    Thy Prospero I'll be.

Over the humped and fishy sea;
    Over the Caliban sea,
O cloud in the West, like a thought in the heart
Of pardon, loose thy wing and start,
    And do a grace for me.

Over the huge and huddling sea,
    Over the Caliban sea,
Bring hither my brother Antonio,—Man,—
My injurer: night breaks the ban;
    Brother, I pardon thee.

Henry James

(1843–1916)

Born in New York City, raised in Albany and Newport and Boston, among other places, James was taken to Europe when he was not a year old, for his philosopher father wanted to make sure his children were internationally bred and widely educated. As a result, young James became fluent in French and a master of cultural nuances at an early age. A back injury—the subject of much biographical speculation—exempted him from enlisting during the Civil War, and in 1862 he entered Harvard Law School, where he stayed for just a semester. Three years later, he published for the first time under his name in the *Atlantic Monthly*, the magazine of the moment, and thus launched, he continued writing reviews and stories. In 1875 he published *Roderick Hudson*, a novel, as well as a travel book, *Transatlantic Sketches* and his first collection of tales, *A Passionate Pilgrim*. Books such as *The American* (1877) and *The Europeans* (1878) followed, along with his best-selling *Daisy Miller* (1878), a book said to "insult" American girlhood. But James's scope was broader: he investigated the moral culpability of Americans abroad, the vaunted and sometimes desiccated sophistication of Europeans, the over-arching sense of culture, the delicacy of self-deception, both cultural and personal. In the 1880s he enlarged and enriched the novel with *The Portrait of a Lady* (1881), *The Bostonians* (1886), *The Princess Casamassima* (1886), and *The Tragic Muse* (1890). He also experimented in theater and with the short story, and his late, great period includes such novels as *The Wings of the Dove* (1902), *The Ambassadors* (1903), and *The Golden Bowl* (1904).

Listing such books and sketches cannot suffice, for of all writers in the nineteenth century, James took writing and its craft so seriously that he wrote on it eloquently and often in his various reviews and essays and in his prefaces to his novels, revealing subtlety, generosity, sensibility, and a passion to reach further, higher, deeper all at the same time in a prose that is sinuous and sly. "You are our Turgenev," said his friend Constance Woolson after Turgenev's death, and T.S. Eliot called James the most intelligent man of his generation, claiming James had a "mind so fine that no idea could violate it." In fact, his very name is synonymous with the practice—the art—of fiction, which he described in one of his best-known essays, "The Art of Fiction" (1884), which is worth excerpting at length. (Written in response to the published lecture about fiction by a cheerfully popular novelist, Walter Besant, James's reply is one of his most insightful and moving expressions of what the novel is and can do.) But James on the art of fiction and the meaning of it as well is an embarrassment of riches, so what follows, also, are some of his other comments, in stories and letters, that all writers could usefully pin over their desks.

FROM *HENRY JAMES: THE YOUNG MASTER*

To Grace Norton
APRIL 13, 1871

The more I think of it, the more I deprecate the growing tendency—born of the very desperation of the writer—to transfer directly and bodily, without any intellectual transmutation, all the crude accidents of his life as they encursively befall, into the subject matter of literature. Before we are fairly launched here we are being swamped by the dire vulgarity of it.

FROM *WILLIAM AND HENRY JAMES,*
SELECTED LETTERS

To William James
SEPTEMBER 22 [1871]

Your criticism of my *Nation* letters was welcome & just: their tendency is
certainly to over-refinement. Howells wrote to me to the same effect & you
are both right. But I am not afraid of being able, on the whole, & insofar
as this is deeply desirable, to work it off with practise. Beyond a certain
point this would not be desirable, I think—for me at least who must give
up the ambition of being a free-going & light paced enough writer to please
the multitude. The multitude, I am more & more convinced, has absolutely no taste—none at least that a thinking man is bound to defer to. To
write for the few who have is bound to lose money, but I am not afraid of
starving. Au point où nous en sommes all writing not really leavened with
thought—of some sort or other—is terribly unprofitable, & to try & work
one's material closely is the only way to form a manner on which one can
keep afloat—without intellectual bankruptcy at least. I have a mortal horror of seeming to write thin—& if I ever feel my pen beginning to scratch,
shall consider that my death-knell has rung.

FROM "IVAN TURGÉNIEFF"

Evil is insolent and strong; beauty enchanting but rare; goodness very
apt to be weak; folly very apt to be defiant; wickedness to carry the day;
imbeciles in great places, people of sense in small, and mankind generally,
unhappy. But the world as it stands is no illusion, no phantasm, no evil
dream of a night; we wake up to it again for ever and ever; we can neither
forget it nor deny it nor dispense with it. We can welcome experience as it
comes, and give what it demands, in exchange for something which it is idle
to pause to call much or little so long as it contributes to swell the volume
of consciousness. In this there is mingled pain and delight, but over the
mysterious mixture there hovers a visible rule, that bids us to learn to will
and seek to understand.

FROM *THE SPOILS OF POYNTON*

The very source of interest for the artist [. . .] resides in the strong consciousness of his seeing all for himself. He has to borrow his motive, and this certainly is half the battle; and this motive is his ground, his site, and his foundation. But after that he only lends and gives, builds and piles high, lays together
the blocks quarried in the deeps of his imagination. He thus remains all the
while in intimate commerce with his motive, and can say to himself—what
really more than anything inflames and sustains him—that he alone has
the *secret* of the particular case, that he alone can measure the truth of the
direction to be taken by his particular idea. There can be for him, evidently,
only one logic for these things; there can be for him only one truth and one
direction—the quarter in which his subject most completely expresses itself.
The careful ascertainment of how it shall do so, and the art of guiding it
with consequent authority—since this sense of "authority" is for the master-
builder the treasure of treasures, or at least the joy of joys—renews in the
modern alchemist something like the dream of the secret of life.

Extravagant as the mere statement sounds, one seemed accordingly to
handle the secret of life in drawing the positive right truth out of the so
easy muddle of wrong truths.

FROM "THE ART OF FICTION"

The only obligation to which in advance we may hold a novel without
incurring the accusation of being arbitrary, is that it be interesting. That
general responsibility rests upon it, but it is the only one I can think of.
The ways in which it is at liberty to accomplish this result (of interesting
us) strike me as innumerable and such as can only suffer from being marked
out, or fenced in, by prescription. They are as various as the temperament
of man, and they are successful in proportion as they reveal a particular
mind, different from others. A novel is in its broadest definition a personal
impression of life; that, to begin with, constitutes its value, which is greater
or less according to the intensity of the impression. But there will be no
intensity at all, and therefore no value, unless there is freedom to feel and
say. The tracing of a line to be followed, of a tone to be taken, of a form

to be filled out, is a limitation of that freedom and a suppression of the very thing that we are most curious about. The form, it seems to me, is to be appreciated after the fact; then the author's choice has been made, his standard has been indicated; then we can follow lines and directions and compare tones. Then, in a word, we can enjoy one of the most charming of pleasures, we can estimate quality, we can apply the test of execution. The execution belongs to the author alone; it is what is most personal to him, and we measure him by that. The advantage, the luxury, as well as the torment and responsibility of the novelist, is that there is no limit to what he may attempt as an executant—no limit to his possible experiments, efforts, discoveries, successes. Here it is especially that he works, step by step, like his brother of the brush, of whom we may always say that he has painted his picture in a manner best known to himself. His manner is his secret, not necessarily a deliberate one. He cannot disclose it, as a general thing, if he would; he would be at a loss to teach it to others. I say this with a due recollection of having insisted on the community of method of the artist who paints a picture and the artist who writes a novel. The painter *is* able to teach the rudiments of his practice, and it is possible, from the study of good work (granted the aptitude), both to learn how to paint and to learn how to write. Yet it remains true, without injury to the *rapprochement*, that the literary artist would be obliged to say to his pupil much more than the other, "Ah, well, you must do it as you can!" It is a question of degree, a matter of delicacy. If there are exact sciences there are also exact arts, and the grammar of painting is so much more definite that it makes the difference. [. . .] The characters, the situation, which strike one as real [in the novel] will be those that touch and interest one most, but the measure of reality is very difficult to fix. The reality of Don Quixote or of Mr. Micawber is a very delicate shade; it is a reality so coloured by the author's vision that, vivid as it may be, one would hesitate to propose it as a model; one would expose one's self to some very embarrassing questions on the part of a pupil. It goes without saying that you will not write a good novel unless you possess the sense of reality; but it will be difficult to give you a recipe for calling that sense into being. Humanity is immense and reality has a myriad forms; the most one can affirm is that some of the flowers of fiction have the odour of it, and others have not; as for telling you in advance how your nosegay should be composed, that is another affair. It is equally excellent and inconclusive to say that one must write from experience; to our supposititious aspirant such a declaration might savour of mockery. What kind of experience is intended, and where does it begin and end? Experience is never limited and it is never complete; it is an immense sensibility, a kind of huge spider-web, of the finest silken threads, suspended in the chamber of consciousness and catching every air-borne particle in its tissue. It is the very atmosphere of the mind; and when the mind is imaginative — much more when it happens to be that of a man of genius — it takes to itself the faintest hints of life, it converts the very pulses of the air into revelations. The young lady living in a village has only to be a damsel upon whom nothing is lost to make it quite unfair (as it seems to me) to declare to her that she shall have nothing to say about the military. Greater miracles have been seen than that, imagination assisting, she should speak the truth about some of these gentlemen. I remember an English novelist, a woman of genius, telling me that she was much commended for the impression she had managed to give in one of her tales of the nature and way of life of the French Protestant youth. She had been asked where she learned so much about this recondite being, she had been congratulated on her peculiar opportunities. These opportunities consisted in her having once, in Paris, as she ascended a staircase, passed an open door where, in the household of a *pasteur*, some of the young Protestants were seated at table round a finished meal. The glimpse made a picture; it lasted only a moment, but that moment was experience. She had got her impression, and she evolved her type. She knew what youth was, and what Protestantism; she also had the advantage of having seen what it was to be French; so that she converted these ideas into a concrete image and produced a reality. Above all, however, she was blessed with the faculty which when you give it an inch takes an ell, and which for the artist is a much greater source of strength than any accident of residence or of place in the social scale. The power to guess the unseen from the seen, to trace the implication of things, to judge the whole piece by the pattern, the condition of feeling life, in general, so completely that you are well on your way to knowing any particular corner of it — this cluster of gifts may almost be said to constitute experience, and they occur in country and in town, and in the most differing stages of education. If experience consists of impressions, it may be said that impressions are experience, just as (have we not seen it?) they are the very air we breathe.

Therefore, if I should certainly say to a novice, "Write from experience, and experience only," I should feel that this was a rather tantalising monition if I were not careful immediately to add, "Try to be one of the people on whom nothing is lost!"

I am far from intending by this to minimise the importance of exactness—of truth of detail. One can speak best from one's own taste, and I may therefore venture to say that the air of reality (solidity of specification) seems to me to be the supreme virtue of a novel—the merit on which all its other merits (including that conscious moral purpose of which Mr. Besant speaks) helplessly and submissively depend. If it be not there, they are all as nothing, and if these be there, they owe their effect to the success with which the author has produced the illusion of life. The cultivation of this success, the study of this exquisite process, form, to my taste, the beginning and the end of the art of the novelist. They are his inspiration, his despair, his reward, his torment, his delight. It is here, in very truth, that he competes with life; it is here that he competes with his brother the painter in *his* attempt to render the look of things, the look that conveys their meaning, to catch the colour, the relief, the expression, the surface, the substance of the human spectacle. It is in regard to this that Mr. Besant is well inspired when he bids him take notes. He cannot possibly take too many, he cannot possibly take enough. All life solicits him, and to "render" the simplest surface, to produce the most momentary illusion, is a very complicated business. His case would be easier, and the rule would be more exact, if Mr. Besant had been able to tell him what notes to take. But this I fear he can never learn in any hand-book; it is the business of his life. He has to take a great many in order to select a few, he has to work them up as he can, and even the guides and philosophers who might have most to say to him must leave him alone when it comes to the application of precepts, as we leave the painter in communion with his palette. That his characters "must be clear in outline," as Mr. Besant says—he feels that down to his boots; but how he shall make them so is a secret between his good angel and himself. It would be absurdly simple if he could be taught that a great deal of "description" would make them so, or that, on the contrary, the absence of description and the cultivation of dialogue, or the absence of dialogue and the multiplication of "incident," would rescue him from his difficulties. Nothing, for instance, is more possible than that he be of a turn of mind for which this odd, literal opposition of description and dialogue, incident and description, has little meaning and light. People often talk of these things as if they had a kind of internecine distinctness, instead of melting into each other at every breath and being intimately associated parts of one general effort of expression. I cannot imagine composition existing in a series of blocks, nor conceive, in any novel worth discussing at all, of a passage of description that is not in its intention narrative, a passage of dialogue that is not in its intention descriptive, a touch of truth of any sort that does not partake of the nature of incident, and an incident that derives its interest from any other source than the general and only source of the success of a work of art—that of being illustrative. A novel is a living thing, all one and continuous, like every other organism, and in proportion as it lives will it be found, I think, that in each of the parts there is something of each of the other parts. The critic who over the close texture of a finished work will pretend to trace a geography of items will mark some frontiers as artificial, I fear, as any that have been known to history. There is an old-fashioned distinction between the novel of character and the novel of incident, which must have cost many a smile to the intending romancer who was keen about his work. It appears to me as little to the point as the equally celebrated distinction between the novel and the romance—to answer as little to any reality. There are bad novels and good novels, as there are bad pictures and good pictures; but that is the only distinction in which I see any meaning, and I can as little imagine speaking of a novel of character as I can imagine speaking of a picture of character. When one says picture, one says of character, when one says novel, one says of incident, and the terms may be transposed. What is character but the determination of incident? What is incident but the illustration of character? What is a picture or a novel that is not of character? What else do we seek in it and find in it? It is an incident for a woman to stand up with her hand resting on a table and look out at you in a certain way; or if it be not an incident, I think it will be hard to say what it is. At the same time it is an expression of character. If you say you don't see it (character in that *allons donc!*) this is exactly what the artist who has reasons of his own for thinking he *does* see it undertakes to show you. When a young man makes up his mind that he has not faith enough, after all, to enter the Church, as he intended, that is an incident, though you may not hurry to the end of the chapter to see whether perhaps he doesn't change once more. I do not say that these are extraordinary or startling incidents. I do not pretend to estimate the degree of interest proceeding from them, for this will depend upon the skill of the painter. It sounds almost puerile to say that some incidents are intrinsically much more important than others, and I need not take this precaution after having professed my sympathy for the major ones in remarking that the only classification of the novel that I can understand is into the interesting and the uninteresting. [. . .]

Of course it is of execution that we are talking—that being the only point of a novel that is open to contention. This is perhaps too often lost sight of, only to produce interminable confusions and cross-purposes. We must grant the artist his subject, his idea, what the French call his *donnée;* our criticism is applied only to what he makes of it. Naturally I do not mean that we are bound to like it or find it interesting: in case we do not our course is perfectly simple—to let it alone. We may believe that of a certain idea even the most sincere novelist can make nothing at all, and the event may perfectly justify our belief; but the failure will have been a failure to execute, and it is in the execution that the fatal weakness is recorded. If we pretend to respect the artist at all we must allow him his freedom of choice, in the face, in particular cases, of innumerable presumptions that the choice will not fructify. Art derives a considerable part of its beneficial exercise from flying in the face of presumptions, and some of the most interesting experiments of which it is capable are hidden in the bosom of common things. Gustave Flaubert has written a story about the devotion of a servant-girl to a parrot, and the production, highly finished as it is, cannot on the whole be called a success. We are perfectly free to find it flat, but I think it might have been interesting; and I, for my part, am extremely glad he should have written it; it is a contribution to our knowledge of what can be done or what cannot. Ivan Turgénieff has written a tale about a deaf and dumb serf and a lap-dog, and the thing is touching, loving, a little masterpiece. He struck the note of life where Gustave Flaubert missed it—he flew in the face of a presumption and achieved a victory.

Nothing, of course, will ever take the place of the good old fashion of "liking" a work of art or not liking it; the more improved criticism will not

abolish that primitive, that ultimate, test. [. . .] [But] I am quite at a loss to
imagine anything (at any rate in this matter of fiction) that people *ought* to
like or to dislike. Selection will be sure to take care of itself, for it has a constant motive behind it. That motive is simply experience. As people feel life,
so they will feel the art that is most closely related to it. This closeness of
relation is what we should never forget in talking of the effort of the novel.
Many people speak of it as a factitious, artificial form, a product of ingenuity, the business of which is to alter and arrange the things that surround us,
to translate them into conventional, traditional moulds. This, however, is a
view of the matter which carries us but a very short way, condemns the art
to an eternal repetition of a few familiar *clichés*, cuts short its development,
and leads us straight up to a dead wall. Catching the very note and trick,
the strange irregular rhythm of life, that is the attempt whose strenuous
force keeps Fiction upon her feet. In proportion as in what she offers us we
see life *without* rearrangement do we feel that we are touching the truth; in
proportion as we see it *with* rearrangement do we feel that we are being put
off with a substitute, a compromise and convention. It is not uncommon
to hear an extraordinary assurance of remark in regard to this matter of
rearranging, which is often spoken of as if it were the last word of art. Mr.
Besant seems to me in danger of falling into this great error with his rather
unguarded talk about "selection." Art is essentially selection, but it is a
selection whose main care is to be typical, to be inclusive. For many people
art means rose-coloured windows, and selection means picking a bouquet
for Mrs. Grundy. They will tell you glibly that artistic considerations have
nothing to do with the disagreeable, with the ugly; they will rattle off shal-
low commonplaces about the province of art and the limits of art, till you
are moved to some wonder in return as to the province and the limits of
ignorance. It appears to me that no one can ever have made a seriously artistic attempt without becoming conscious of an immense increase—a kind
of revelation—of freedom. One perceives, in that case—by the light of a
heavenly ray—that the province of art is all life, all feeling, all observation,
all vision. As Mr. Besant so justly intimates, it is all experience. That is a
sufficient answer to those who maintain that it must not touch the painful,
who stick into its divine unconscious bosom little prohibitory inscriptions
on the end of sticks, such as we see in public gardens—"It is forbidden to
walk on the grass; it is forbidden to touch the flowers; it is not allowed to

introduce dogs, or to remain after dark; it is requested to keep to the right."
The young aspirant in the line of fiction, whom we continue to imagine,
will do nothing without taste, for in that case his freedom would be of little
use to him; but the first advantage of his taste will be to reveal to him the
absurdity of the little sticks and tickets. If he have taste, I must add, of
course he will have ingenuity, and my disrespectful reference to that quality
just now was not meant to imply that it is useless in fiction. But it is only a
secondary aid; the first is a vivid sense of reality.

Mr. Besant has some remarks on the question of "the story," which I
shall not attempt to criticise, though they seem to me to contain a singular
ambiguity, because I do not think I understand them. I cannot see what
is meant by talking as if there were a part of a novel which is the story and
part of it which for mystical reasons is not—unless indeed the distinction
be made in a sense in which it is difficult to suppose that anyone should
attempt to convey anything. "The story," if it represents anything, represents the subject, the idea, the data of the novel; and there is surely no
"school"—Mr. Besant speaks of a school—which urges that a novel should
be all treatment and no subject. There must assuredly be something to
treat; every school is intimately conscious of that. This sense of the story
being the idea, the starting-point, of the novel is the only one that I see in
which it can be spoken of as something different from its organic whole;
and since, in proportion as the work is successful, the idea permeates and
penetrates it, informs and animates it, so that every word and every punc-
tuation-point contribute directly to the expression, in that proportion do
we lose our sense of the story being a blade which may be drawn more or
less out of its sheath. The story and the novel, the idea and the form, are the
needle and thread, and I never heard of a guild of tailors who recommended
the use of the thread without the needle or the needle without the thread.
Mr. Besant is not the only critic who may be observed to have spoken as if
there were certain things in life which constitute stories and certain others
which do not. I find the same odd implication in an entertaining article in
the *Pall Mall Gazette*, devoted, as it happens, to Mr. Besant's lecture. "The
story is the thing!" says this graceful writer, as if with a tone of opposition
to another idea. I should think it was, as every painter who, as the time for
"sending in" his picture looms in the distance, finds himself still in quest of

a subject—as every belated artist, not fixed about his *donnée*, will heartily agree. There are some subjects which speak to us and others which do not, but he would be a clever man who should undertake to give a rule by which the story and the no-story should be known apart. It is impossible (to me at least) to imagine any such rule which shall not be altogether arbitrary. The writer in the *Pall Mall* opposes the delightful (as I suppose) novel of *Margot la Balafrée* to certain tales in which "Bostonian nymphs" appear to have "rejected English dukes for psychological reasons." I am not acquainted with the romance just designated, and can scarcely forgive the *Pall Mall* critic for not mentioning the name of the author, but the title appears to refer to a lady who may have received a scar in some heroic adventure. I am inconsolable at not being acquainted with this episode, but am utterly at a loss to see why it is a story when the rejection (or acceptance) of a duke is not, and why a reason, psychological or other, is not a subject when a cicatrix is. They are all particles of the multitudinous life with which the novel deals, and surely no dogma which pretends to make it lawful to touch the one and unlawful to touch the other will stand for a moment on its feet. It is the special picture that must stand or fall, according as it seems to possess truth or to lack it. Mr. Besant does not, to my sense, light up the subject by intimating that a story must, under penalty of not being a story, consist of "adventures." Why of adventures more than of green spectacles? He mentions a category of impossible things, and among them he places "fiction without adventure." Why without adventure, more than without matrimony, or celibacy, or parturition, or cholera, or hydropathy, or Jansenism? This seems to me to bring the novel back to the hapless little *rôle* of being an artificial, ingenious thing—bring it down from its large, free character of an immense and exquisite correspondence with life. And what *is* adventure, when it comes to that, and by what sign is the listening pupil to recognise it? It is an adventure—an immense one—for me to write this little article; and for a Bostonian nymph to reject an English duke is an adventure only less stirring, I should say, than for an English duke to be rejected by a Bostonian nymph. I see dramas within dramas in that, and innumerable points of view. A psychological reason is, to my imagination, an object adorably pictorial; to catch the tint of its complexion—I feel as if that idea might inspire one to Titianesque efforts. There are few things more exciting to me, in short, than a psychological reason, and yet, I protest, the novel seems to me the most magnificent form of art. I have just been reading, at the same time, the delightful story of *Treasure Island*, by Mr. Robert Louis Stevenson, and the last tale from M. Edmond de Goncourt, which is entitled *Chérie*. One of these works treats of murders, mysteries, islands of dreadful renown, hairbreadth escapes, miraculous coincidences and buried doubloons. The other treats of a little French girl who lived in a fine house in Paris and died of wounded sensibility because no one would marry her. I call *Treasure Island* delightful, because it appears to me to have succeeded wonderfully in what it attempts; and I venture to bestow no epithet upon *Chérie*, which strikes me as having failed in what it attempts—that is, in tracing the development of the moral consciousness of a child. But one of these productions strikes me as exactly as much of a novel as the other, and as having a "story" quite as much. The moral consciousness of a child is as much a part of life as the islands of the Spanish Main, and the one sort of geography seems to me to have those "surprises" of which Mr. Besant speaks quite as much as the other. For myself (since it comes back in the last resort, as I say, to the preference of the individual), the picture of the child's experience has the advantage that I can at successive steps (an immense luxury, near to the "sensual pleasure" of which Mr. Besant's critic in the *Pall Mall* speaks) say Yes or No, as it may be, to what the artist puts before me. I have been a child, but I have never been on a quest for a buried treasure, and it is a simple accident that with M. de Goncourt I should have for the most part to say No. With George Eliot, when she painted that country, I always said Yes.

[. . .] No good novel will ever proceed from a superficial mind; that seems to me an axiom which, for the artist in fiction, will cover all needful moral ground; if the youthful aspirant take it to heart it will illuminate for him many of the mysteries of "purpose." There are many other useful things that might be said to him, but I have come to the end of my article, and can only touch them as I pass. The critic in the *Pall Mall Gazette*, whom I have already quoted, draws attention to the danger, in speaking of the art of fiction, of generalizing. The danger that he has in mind is rather, I imagine, that of particularizing, for there are some comprehensive remarks which, in addition to those embodied in Mr. Besant's suggestive lecture, might, without fear of misleading him, be addressed to the ingenuous student. I should remind him first of the magnificence of the form that is open to him, which offers to sight so few restrictions and such innumerable opportunities. The other arts, in comparison, appear confined and hampered; the various conditions under which they are exercised are so rigid and definite. But the only condition that I can think of attaching to the composition of the novel is, as I have already said, that it be interesting. This freedom is a splendid privilege, and the first lesson of the young novelist is to learn to be worthy of it. "Enjoy it as it deserves," I should say to him; "take possession of it, explore it to its utmost extent, reveal it, rejoice in it. All life belongs to you, and don't listen either to those who would shut you up into corners of it and tell you that it is only here and there that art inhabits, or to those who would persuade you that this heavenly messenger wings her way outside of life altogether, breathing a superfine air and turning away her head from the truth of things. There is no impression of life, no manner of seeing it and feeling it, to which the plan of the novelist may not offer a place; you have only to remember that talents so dissimilar as those of Alexandre Dumas and Jane Austen, Charles Dickens and Gustave Flaubert, have worked in this field with equal glory. Don't think too much about optimism and pessimism; try and catch the colour of life itself. In France to-day we see a prodigious effort (that of Émile Zola, to whose solid and serious work no explorer of the capacity of the novel can allude without respect), we see an extraordinary effort vitiated by a spirit of pessimism on a narrow basis. M. Zola is magnificent, but he strikes an English reader as ignorant; he has an air of working in the dark; if he had as much light as energy his results would be of the highest value. As for the aberrations of a shallow optimism, the ground (of English fiction especially) is strewn with their brittle particles as with broken glass. If you must indulge in conclusions let them have the taste of a wide knowledge. Remember that your first duty is to be as complete as possible—to make as perfect a work. Be generous and delicate, and then, in the vulgar phrase, go in!

FROM "THE MIDDLE YEARS"

We work in the dark—we do what we can—we give what we have. Our doubt is our passion and our passion is our task. The rest is the madness of art.

George Washington Cable

(1844–1925)

Born in New Orleans, which he called "a hybrid city," the diminutive George Washington Cable (five feet tall) joined the Confederate army in 1863. After the war he returned to New Orleans, where he worked as a surveyor and grocery clerk and bookkeeper and then as a popular stringer for the *Picayune* covering literary and social issues. In 1873 he published his first story in *Scribner's;* it was as if Nathaniel Hawthorne had moved to the French Quarter. But when his nationally acclaimed *Old Creole Days* (1879), his first collection of such stories, exposed in radical ways the racially mixed history of southern culture, it was a scandal. Cable was the most hated man in town (it was said)—and Lafcadio Hearn and Mark Twain both sought him out. As he'd done in novels such as *The Grandissimes* (1880) and *Madame Delphine* (1881), Cable vehemently protested in prose the besetting racism of the South, particularly in such works as *The Negro Question* (1890): no midnight and magnolias for him. By then he had moved to Massachusetts.

The excerpt below is taken from an enchanting, intelligent essay, "The Speculations of a Story-Teller" (1896), in which Cable presents a dialogue between the storyteller and the public in which he says the storyteller, though not one to proffer a formula for fiction, will allow the public to peer into his workshop and learn, among other things, how he juggles fact and fiction and the truths of the deeply haunted human heart.

FROM "THE SPECULATIONS OF A STORY-TELLER"

There never was a bunch of facts which would not have been more interesting if, just as they were, they could have possessed all, and only, the features and arrangement the story-teller would have liked them to have. His main purpose, however grave, however playful he may be, is to convey, not weighty information, but welcome emotions, thereby to establish, for the moment at least, and as much longer as he may, spiritual facts of life, in the sensibilities, sentiments, and affections of his readers. For him fact and fiction alike are but means to this end. He draws no distinctions between them. As long as facts serve him best he will use them, disguised as fiction. When fictions suit better he will use them, in the guise of facts. And when the improbable is his best instrument, as at times it may be, he does well to use it, if he can so wield it that in the end it is cheerfully forgiven by the head for the good it has brought to the heart. [. . .]

Fiction that is only fiction has no pleasing interest whatever. Nor is any such thing to be found in literature. It is the facts in the fiction,—not mixed with it, as some boor may mix sand with sugar, but the facts *in* the fiction, as our life is in our blood,—it is this that holds our interest. Every fact is interesting to every one interested in the group of facts to which it belongs, and every fact of the heart's experience is interesting to every true heart; so interesting that only by taking on the drapery of art can fiction compete with naked fact at all. Even in its most extravagant phases it is, after all, both spiritually and materially, mostly facts,—facts simply turned inside out and swapped about among their owners, as boys play at swapping caps and coats; or rather, made over into artistic form,—reshaped, that is, into clearer and more powerful relation than accident could ever work, to the whole mass of the world's facts, and especially to its great verities.

FROM "AFTER-THOUGHTS OF A STORY-TELLER"

1894

Not actual experience, not actual observation, but the haunted heart; that is what makes the true artist, of every sort. [. . .]

On the other hand, the story-teller finds that what he reveals of himself comes not from what is himself alone, but which is only, and recognizably, so many phases of the universal self. These he clothes in any idiosyncrasies, whether of self or of others, which, as a cunning costumer, he finds will so drape them in the garments of individuality as not to conceal, but exaltedly to adorn, emphasize, and reveal, the humanity within. The artistic necessity that he should be wholly free to do this is what so often makes the marriage of fiction to biography an unhappy match. It is only in its eclectic use of the idiosyncratic that fiction needs to be fiction at all. In its presentiments of the universal self it is as firmly bound by art as history is by morals to be true to the very white of truth. Seest then a man free in the one realm and faithful in the other? He shall stand before kings; he shall not stand before Sunday-school library committees.

Alice James

(1848–1892)

Besides Mary Chesnut, one of the great diarists of the nineteenth century
was a woman: Alice James, who originally kept a diary to chronicle a war
within, not without. "I think that if I get into the habit of writing a bit about
what happens, or rather doesn't happen, I may lose a little of the sense of
loneliness and desolation which abides with me," she begins (as excerpted
below). Writing is not just relief, though, for this longtime invalid, who suffered from depression and later cancer; it is power, it is force, it is what her
eldest brother, William, called "a unique and tragic impression of personal
power venting itself on no opportunity": a woman's dilemma—and one exac-
erbated by an environment steeped in male genius, particularly that of her
brothers William and Henry, to say nothing of that of her difficult father. But
with gimlet eye and tart prose style, her sense of satiric self-assessment and
her acerbic measure of the world, she converted her lifelong flirtation with
death into a work of chiseled proportions, one that resides right between
the interests of her psychologically and novelistically minded siblings.

FROM *THE DIARY OF ALICE JAMES*

MAY 31, 1889

I think that if I get into the habit of writing a bit about what happens, or
rather doesn't happen, I may lose a little of the sense of loneliness and desolation which abides with me. My circumstances allowing of nothing but the
ejaculation of one-syllabled reflections, a written monologue by that most
interesting being, myself, may have its yet to be discovered consolations.
I shall at least have it all my own way and it may bring relief as an outlet
to that geyser of emotions, sensations, speculations and reflections which
ferments perpetually within my poor old carcass for its sins; so here goes,
my first Journal!

JULY 12 [1889]

It's amusing to see how, even on my microscopic field, minute events are
perpetually taking place illustrative of the broadest facts of human nature.
Yesterday Nurse and I had a good laugh but I must allow that decidedly
she "had" me. I was thinking of something that interested me very much
and my mind was suddenly flooded by one of those luminous waves that
sweep out of consciousness all but the living sense and overpower one with
joy in the rich, throbbing complexity of life, when suddenly I looked up at
Nurse, who was dressing me, and saw her primitive, rudimentary expression (so common here) as of no inherited quarrel with her destiny of putting
petticoats over my head; the poverty and deadness of it contrasted to the
tide of speculation that was coursing thro' my brain made me exclaim,
"Oh! Nurse, don't you wish you were inside of *me*!"—her look of dismay
and vehement disclaimer—"Inside of you, Miss, when you have had a sick
head-ache for five days!"—gave a greater blow to my vanity, than that much
battered article has ever received. The headache had gone off in the night
and I had clean forgotten it—when the little wretch confronted me with
it, at this sublime moment when I was feeling within me the potency of
a Bismarck, and left me powerless before the immutable law that however great we may seem to our own consciousness no human being would
exchange his for ours, and before the fact that *my* glorious role was to stand
for Sick headache to mankind!

Sarah Orne Jewett

(1849–1909)

Born in South Berwick, Maine, the daughter of a well-known and prosper-
ous physician whom she accompanied on his local rounds, Sarah Orne Jewett
published her first collection of sketches, *Deephaven*, in 1877. Encouraged by
William Dean Howells and later by the *Atlantic Monthly* editor Horace Scud-
der—and financially comfortable—she then published several more collections of her tales; *A White Heron and Other Stories* (1886) is considered her
best. Her first novel, *A Country Doctor* (1884), was followed by the renowned
The Country of the Pointed Firs (1896). "Country" is in fact at the heart of
her oeuvre: the concerns of the local villagers, closely observed, as well as
the lives of the women who live their lives in rural places with little fanfare
and a great deal of strength. Willa Cather, much influenced by Jewett, whom
she knew, characterized the older woman's work as an "earnest endeavor to
tell truly the thing that haunts the mind" and dedicated *O! Pioneers* (1913) to
her. Women such as Jewett and Cather, as Jewett's correspondence indicates,
were self-conscious and meticulous artists committed to perfecting their
craft. And in her preface to *Alexander's Bridge* (1922), Cather recalled that
"one of the few really helpful words I ever heard from an older writer, I had
from Sarah Orne Jewett when she said to me: 'Of course, one day you will
write about your own country. In the meantime, get all you can. One must
know the world so well before one can know the parish.'"

   As one of the authors in the *Atlantic Monthly*, Jewett met James T.

Fields and his literary wife, Annie, who became Jewett's life partner, even at long distance, after James Fields's sudden death in 1881. The two traveled extensively, visited Henry James, and lived part of the year in the Fields's hospitable home in Boston. But a carriage accident in 1902 effectively ended Jewett's career as an author of fiction. In 1911 Annie Fields edited Jewett's letters; the excerpts from them reveal how deeply Jewett cared about the writing, for over and over she makes the point, long before Hemingway's famous dictum to "tell it like it is," that one must just tell the truth, no easy thing to do.

FROM *Sarah Orne Jewett Letters*

To Laura Bellamy

August 31, 1885

It isn't for me to decide whether you must keep on writing; that belongs to your own heart and conscience. But I know one thing—that you will not be left in the dark about it. Do not be misled either by a difficulty or a facility of expression. If you have something to say, it will and must say itself, and the people will listen to whom the message is sent. [. . .]

My dear father used to say to me very often, "Tell things just as they are!" and used to show me what he meant in *A Sentimental Journey*! The great messages and discoveries of literature come to us, they write us, and we do not control them in a certain sense. [. . .]

I fear that I cannot help you much, but I hope and believe that you are equal to helping yourself, for it is what we ourselves put into our own lives that really counts. [. . .] I only wish that I could be as kind a friend to younger writers as those friends whom I found when I was beginning. But they all said, "Work away!"

With best wishes, believe me

Yours sincerely,

Sarah O. Jewett

FROM *THE LETTERS OF SARAH ORNE JEWETT*

To Rose Lamb

1896

My dear Rose,

[. . .] One must have one's own method: it is the personal contribution that makes true value in any form of art or work of any sort.

I could write much about these things, but I do not much believe that it is worth while to say anything, but keep at work! If something comes into a writer's or a painter's mind the only thing is to try it, to see what one can do with it, and give it a chance to show if it has real value. Story-writing is always experimental, just as a water-color sketch is, and that something which does itself is the vitality of it. I think we must know what good work is, before we can do good work of our own, and so I say, study work that the best judges have called good and see why it is good; whether it is in that particular story, the reticence or the bravery of speech, the power of suggestion that is in it, or the absolute clearness and finality of revelation; whether it sets you thinking, or whether it makes you see a landscape with a live human figure living its life in the foreground.

To Willa Cather

DECEMBER 13, 1908

My dear Willa,

I have been thinking about you and hoping that things are going well. I cannot help saying what I think about your writing and its being hindered by such incessant, important, responsible work as you have in your hands now. I do think that it is impossible for you to work so hard and yet have your gifts mature as they should—when one's first working power has spent itself nothing ever brings it back just the same, and I do wish in my heart that the force of this very year could have gone into three or four stories. In the "Troll-Garden" the Sculptor's Funeral stands alone a head higher than the rest, and it is to that level you must hold and take for a starting-point. You are older now than that book in general; you have been living and reading and knowing new types; but if you don't keep and guard and mature your force, and above all, have time and quiet to perfect your work, you will be writing things not much better than you did five years ago. This you are anxiously saying to yourself! but I am wondering how to get at the right conditions. I want you to be surer of your backgrounds,—you have your Nebraska life,—a child's Virginia, and now an intimate knowledge of what we are pleased to call the "Bohemia" of newspaper and magazine-office life. These are uncommon equipment, but you don't see them yet quite enough from the outside,— you stand right in the middle of each of them when you write, without having the standpoint of the looker-on who takes them each in their relations to letters, to the world. Your good schooling and your knowledge of "the best that has been thought and said in the world," as Matthew Arnold put it, have helped you, but these you wish and need to deepen and enrich still more. You must find a quiet place near the best companions (not those who admire and wonder at everything one does, but those who know the good things with delight!). You do need reassurance,—every artist does!—but you need still more to feel "responsible for the state of your conscience" (your literary conscience, we can just now limit that quotation to), and you need to dream your dreams and go on to new and more shining ideals, to be aware of "the gleam" and to follow it; your vivid, exciting companionship in the office must not be your audience, you must find your own quiet centre of life, and write from that to the world that holds offices, and all society, all Bohemia; the city, the country—in short, you must write to the human heart, the great consciousness that all humanity goes to make up. Otherwise what might be strength in a writer is only crudeness, and what might be insight is only observation; sentiment falls to sentimentality—you can write about life, but never write life itself. And to write and work on this level, we must live on it—we must at least recognize it and defer to it at every step. We must be ourselves, but we must be our best selves. If we have patience with cheapness and thinness, as Christians must, we must know that it is cheapness and not make believe about it. To work in silence and with all one's heart, that is the writer's lot; he is the only artist who must be a solitary, and yet needs the widest outlook upon the world. But you have been growing I feel sure in the very days when you felt most hindered, and this will be counted to you. You need to have time to yourself and time to read and add to your recognitions. I do not know when a letter has grown so long and written itself so easily, but I have been full of thought about you. You will let me hear again from you before long?

Emma Lazarus

(1849–1887)

"Give me your tired, your poor, / Your huddled masses yearning to breathe free": these lines famously etched on the Statue of Liberty in New York harbor are from Emma Lazarus's finely made sonnet "The New Colossus" (1883), which had been commissioned to help raise funds for a pedestal for Bartholdi's statue. But until recently and except for this sonnet, Lazarus, who died quite young, had fallen into obscurity—in spite of the passion and craft of much of her verse and the fact that, as it matured, she sought a way to write about the fate of the Jews, particularly after news of the Russian pogroms spread to America: "What! can these dead bones live, whose sap is dried / By twenty scorching centuries of wrong?" Born in New York to Sephardic and German Jewish parents, well read, musical, and with an ear for several languages, Emma Lazarus presumably began to write poetry during the Civil War; she continued honing her craft in verse drama, in poetry, and in several essays, and she also translated Hugo, Dumas, Schiller, and Heinrich Heine, a favorite, as well as medieval Hebrew poetry from its German versions and the Jewish poets of medieval Spain.

In her writing she embraces and explores the complexities of what, today, we call identity, whether it be the identity of an American, a Jew, a woman, or all three. She argues forcefully against the stiff Victorian assumption that American literature is empty and derivative by suggesting that

place matters, and in the pristine sonnet "Long Island Sound" (1869), she
shows how she makes place, in a traditional form, "my own." At the same
time, she began to see her role of poet as a political one that, as she says,
revitalizes the rich Jewish tradition of literature and history.

LONG ISLAND SOUND

I see it as it looked one afternoon
In August,—by a fresh soft breeze o'erblown.
The swiftness of the tide, the light thereon,
A far-off sail, white as a crescent moon.
The shining waters with pale currents strewn,
The quiet fishing-smacks, the Eastern cove,
The semi-circle of its dark, green grove.
The luminous grasses, and the merry sun
In the grave sky; the sparkle far and wide,
Laughter of unseen children, cheerful chirp
Of crickets, and low lisp of rippling tide,
Light summer clouds fantastical as sleep
Changing unnoted while I gazed thereon.
And these fair sounds and sights I made my own.

FROM INTRODUCTION TO
THE POEMS OF EMMA LAZARUS

My chief aim has been to contribute my mite towards arousing that spirit
of Jewish enthusiasm which might manifest itself: First, in a return to
varied pursuits and broad system of physical and intellectual education
adopted by our ancestors; Second, in a more fraternal and practical movement towards alleviating the sufferings of oppressed Jews in countries less
favored than our own; Third, in a closer and wider study of Hebrew literature and history; and finally, in a truer recognition of the large principles of
religion, liberty, and law upon which Judaism is founded, and which should
draw into harmonious unity Jews of every shade of opinion.

Kate Chopin

(1850–1904)

An admirer of the work of Sarah Orne Jewett and Guy de Maupassant (whose stories she translated), Kate Chopin wrote of different milieus than either: that of the Creole, Cajun, and African American cultures mixed together in New Orleans and rural Louisiana. Yet she shared with Jewett and de Maupassant a passion for *le mot juste*, which is the hallmark of all her work. She began to write after the death of her husband, a Louisiana cotton dealer, and her mother; her first novel, *At Fault* (1890), privately published, was a somewhat autobiographical account of a young Creole widow, set in both Louisiana and St. Louis (Chopin's birthplace and the place to which she returned after the death of her husband). *Bayou Folk* (1894), a collection of short stories, catapulted her to fame, though she never felt that her stories were quite understood by the buttoned-up editors who balked at the sensuality of her subject matter and her sympathetic portrayal of women's passionate inner lives. *The Awakening* (1899), now considered her masterpiece, was deemed unhealthy and morbid; and after her death in 1904, her fiction was largely forgotten, not to be rediscovered—and admired—until the 1960s.

As these excerpts from various interviews or unfinished sketches reveal, the rather brilliant and witty Chopin well understood her anomalous place in American letters, and though she may have regretted it or the society that surrounded and often stymied her, she would never change herself to suit the moral didacticism of the day that passed for literary criticism.

FROM "ON CERTAIN BRISK, BRIGHT DAYS"

1899

Eight or nine years ago I began to write stories—short stories which appeared in the magazines, and I forthwith began to suspect I had the writing habit. The publisher shared this impression, and called me an author. Since then, though I have written many short stories and a novel or two, I am forced to admit that I have not the writing habit. But it is hard to make people with the questioning habit believe this.

"Now, where, when, why, what do you write?" are some of the questions that I remember. How do I write? On a lapboard with a block of paper, a stub pen and a bottle of ink bought at the corner grocery, which keeps the best in town.

Where do I write? In a Morris chair beside the window, where I can see a few trees and a patch of sky, more or less blue.

When do I write? I am greatly tempted here to use slang and reply "any old time," but that would lend a tone of levity to this bit of confidence, whose seriousness I want to keep intact if possible. So I shall say I write in the morning, when not too strongly drawn to struggle with the intricacies of a pattern, and in the afternoon, if the temptation to try a new furniture polish on an old table leg is not too powerful to be denied; sometimes at night, though as I grow older I am more and more inclined to believe that night was made for sleep.

"Why do I write?" is a question which I have often asked myself and never very satisfactorily answered. Story-writing—at least with me—is the spontaneous expression of impressions gathered goodness knows where. To seek the source, the impulse of a story is like tearing a flower to pieces for wantonness.

What do I write? Well, not everything that comes into my head, but much of what I have written lies between the covers of my books.

There are stories that seem to write themselves, and others which positively refuse to be written—which no amount of coaxing can bring to anything. I do not believe any writer has ever made a "portrait" in fiction. A trick, a mannerism, a physical trait or mental characteristic go a very short way towards portraying the complete individual in real life who suggests the individual in the writer's imagination. The "material" of a writer is to the last degree uncertain, and I fear not marketable. I have been told stories which were looked upon as veritable gold mines by the generous narrators who placed them at my disposal. I have been taken to spots supposed to be alive with local color. I have been introduced to excruciating characters with frank permission to use them as I liked, but never, in any single instance, has such material been of the slightest service. I am completely at the mercy of unconscious selection. To such an extent is this true, that what is called the polishing up process has always proved disastrous to my work, and I avoid it, preferring the integrity of crudities to artificialities.

FROM "AS YOU LIKE IT"

1897

Editors are really a singular class of men; they have such strange and incomprehensible ways with them.

I once submitted a story to a prominent New York editor, who returned it promptly with the observation that "the public is getting very tired of that sort of thing." I felt very sorry for the public; but I wasn't willing to take one man's word for it, so I clapped the offensive document into an envelope and sent it again—this time to a well-known Boston editor.

"I am delighted with the story," read the letter of acceptance, which came a few weeks later, "and so I am sure, will be our readers." (!)

When an editor says a thing like that it is at his own peril. I at once sent him another tale, thinking thereby to increase his delight and add to it ten-fold.

"Can you call this a story, dear madam?" he asked when he sent it back.

"Really, there seems to me to be no story at all; what is it all about?" I could see his pale smile.

It was getting interesting, like playing battledore and shuttlecock. Off went the would-be story by the next mail to the New York editor—the one who so considerately gauged the ennui of the public.

"It is a clever and excellent piece of work," he wrote me; "the story is well told." I wonder if the editor, the writer, and the public are ever at one.

from "In the Confidence of a Story-Writer"

1899

I had heard so often reiterated that "genius is a capacity for taking pains" that the axiom had become lodged in my brain with the fixedness of a fundamental truth. I had never hoped or aspired to be a genius. But one day the thought occurred to me, "I will take pains." Thereupon I proceeded to lie awake at night plotting a tale that should convince my limited circle of readers that I could rise above the commonplace. As to choice of "time," the present century offered too prosaic a setting for a tale intended to stir the heart and the imagination. I selected the last century. It is true I know little of the last century, and have a feeble imagination. I read volumes bearing upon the history of the times and people that I proposed to manipulate, and pored over folios depicting costumes and household utensils then in use, determined to avoid inaccuracy. For the first time in my life I took notes,—copious notes,—and carried them bulging in my jacket pockets, until I felt as if I were wearing Zola's coat. I have never seen a craftsman at work upon a fine piece of mosaic, but I fancy that he must handle the delicate bits much as I handled the words in that story, picking, selecting, grouping, with an eye to color and to artistic effect,—never satisfied. The story completed, I was very, very weary; but I had the satisfaction of feeling that for once in my life I had worked hard, I had achieved something great, I had taken pains.

But the story failed to arouse enthusiasm among the editors. It is at present lying in my desk. Even my best friend declined to listen to it, when I offered to read it to her.

I am more than ever convinced that a writer should be content to use his own faculty, whether it be a faculty for taking pains or a faculty for reaching his effects by the most careless methods. Every writer, I fancy, has his group of readers who understand, who are in sympathy with his thoughts or impressions or whatever he gives them. And he who is content to reach his own group, without ambition to be heard beyond it, attains, in my opinion, somewhat to the dignity of a philosopher.

Lafcadio Hearn

(1850–1904)

Born in Greece of Irish and Greek parents, shuttled off to Ireland and France
and then Wales in his youth, where the undersized youth was partially
blinded in an accident, Hearn ran away to the United States in 1869, and
though not a native, he was an American original: self-made in that new and
raucous country, where during the Gilded Age he slept on floors and then
worked his way up to journalist (he learned his trade much as Whitman and
Harte learned theirs) and to translator of Flaubert, Gautier, and de Maupassant; he wrote of New Orleans for a Cincinnati paper, traveled to the West
Indies, and later settled in Japan, where he lived the last fourteen years of
his life. His miscellaneous narrative essays, travel sketches, and tales of ghosts
are meditations of rare discernment on life and the human soul, for as a
superb prose stylist, Hearn was also a latter-day Thoreau in his solitariness,
his fixity, and his poise. In his penchant for sensuous beauty, he was also the
descendant of Edgar Allan Poe, whom he admired. Add this to his agnosti-
cism and his Buddhism, his fine writing on Japan, his pantheism, and his
dedication to craft, and you have Lafcadio Hearn.

These excerpts, from Hearn's letters, need no other explanation than
that they speak directly of his dedication to and understanding of the scru-
pulous work that good writing entails. And to his passion for the heft and
color and form of words.

FROM *The Japanese Letters of Lafcadio Hearn*

To Basil Hall Chamberlain

February 6, 1893

I have had to rewrite pages fifty times. It is like a groping for something you know is inside the stuff, but the exact shape of which you don't know. That is, I think, also the explanation of the sculptor's saying that the figure was already in the marble; the art was only to "disengage it." [. . .]

And as you excellently observe, the effect of the work is in direct ratio to the pains taken to produce it by a master hand. This takes no small time to learn. What apparent ease in writing really means I regret to say that I only learned a few years ago; if I had learned sooner, it would have done me much good.

Otherwise your method is in all points like mine. I have to do much excision of "verys," "thats" and "whiches,"—to murder adjectives and adverbs,—to modify verbs. Every important word seems to me to have three qualities: form, sound, and colour. After the first and last have been considered, follows the question of the rhythm of the sentence. This I think may approach blank verse, at the termination of paragraphs, if a strong emotion be expressed. It may be smooth as oil if the effect to be produced is smooth,—or rough,—or violent as may be. But all this is never done by rule,—only by instinctive feeling, half unconsciously. In the body of a paragraph too much flow and rhythm seems to hurt the effect. Full force is best reserved for the casting-throw of the whole thought or emotion. I should like now to go through many paragraphs written years ago, and sober them down.

Print, of course, is the great test. Colour only comes out in proof,—never in MS. I can't get anything perfect in MS. A friend is invaluable. [. . .]

Then I keep note-books. I have no memory to speak of, since my experiences with tropical fevers and other sickness. I note down every sensation or idea, as you say au vol. And I have classified notebooks,—with indexes; must show you some one of these days.

To Basil Hall Chamberlain
JUNE 5, 1893

For me words have colour, form, character: They have faces, ports, manners, gesticulations;—they have moods, humours, eccentricities:— they have tints, tones, personalities. That they are unintelligible makes no difference at all. Whether you are able to speak to a stranger or not, you can't help being impressed by his appearance sometimes,—by his dress,— by his air,—by his exotic look. He is also unintelligible, but not a whit less interesting. Nay he is interesting *because* he is unintelligible.—I won't cite other writers who have felt the same way about African, Chinese, Arabian, Hebrew, Tartar, Indian and Basque words,—I mean novelists and sketch-writers.

To such it has been justly observed:—"The readers do not feel as you do about words. They can't be supposed to know that you think the letter A is blush-crimson, and the letter E pale sky-blue. They can't be supposed to know that you think KH wears a beard and a turban; that the initial X is a mature Greek with wrinkles;—or that '—NO—' has an innocent, lovable, and childlike aspect." All this is true from the critic's standpoint.

But from ours,—the standpoint of—

the Dreamer of Dreams
To whom what is and what seems
Is often one and the same,—
to us the idea is thus:—

"Because people cannot see the colour of words, the tints of words, the secret ghostly motions of words;—

"Because they cannot hear the whispering of words, the rustling of the procession of letters, the dream-flutes and dream-drums which are thinly and weirdly-played by words;—

"Because they cannot perceive the pouting of words, the frowning and fuming of words, the weeping, the raging and racketing and rioting of words;—

"Because they are insensible to the phosphorescing of words, the fragrance of words, the noisomeness of words, the tenderness or hardness, the dryness or juiciness of words,—the interchange of values in the gold, the silver, the brass and the copper of words:—

"Is that any reason why we should not try to make them hear, to make them see, to make them feel?—Surely one who has never heard Wagner, cannot appreciate Wagner without study. Why should the people not be forcibly introduced to foreign words,—as they were introduced to tea and coffee and tobacco?"

Unto which the friendly reply is,—"Because they won't buy your book, and you won't make any money."

And I say:—"Surely I have never yet made, and never expect to make any money. Neither do I expect to write ever for the multitude. I write for beloved friends who can see colour in words, can smell the perfume in syllables in blossom, can be shocked with the fine elfish electricity of words. And in the eternal order of things, words will eventually have their rights recognized by the people."

All this is heresy. But a bad reason, you will grant, is better than—&c.
Faithfully,
Lafcadio Hearn

Harold Frederic

(1856–1898)

Born in upstate New York, where he became well known as an independent-minded journalist, Harold Frederic considered his literary parents to be Erck-mann-Chatrian and Hawthorne, each of whom helped Frederic travel beyond the pictorial realism touted in his day toward a psychological comprehension of character, a more aesthetic definition of the novel itself, and toward the un-Howellsian intuition of what Melville called the "power of blackness": humans are "savages in a dangerous wood in the dark, telling one another ghost stories around a camp-fire," says one of Frederic's characters. Himself alternating between journalism and writing novels, like Stephen Crane, Frederic was appointed chief London correspondent for the *New York Times*, though once in England, he abandoned his unhappy marriage and moved in with Kate Lyons, a Christian Scientist later tried for manslaughter after she attempted (and failed) to heal Frederic, who suffered a stroke in 1898 and subsequently died. By then, his best-selling masterwork, *The Damnation of Theron Ware* (1896), far outstripped Frederic's other novels (he wrote ten) in conception and execution, for as the story of a young self-deluded minister in upstate New York, it sharply defined the so-called American character as a rube on the social, sexual, and cultural make.

The excerpts here include Frederic's first comments on his own method of composition, which includes research, particularly for *The Damnation of Theron Ware*, and his singular commentary on Stephen Crane's *The Red Badge of Courage* (1896). This novel of war reveals yet again his commitment to the technique of the novel—and his ability to distinguish literary writing and journalism: "At last," he concludes, "along comes a Muybridge, with his instantaneous camera, and shows that the real motion is entirely different."

FROM "AN AMERICAN JOURNALIST IN LONDON"

1895

I am now writing a novel, the people of which I have been carrying about with me, night and day, for fully five years. After I had got them grouped together in my mind, I set myself the task of knowing everything they know. As four of them happen to be specialists in different professions, the task has been tremendous. For instance, one of them is a biologist, who, among many other things, is experimenting on Lubbock's and Darwin's lines. Although these pursuits are merely mentioned, I have got up masses of stuff on bees and the cross-fertilization of plants. I have had to teach myself all the details of a Methodist minister's work, obligations, and daily routine, and all the machinery of his Church. Another character is a priest, who is a good deal more of a pagan than a simple-minded Christian. He loves luxury and learning. I have studied the arts he loves as well as his theology; I have waded in Assyriology and Schopenhauer; pored over palimpsests and pottery; and, in order to write understandingly about a musician who figures in the story, I have bored a professional friend to death getting technical musical stuff from him. I don't say this is the right way to build novels; only, it is my way.

FROM *THE NEW YORK TIMES*

JANUARY 26, 1896

If there were in existence any books of a similar character, one could start confidently by saying that it [*The Red Badge of Courage*] was the best of its kind. But it has no fellows. It is a book outside of all classification. So unlike anything else is it that the temptation rises to deny that it is a book at all. When one searches for comparisons, they can only be found by culling out selected portions from the trunks of masterpieces, and considering these detached fragments, one by one, with reference to the Red Badge, which is itself a fragment, and yet is complete.

Thus one lifts the best battle pictures from Tolstoi's great *War and Peace*, from Balzac's *Chouans*, from Hugo's *Les Misérables*, and the forest fight in "93," from Prosper Mérimée's assault of the redoubt, from Zola's *La Débâcle* and *Attack on the Mill*, (it is strange enough that equivalents in the literature of our own language do not suggest themselves) and studies them side by side with this tremendously effective battle painting by the unknown youngster. Positively they are cold and ineffectual beside it. The praise may sound exaggerated, but really it is inadequate. These renowned battle descriptions of the big men are made to seem all wrong. *The Red Badge* impels the feeling that the actual truth about a battle has never been guessed before.

In construction the book is as original as in its unique grasp of a new grouping of old materials. [. . .] We begin with the young raw recruit, hearing that at last his regiment is going to see some fighting, and brooding over the problem of his own behavior under fire. We follow his perturbed meditations through thirty pages, which cover a week or so of this menace of action. Then suddenly, with one gray morning, the ordeal breaks abruptly over the youngster's head. We go with him, so close that he is never out of sight, for two terribly crowded days, and then the book is at an end. This cross-section of his experience is made a part of our own. We see with his eyes, think with his mind, quail or thrill with his nerves. He strives to argue himself into the conventional soldier's bravery; he runs ingloriously away; he excuses, defends, and abhors himself in turn; he tremblingly yields to the sinister fascination of creeping near the battle; he basely allows his comrades to ascribe to heroism the wound he received in the frenzied "sauve qui peut" [stampede] of the fight, he gets at last the fire of combat in his veins, and blindly rushing in deports himself with such hardy and temerarious valor that even the Colonel notes him, and admits that he is a "jimbickey." These sequent processes, observed with relentless minutiae, are so powerfully and speakingly portrayed that they seem the veritable actions of our own minds. To produce the effect is a notable triumph, but it is commonplace by comparison with the other triumph of making us realize what Henry saw and heard as well as what he felt. The value of the former feat has the limitations of the individual. No two people are absolutely alike; any other young farm boy would have passed through the trial with something different somewhere. Where Henry fluttered, he might have been obtuse; neither the early panic nor the later irrational ferocity would necessarily have been just the same. But the picture of the trial itself seems to me never to have been painted as well before.

Oddly enough, *The Saturday Review* and some other of the commentators take it for granted that the writer of the *Red Badge* must have seen real warfare. "The extremely vivid touches of detail convince us," says *The Review*, "that he has had personal experience of the scenes he depicts. Certainly, if his book were altogether a work of imagination, unbased on personal experience, his realism would be nothing short of a miracle." This may strike the reader who has not thought much about it as reasonable, but I believe it to be wholly fallacious. Some years ago I had before me the task of writing some battle chapters in a book I was at work upon. The novel naturally led up to the climax of a battle, and I was excusably anxious that when I finally got to this battle, I should be as fit to handle it as it was possible to make myself. A very considerable literature existed about the actual struggle, which was the Revolutionary battle of Oriskany, fought only a few miles from where I was born. This literature was in part the narratives of survivors of the fight, in part imaginative accounts based on these by later writers. I found to my surprise that the people who were really in the fight gave one much less of an idea of a desperate forest combat than did those who pictured it in fancy. Of course, here it might be that the veterans were inferior in powers of narration to the professional writer. Then I extended the test to writers themselves. I compared the best accounts of Franco-German battles, written for the London newspapers by trained correspondents of distinction who were on the spot, with the choicest imaginative work of novelists, some of them mentioned above, who had never seen a gun fired in anger.

There was literally no comparison between the two. The line between journalism and literature obtruded itself steadily. Nor were cases lacking in which some of these war correspondents had in other departments of work showed themselves capable of true literature. [. . .] When Warren Lee Goss began his *Personal Recollections of a Private*, his study of the enlistment, the early marching and drilling, and the new experiences of camp life were so piquant and fresh that I grew quite excited in anticipation. But when he came to the fighting, he fell flat. The same may be said, with more reservations, about the first parts of Judge Tourgée's more recent *Story of a Thousand*. It seems as if the actual sight of a battle has some dynamic quality in it which overwhelms and crushes the literary faculty in the observer. At best, he gives us a conventional account of what happened; but on analysis you find that this is not what he really saw, but what all his reading has taught him that he must have seen. In the same way battle painters depict horses in motion, not as they actually move, but as it has been agreed by numberless generations of draughtsmen to say that they move. At last, along comes a Muybridge, with his instantaneous camera, and shows that the real motion is entirely different. It is this effect of a photographic revelation which startles and fascinates one in *The Red Badge of Courage*. The product is breathlessly interesting, but still more so is the suggestion behind it that a novel force has been disclosed, which may do all sorts of other remarkable things. Prophecy is known of old as a tricky and thankless hag, but all the same I cannot close my ears to her hint that a young man who can write such a first book as that will make us all sit up in good time.

Charles Chesnutt

(1858–1932)

Henry James may have been the chief and most eloquent proponent of
execution as the *sine qua non* of the novel, but a writer like Charles Chesnutt
knew that the reading public was addicted to—and would judge—subject
matter. And if the subject matter was race, as it is in Chesnutt's novels, then
the novels, however well crafted or subtle, were going to suffer from the
vagaries of prejudice and time. The sales of his own fine novels plummeted
when Jim Crow raised his head at the turn of the nineteenth century, and
in the twentieth century, during the 1960s, the intricate realism of Chesnutt
was dismissed, ironically, as not being quite militant enough. Yet in publishing two volumes of short stories and two novels between 1899 and 1901
(*The Conjure Woman*, *The Wife of His Youth and Other Stories of the Color
Line*, *The House Behind the Cedars*, and *The Marrow of Tradition*), Chesnutt
broke through a color line even while he wrote of it in his fiction, where he
explored its complexity, investigating, as he did, what color might actually
mean. In this he is the first. Plus, this well-read former teacher, stenographer,
and lawyer was thoroughly committed to the study of writing as a craft.
Chesnutt in his journals, for instance, records his impressions of various writers and their styles; his evaluations of books, particularly about the African
American as depicted by northern writers such as Albion Tourgée; and his

decision as well as his growing determination to write of the racial complexities he knows so well: "I intend to record my impressions of men and things,
and such incidents or conversations which take place within my knowledge,
with a view to future use in literary work," he promised himself. "I shall not
record stale minstrel jokes, or worn out newspaper squibs on the 'man and
brother.'" In the sections from his journals excerpted here, one can read of
his definition of a novel—subtle, serious, purposeful—and, from his letters,
his careful consideration of what writing means, what it entails, what one
needs in order to undertake it, what it can and what it may not, ultimately,
accomplish.

FROM *THE JOURNALS OF CHARLES W. CHESNUTT*
MAY 29, 1880

I think I must write a book. I am almost afraid to undertake a book so early
and with so little experience in composition. But it has been my cherished
dream, and I feel an influence that I cannot resist calling me to the task.
Besides, I do not know but I am as well prepared as some other successful
writers. A fair knowledge of the classics, a speaking acquaintance with
the modern languages, an intimate friendship with literature, etc.; seven
years experience in the school room, two years of married life, and a habit
of studying character have I think, left me not entirely unprepared to
write even a book. Fifteen years of life in the South, in one of the most
eventful eras of its history; among a people whose life is rich in the elements of romance; under conditions calculated to stir one's soul to the very
depths;—I think there is here a fund of experience, a supply of material,
which a skillful pers[on] could work up with tremendous effect. Besides,
if I do write, I shall write for a purpose, a high, holy purpose, and this will
inspire me to greater efforts. The object of my writings would be not so
much the elevation of the colored people as the elevation of the whites,—
for I consider the unjust spirit of caste which is so insidious as to pervade a

whole nation, and so powerful as to subject a whole race and all connected with it to scorn and social ostracism—I consider this a barrier to the moral progress of the American people; and I would be one of the first to head a determined, organized crusade against it. Not a fierce indiscriminate onslaught; not an appeal to force, for this is something that force can but slightly affect; but a moral revolution which must be brought about in a different manner. [. . .] The subtle almost indefinable feeling of repulsion toward the negro, which is common to most Americans—and easily enough accounted for—, cannot be stormed and taken by assault; the garrison will not capitulate: so their position must be mined, and we will find ourselves in their midst before they think it.

FROM *"To Be an Author"*: THE LETTERS OF CHARLES W. CHESNUTT

To George Washington Cable

JUNE 13, 1890

Self-confidence is a good thing, but recognition is better; and next to an accepted MS, there is nothing so encouraging as the recognition of those who have proved their right to criticize. [. . .] I shall write to please the editors, and the public, and who knows but that perhaps at some future day I may be best able to please others by pleasing myself?

To editors at Houghton, Mifflin & Co.

DECEMBER 30, 1901

I am beginning to suspect that the public as a rule does not care for books in which the principal characters are colored people, or with a striking sympathy with that race as contrasted with the white race. I find a number of my friends advise me to break away from this theme for a while and write something which is entirely dissociated from it. They suggest that the line between zeal and fanaticism is a very narrow one and I gather that they suspect me of being perilously near it in my latest book; they suggest further that considering the extent to which I have been advertised as a member of

that race I might do it just as much good by a worthy achievement in some
other fields, as by writing books about it which the public does not care
for. I am beginning to think somewhat the same way. If a novel which is
generally acknowledged to be interesting, dramatic, well constructed, well
written—all of which qualities have been pretty generally ascribed to *The
Marrow of Tradition*, of which in addition, both the author and the publishers have good hopes—cannot sell 5,000 copies within three months after
its publication, there is something radically wrong somewhere, and I do not
know where it is unless it be in the subject. My friend Mr. Howells, who has
said many nice things about my writing [. . .] has remarked several times
that there is no color line in literature. On that point I take issue with
him. I am fairly convinced that the color line runs everywhere so far as
the United States is concerned, and I am even now wondering whether the
reputation I have made would help or hinder a novel that I might publish
along an entirely different line.

Hamlin Garland

(1860–1940)

Though he lived far into the twentieth century, I consider the radical writer Hamlin Garland to be a nineteenth-century author in style and subject matter, although he certainly anticipates the realists and naturalists of a later age. Born in the Midwest, he wrote of its prairies and its people in works of startling realism about "sorrow, resignation, and a sort of dumb despair," as he notes in the stories of *Main-Travelled Roads* (1891). A social realist and memoirist of certain force (he won the Pulitzer Prize for his *Daughter of the Middle Border* [1921]), Garland consistently depicts the harsher side of western life, especially for the women who must endure it, and though writing in the twentieth century, he is constantly looking backward to the time and place of his youth. But not in his literary criticism, in which he insisted that "the reign of justice should everywhere be the design and intent of the artist." His *Crumbling Idols* (1894), which he dedicated to "the men and women of America who have the courage to be artists," and from which the excerpt below is taken, contains his democratic and Emersonian credo: that the individual has a right, even a duty, to throw off the dry bones of the crumbling past and "create in the image of life," whatever and wherever that may be, and however local or seemingly cramped and "provincial."

FROM *CRUMBLING IDOLS*

The consideration of success [. . .] is not the power which makes the true artist. Deeper yet must be the keen creative delight, the sweetest, deepest pleasure the artist knows; the passion which sends him supperless to bed in order that his story shall reflect his own ideal, his own concept of life.

But it may be concluded that the encouragement of this local fiction will rob our literature of its dignity. There is no dignity in imitation, it is mere pretence; to seek dignity in form is like putting on stilts. The assumption of the epic by an American poet is like putting a chimney-pot hat on a child. If we insist on sincerity, the question of dignity will take care of itself. Truth is a fine preparation for dignity, and for beauty as well.

Art, I must insist, is an individual thing,—the question of one man facing certain facts and telling his individual relations to them. His first care must be to present his own concept. This is, I believe, the essence of veritism: "Write of those things of which you know most, and for which you care most. By so doing you will be true to yourself, true to your locality, and true to your time."

I am a Western man; my hopes and ambitions for the West arise from absolute knowledge of its possibilities. I want to see its prairies, its river banks and coulees, its matchless skies, put upon canvas. I want to see its young writers writing better books, its young artists painting pictures that are true to the life they live and the life they know. I want to see the West supporting its own painters and musicians and novelists; and to that end I want to state my earnest belief, which I have carefully matched with the facts of literary history, that, to take a place in the long line of poets and artists in the English language, the Western writer must, above all other things, be true to himself and to his time. To imitate is fatal. Provincialism (that is to say, localism) is no ban to a national literature.

John Jay Chapman

(1862–1933)

Essayist, poet, literary critic, biographer, playwright, and reformer, the
brilliant John Jay Chapman was a man of stunning perception and wit; he
expressed himself with immediacy, force, and high color. A moralist (his
grandmother Maria Weston Chapman had been a staunch abolitionist),
he also understood passion and self-punishment: famously, he put his left
hand into a fire after assaulting a man who presumably had insulted his
girlfriend; the hand had to be amputated. A lawyer, he also participated in
reform politics, supported Theodore Roosevelt's candidacy for president, and
edited the monthly *Political Nursery* (1897–1901), a journal, as well as essays
collected into two volumes, *Causes and Consequences* (1898) and *Practical
Agitation* (1900). In 1911 he became actively involved in the prosecution of
those responsible for a lynching in Coatsville, Pennsylvania, and his excellent speech on the subject is still anthologized today. Greatly influenced by
Emerson—"he reviews the world like a search light placed on the top of a
tall tower," Chapman wrote—he eventually gave up the law to write full-
time and composed a biography of abolitionist William Lloyd Garrison (his
grandmother's friend) as well as incisive literary criticism on Whitman, Dante,
Shakespeare, Plato, Robert Louis Stevenson, and others; and he composed
verse. His writing is coruscating, imaginative, concentrated, and Emersonian;

it was collected in twelve volumes at the time of his death, and Edmund
Wilson praised him as one of the greatest American critics and letter writers, but for some reason, his star has dimmed, and he has become a writer's
writer rather than a popular one. But as these excerpts suggest, Chapman
understood the essentials of art and literature, which he unabashedly loved
and whose lamp he keeps lit.

FROM *JOHN JAY CHAPMAN AND HIS LETTERS*

My reading was apt to arouse ideas and questions in my mind that did not
interest my family or my companions and were met with set indifference.
I said to myself, "But unless I say these things, I shall lose them and lose
the source and habit of them." Therefore I continued to talk without the
expectation of being understood, and I have done this ever since.

FROM *LEARNING AND OTHER ESSAYS*

The artist gets his experience of art by working directly and immediately
in the art; and the problems he works on can neither be stated nor solved
except in the terms of his art. The critic, meanwhile, believes that he himself has stated and solved those problems; but what he says is folly to the
ears of the artist.

FROM *MEMORIES AND MILESTONES*

The great artist is the most educative influence upon the globe. But he
must not and he will not care for educating or for uplifting other people.
He cares for truth, and leaves that to do the work.
[. . .]
    We may regard art as all technique. Certainly all of these matters con-
sist of doing or of arranging some mechanical thing which gives a certain
effect; of screwing up a peg, darkening a shadow, lengthening a pause. But

if you insist upon regarding art from this point of view, nevertheless you have to confess ignorance as to what it is that produces the thing we want. All of the rules and regulations may be obeyed and yet in the outcome we are not satisfied. The rules give us a Barmecide feast, because that technique which does the magic is un-get-at-able. We thus find ourselves farther away from an understanding of the matter than if we had accepted its mystery at the beginning.

It is, perhaps, from some such point of view as the foregoing that we ought to approach the great subject; although it would be absurd to stop here and neglect other aspects of the case. Most men have nothing to say. They will under no circumstances become artists. They may hope to be craftsmen; they may gain a little insight into the subject which shall tinge their general education. Or they may become teachers or writers. A school of art besides developing creative artists, enlightens the community in many other ways. It is a focus of pure intellect, and qualifies society. It sends out journeymen, critics, experts, evangelists, heralds of freedom, men of courage, men of knowledge, standard bearers of civilization. It is a school of character and of philosophy; of language and articulation; of religion and progress. The great artist implies and requires this whole hierarchy, which exists beneath him, of equally sincere but less gifted persons.

Let no one undervalue the aesthetic impulse, or disparage the crude beginnings of art. Any finger-post of art shines with ethereal fire though it be "flute-playing taught here," on a signboard in Omaha. How much is any mind liberalized by even a short apprenticeship to any branch of art! An academy of design does as much for the cause of clear thinking as a college of philosophy. Nothing so stimulates the mind as creative endeavor; and the methods of study in science should be modeled after those of a good art-school. Here we have the cue to any pupil's approach towards any study, namely: it should be through successive original investigations tempered by text books. The psychological problem is the same in the study of science as of art—to keep the old formulations fluid, to possess them and use them, without being possessed or ruled by them. In the realm of science and of art nothing is fact, all is hypothesis, all is symbol.

FROM *EMERSON AND OTHER ESSAYS*

It is a pity that truth and beauty turn to cant on the second delivery, for it makes poetry, as a profession, impossible. The lyric poets have always spent most of their time in trying to write lyric poetry, and the very attempt disqualifies them.

A poet who discovers his mission is already half done for; and even Wordsworth, great genius though he was, succeeded in half drowning his talents in his parochial theories, in his own self-consciousness and self-conceit.

Edith Wharton

(1862–1937)

"Do New York," Henry James told Edith Wharton, urging her to become the American Balzac; in a way, she did. Edith Newbold Jones Wharton, born to a very well-to-do New York family, largely broke free from the habits of her class and kin to become a first-rate and tough-minded novelist who chronicled in exquisite style and with deep compassion its foibles and cruelties; her prose and vision matched those of Hardy and de Maupassant, though for many years she was compared to her friend Henry James and considered a lesser writer than the Master. That view has thankfully changed.

Friendships were a significant part of life to Wharton, who speaks in her autobiography, *A Backward Glance* (1934), of how much she learned about her craft from the sympathetic and brilliant Walter Berry. Here, too, she recounts the horrific and formative episode (also excerpted) that inaugurated her literary career. Yet Wharton nonetheless went on to write travel articles, later collected, and stories for magazines such as *Scribner's* and *The Century* at an early age, and in 1899 her very first volume of stories sold well, tamping down bouts of insecurity and (psychosomatic) illness. In the next five years she steamed ahead, publishing two novellas, two more story collections, a two-volume novel, a translation, and two books on Italy. She handled editors, advertising, contracts, and illustrations with professional aplomb, and her sleek, searing novel *The House of Mirth* (1905) earned

twenty thousand dollars off the bat—and was a *succès d'estime*. And though
her other fine novels include *Ethan Frome* (1911), *The Custom of the Country*
(1913), the tragic *Summer* (1917), and the Pulitzer Prize–winning *Age of Inno-
cence* (1920)—all twentieth-century books—Wharton was firmly planted in
the later part of the nineteenth century both in style and subject matter. She
was a novelist of manners par excellence, who understood that the depiction
of manners is a depiction of the human condition, and though she seemed a
bit outmoded to the modernists, her staying power, her talent, and the acuity of her vision precedes and extends far beyond them.

Excerpted here are selections from her letters and from a well-known
section of her autobiography. Also, there is an excerpt from her fine book
The Writing of Fiction (1924), in which she talks about the significance, never
to be gainsaid, of the perceiving consciousness.

FROM *The Letters of Edith Wharton*

To William Crary Brownell
June 25 [1904]

The continued cry that I am an echo of Mr. James (whose books of the last
ten years I can't read, much as I delight in the man), & the assumption that
the people I write about are not "real" because they are not navvies & char-
women, makes me feel rather hopeless. I write about what I see, what I
happen to be nearest to, which is surely better than doing cowboys de chic.

To Morgan Dix
December 5 [1905]

Lightly as I think of my own equipment, I could not do anything if I did
not think seriously of my trade; & the more I have considered it, the more
has it seemed to me valuable & interesting only in so far as it is "a criticism
of life."—It almost seems to me that bad & good fiction (using the words in

their ethical sense) might be defined as the kind which treats of life trivially & superficially, & that which probes deeply enough to get at the relation with the eternal laws; & the novelist who has this feeling is so often discouraged by the comments of readers & critics who think a book "unpleasant" because it deals with unpleasant conditions, that it is a high solace & encouragement to come upon the recognition of one's motive. *No* novel worth anything can be anything but a novel "with a purpose," & if anyone who cared for the moral issue did not see in my work that *I* care for it, I should have no one to blame but myself—or at least my inadequate means of rendering my effects.

Social conditions as they are just now in our new world, where the sudden possession of money has come without inherited obligations, or any traditional sense of solidarity between the classes, is a vast & absorbing field for the novelist, & I wish a great master could arise to deal with it—

To Corinne Roosevelt Robinson

MARCH 2 [1904]

You know I think criticisms of technique are the only useful ones—the other kind one must draw out of one's self, one's experience, one's comparisons, one's "inward ear." But technique can be cultivated, & chiefly, I think, by reading only the best & rarest things, until one instinctively rejects the easy, accommodating form, where the sentiment helps the verse to dissemble its deficiencies. The cultivation of the rhythmical sense is all the more important because there develops with it, undoubtedly, an acuter sense for the right word, right in sound, significance, colour—& also in expressiveness. The whole thing—all the complex process—is really one, & once one begins to wait attentively on the mysteries of sound in verse, the need of the more expressive word, the more imaginative image, develops also, & one asks more of one's self, one seeks to extract more from each sensation & emotion, & to distil that "more" into fewer & intenser syllables.

FROM *A BACKWARD GLANCE*

A ferment of reading revived my story-telling fever; but now I wanted to write and not to improvise. My first attempt (at the age of eleven) was a novel, which began: "'Oh, how do you do, Mrs. Brown?' said Mrs. Tompkins. 'If only I had known you were going to call I should have tidied up the drawing-room.'" Timorously I submitted this to my mother, and never shall I forget the sudden drop of my creative frenzy when she returned it with the icy comment: "Drawing-rooms are always tidy."

This was so crushing to a would-be novelist of manners that it shook me rudely out of my dream of writing fiction, and I took to poetry instead. It was not thought necessary to feed my literary ambitions with foolscap, and for lack of paper I was driven to begging for the wrappings of the parcels delivered at the house. After a while these were regarded as belonging to me, and I always kept a stack in my room. It never occurred to me to fold and cut the big brown sheets, and I used to spread them on the floor and travel over them on my hands and knees, building up long parallel columns of blank verse headed: "Scene: A Venetian palace," or "Dramatis Personae" (which I never knew how to pronounce).

My dear governess, seeing my perplexity over the structure of English verse, gave me a work called "Quackenbos's Rhetoric," which warned one not to speak of the oyster as a "succulent bivalve," and pointed out that even Shakespeare nodded when he made Hamlet "take arms against a sea of troubles." Mr. Quackenbos disposed of the delicate problems of English metric by squeezing them firmly into the classic categories, so that Milton was supposed to have written in "iambic pentameters," and all superfluous syllables were got rid of (as in the eighteenth century) by elisions and apostrophes. Always respectful of the rules of the game, I tried to cabin my Muse within these bounds, and once when, in a moment of unheard-of audacity, I sent a poem to a newspaper (I think "The World"), I wrote to the editor apologizing for the fact that my metre was "irregular," but adding firmly that, though I was only a little girl, I wished this irregularity to be respected, as it was "intentional." The editor published the poem, and wrote back politely that he had no objection to irregular metres himself; and thereafter I breathed more freely. My poetic experiments, however, were destined to meet with the same discouragement as my fiction. Having vainly attempted a tragedy in five acts I turned my mind to short lyrics, which I poured out with a lamentable facility. My brother showed some of these to one of his friends, an amiable and cultivated Bostonian named

Allen Thorndike Rice, who afterward became the owner and editor of the "North American Review." Allen Rice very kindly sent the poems to the aged Longfellow, to whom his mother's family were related; and on the bard's recommendation some of my babblings appeared in the "Atlantic Monthly." Happily this experiment was not repeated; and any undue pride I might have felt in it was speedily dashed by my young patron's remarking to me one day: "You know, writing lyrics won't lead you anywhere. What you want to do is to write an epic. All the great poets have written epics. Homer . . . Milton . . . Byron. Why don't you try your hand at something like 'Don Juan'?" This was a hard saying to a dreamy girl of fifteen, and I shrank back into my secret retreat, convinced that I was unfitted to be either a poet or a novelist. I did, indeed, attempt another novel, and carried this one to its close; but it was destined for the private enjoyment of a girlfriend, and was never exposed to the garish light of print. [. . .]

I suppose there is one friend in the life of each of us who seems not a separate person, however dear and beloved, but an expansion, an interpretation, of one's self, the very meaning of one's soul. Such a friend I found in Walter Berry, and though the chances of life then separated us, and later his successful professional career, first in Washington, afterward as one of the Judges of the International Tribunal in Cairo, for long years put frequent intervals between our meetings, yet whenever we did meet the same deep understanding drew us together. That understanding lasted as long as my friend lived; and no words can say, because such things are unsayable, how the influence of his thought, his character, his deepest personality, were interwoven with mine.

He alone not only encouraged me to write, as others had already done, but had the patience and the intelligence to teach me how. Others praised, some flattered—he alone took the trouble to analyze and criticize. The instinct to write had always been there; it was he who drew it forth, shaped it and set it free. From my first volume of short stories to "Twilight Sleep," the novel I published just before his death, nothing in my work escaped him, no detail was too trifling to be examined and discussed, gently ridiculed or quietly praised. He never overlooked a defect, and there were times when his silence had the weight of a page of censure; yet I never remember to have been disheartened by it, for he had so deep a respect for the artist's liberty that he never sought to restrict my imagination or to check its flight. His invariable rule, though he prized above all things concision and austerity, was to encourage me to write as my own instinct impelled me; and it was only after the story or the book was done that we set out together on the "adjective hunts" from which we often brought back such heavy bags.

Once I had found my footing and had my material in hand, his criticisms became increasingly searching. With each book he exacted a higher standard in economy of expression, in purity of language, in the avoidance of the hackneyed and the precious. Sometimes I was not able to show him a novel before publication, and in that case he confined himself to friendly generalities, often helping me to avoid, in my next book, the faults he gently hinted at. When he could follow my work in manuscript he left no detail unnoticed; but though I sometimes caught a faint smile over a situation which he did not see from my angle, or a point of view he did not share, his only care was to help me do better whatever I had set out to do.

But perhaps our long, our ever-recurring talks about the masters of fiction, helped me even more than his advice. I had never known any one so instantly and unerringly moved by all that was finest in literature. His praise of great work was like a trumpet-call. I never heard it without discovering new beauties in the work he praised; he was one of those commentators who unseal one's eyes. I remember his once saying to me, when I was very young: "It is easy to see superficial resemblances between things. It takes a first-rate mind to perceive the differences underneath." Nothing has ever sharpened my own critical sense as much as that.

FROM *The Writing of Fiction*

Form might perhaps, for present purposes, be defined as the order, in time and importance, in which the incidents of the narrative are grouped; and style as the way in which they are presented, not only in the narrower sense of language, but also, and rather, as they are grasped and coloured by their medium, the narrator's mind, and given back in his words. It is the quality of the medium which gives these incidents their quality; style, in this sense, is the most personal ingredient in the combination of things out of which any work of art is made. Words are the exterior symbols of thought, and it is only by their exact use that the writer can keep on his subject the close and patient hold which "fishes the murex up," and steeps creating in unfading colours.

Edwin Arlington Robinson

(1869–1935)

Edwin Arlington Robinson, too, is one of those writers perched precariously on the cusp of the twentieth century and whose work actually helps usher in that new, modern century with a look backward as well as forward, as the poem below suggests. For art outlives its century, he says, in his poetic tribute "Walt Whitman" (1896), a poem dedicated not just to Whitman but to art and, more broadly, the artist.

Robinson devoted his life to poetry. Born in Maine, Robinson at first chronicled in verse its inhabitants: commonplace men and women of blighted ambition and unspoken courage who passed lives of quiet desperation in the repressive, puritanical confines of "Tilbury Town." He published at his own expense and with the help of friends *The Torrent and the Night Before* (1896) and the expanded, excellent volume *The Children of the Night* (1897), both mostly ignored by critics as was his long verse narrative in *Captain Craig and Other Poems* (1902). In rigorous verse deftly handled with unforced rhyme and simple speech, Robinson penned poems about tragic dignity. Moreover, Robinson believed in his poetry; he believed in art. He never joined a literary club or movement, but having moved to New York City, where he lived in poverty, Robinson was soon discovered by Theodore Roosevelt (Roosevelt's son Kermit was a fan), who placed him in the New York custom house (where

Melville had also been employed). Roosevelt also urged Scribner's to repub-
lish *Captain Craig*. Robinson dedicated his next book to Roosevelt, which
increased his popular audience. His life devoted not just to poetry but to
traditional verse forms, Robinson was nonetheless embraced by the likes of
the modernist Amy Lowell and increasingly honored, going on to win three
Pulitzer Prizes—one for his *Collected Poems* (1921), one for *The Man Who
Died Twice* (1924), and one for his narrative poem *Tristram* (1927).

WALT WHITMAN

The master-songs are ended, and the man
That sang them is a name. And so is God
A name; and so is love, and life, and death,
And everything.—But we, who are too blind
To read what we have written, or what faith
Has written for us, do not understand:
We only blink, and wonder.

Last night it was the song that was the man,
But now it is the man that is the song.
We do not hear him very much to-day;—
His piercing and eternal cadence rings
Too pure for us—too powerfully pure,
Too lovingly triumphant, and too large;
But there are some that hear him, and they know
That he shall sing to-morrow for all men.
And that all time shall listen.

The master-songs are ended?—Rather say
No songs are ended that are ever sung,
And that no names are dead names. When we write
Men's letters on proud marble or on sand,
We write them there forever.

Frank Norris

(1870–1902)

Born in Chicago, raised in California, educated at Berkeley and Harvard
(though he graduated from neither), the energetic, if not frenetic, Frank
Norris also studied painting in Paris at the Académie Julien, contributed
to various San Francisco magazines, started several novels, went to South
Africa to cover the Boer War, became assistant editor of the *San Francisco
Wave*, and then sailed to Cuba to report on the Spanish-American War for
McClure's Magazine. His novel, the controversial *McTeague* (1899), was the
peculiar story of a San Francisco dentist and his wife who, once the veneer
of civilization wore thin, atavistically descend into obsession and madness.
This was not, as Norris would write in "A Plea for Romantic Fiction" (1904),
excerpted here, the story of drawing-room teacups but of elemental psychic
and sexual force. That is what he valued in the realistic fiction (literary critics
call it "naturalism"), which he now dubbed the "romance," inverting beloved
terms, and that is what he found in Theodore Dreiser's *Sister Carrie* (1900),
which Norris recommended to Frank Doubleday when he read manuscripts
for the latter's publishing company. And so a modern American novel began
to emerge, a book *not* of didactic moral purpose (*vide* "The Novel with a
'Purpose'" [1903], also excerpted here.) Alas, though, Norris did not live long
enough—he died in 1902 of peritonitis—to complete his own modern trilogy

of wheat, which was to include *The Octopus* (1901), about wheat farmers struggling against the Southern Pacific Railroad; *The Pit* (1903), about the Chicago Board of Trade; and the unfinished novel *The Wolf*.

FROM "THE NOVEL WITH A 'PURPOSE'"

Fiction can find expression only in the concrete. The elemental forces, then, contribute to the novel with a purpose to provide it with vigorous action. In the novel, force can be expressed in no other way. The social tendencies must be expressed by means of analysis of the characters of the men and women who compose that society, and the two must be combined and manipulated to evolve the purpose — to find the value of x.

The production of such a novel is probably the most arduous task that the writer of fiction can undertake. Nowhere else is success more difficult; nowhere else is failure so easy. Unskillfully treated, the story may dwindle down and degenerate into mere special pleading, and the novelist become a polemicist, a pamphleteer, forgetting that, although his first consideration is to prove his case, his means must be living human beings, not statistics, and that his tools are not figures, but pictures from life as he sees it. The novel with a purpose is, one contends, a preaching novel. But it preaches by telling things and showing things. Only, the author selects from the great storehouse of actual life the things to be told and the things to be shown, which shall bear upon his problem, his purpose. The preaching, the moralizing, is the result not of direct appeal by the writer, but is made — should be made — to the reader by the very incidents of the story.

But here is presented a strange anomaly, a distinction as subtle as it is vital. Just now one has said that in the composition of the kind of novel under consideration the purpose is for the novelist the all-important thing, and yet it is impossible to deny that the story, as a mere story, is to the story-writer the one great object of attention. How reconcile then these two apparent contradictions?

For the novelist, the purpose of his novel, the problem he is to solve, is to his story what the keynote is to the sonata. Though the musician cannot exaggerate the importance of the keynote, yet the thing that interests him is the sonata itself. The keynote simply coördinates the music, systematizes it, brings all the myriad little rebellious notes under a single harmonious code.

Thus, too, the purpose in the novel. It is important as an end and also as an ever-present guide. For the writer it is as important only as a note to which his work must be attuned. The moment, however, that the writer becomes really and vitally interested in his purpose his novel fails.

Here is the strange anomaly. Let us suppose that Hardy, say, should be engaged upon a story which had for a purpose to show the injustices under which the miners of Wales were suffering. It is conceivable that he could write a story that would make the blood boil with indignation. But he himself, if he is to remain an artist, if he is to write his novel successfully, will, as a novelist, care very little about the iniquitous labour system of the Welsh coal-mines. It will be to him as impersonal a thing as the key is to the composer of a sonata. As a man Hardy may or may not be vitally concerned in the Welsh coal-miner. That is quite unessential. But as a novelist, as an artist, his sufferings must be for him a matter of the mildest interest. They are important, for they constitute his keynote. They are not interesting for the reason that the working out of his story, its people, episodes, scenes and pictures, is for the moment the most interesting thing in all the world to him, exclusive of everything else. Do you think that Mrs. Stowe was more interested in the slave question than she was in the writing of "Uncle Tom's Cabin"? Her book, her manuscript, the page-to-page progress of the narrative, were more absorbing to her than all the Negroes that were ever whipped or sold. Had it not been so, that great purpose-novel never would have succeeded.

[. . .] It must be remembered that the artist has a double personality, himself as a man, and himself as an artist. But, it will be urged, how account for the artist's sympathy in his fictitious characters, his emotion, the actual tears he sheds in telling of their griefs, their deaths, and the like?

The answer is obvious. As an artist his sensitiveness is quickened because they are characters in his novel. It does not at all follow that the same artist would be moved to tears over the report of parallel catastrophes in real life. As an artist, there is every reason to suppose he would welcome

the news with downright pleasure. It would be for him "good material."
He would see a story in it, a good scene, a great character. Thus the artist.
What he would do, how he would feel as a man is quite a different matter.

FROM "A PLEA FOR ROMANTIC FICTION"

Realism stultifies itself. It notes only the surface of things. For it, Beauty
is not even skin deep, but only a geometrical plane, without dimensions
and depth, a mere outside. Realism is very excellent so far as it goes, but
it goes no further than the Realist himself can actually see, or actually
hear. Realism is minute; it is the drama of a broken teacup, the tragedy of
a walk down the block, the excitement of an afternoon call, the adventure
of an invitation to dinner. It is the visit to my neighbour's house, a formal
visit, from which I may draw no conclusions. I see my neighbour and his
friends—very, oh, such very probable people—and that is all. Realism bows
upon the doormat and goes away and says to me, as we link arms on the
sidewalk: "That is life." And I say it is not. It is not, as you would very well
see if you took Romance with you to call upon your neighbour. [. . .]

Let Realism do the entertaining with its meticulous presentation of
teacups, rag carpets, wall-paper and haircloth sofas, stopping with these,
going no deeper than it sees, choosing the ordinary, the untroubled, the
commonplace.

But to Romance belongs the wide world for range, and the unplumbed
depths of the human heart, and the mystery of sex, and the problems of life,
and the black, unsearched penetralia of the soul of man. You, the indolent,
must not always be amused. What matter the silken clothes, what matter
the prince's houses? Romance, too, is a teacher, and if—throwing aside the
purple—she wears the camel's-hair and feeds upon the locusts, it is to cry
aloud unto the people, "Prepare ye the way of the Lord; make straight his
path."

Stephen Crane

(1871–1900)

Stephen Crane insisted that he intended *The Red Badge of Courage* (1895) to be a psychological portrayal of fear written not because he had been in battle himself but because he learned what he needed to know of conflict on the football field. A college dropout who preferred baseball to books, save literature, Crane was a hardscrabble journalist who began publishing stories in 1892; an ardent admirer of Tolstoy who also respected the work of Anatole France and Henry James, Crane said he liked his "art straight"— unmixed, that is, with moralizing or didacticism, even though he himself was the son of a Methodist minister and his church-writing wife. Crane's brand of realism earned the praise of William Dean Howells and Hamlin Garland early on for *Maggie: A Girl of the Streets* (1893), which Crane published at his own expense and which did not sell. But the young man's fortunes radically changed with *The Red Badge of Courage* (1895), a popular book in its own time, internationally acclaimed, and now considered a classic.

Crane was also something of a literary adventurer who covered the Spanish-American War from April to November 1898 for the *New York World* and the *New York Journal;* his ordeal in a ten-foot dinghy with three members of the crew of the *Commodore*, the gun-running tug Crane had boarded in Jacksonville, Florida, inspired his story "The Open Boat," still chilling today.

And in addition to such major stories, he also composed poetry that was clearly influenced by Dickinson, who had just been published in book form in 1891. Crane valued his verse more than his novel *Red Badge*, for, as he says in the excerpt below, in it "I aim to give my ideas of life as a whole." Two of the excerpts are taken from interviews with Crane, who had become a celebrity of sorts. The other comes from *The Black Riders and Other Lines* (1895) and speaks to his sensibility.

In 1899 Crane and his common-law wife, Cora Taylor Crane, settled in Sussex, England, but by then Crane had contracted tuberculosis. He died in the spring of 1900. "It was his fate," mourned Joseph Conrad, "to fall early in the fray."

FROM "STEPHEN CRANE" (AN INTERVIEW)

As far as myself and my own meagre success are concerned, I began the battle of life with no talent, no equipment, but with an ardent admiration and desire. I did little work at school, but confined my abilities, such as they were, to the [baseball] diamond. Not that I disliked books, but the cut-and-dried curriculum of the college did not appeal to me. Humanity was a much more interesting study. When I ought to have been at recitations I was studying faces on the streets, and when I ought to have been studying my next day's lessons I was watching the trains roll in and out of the Central Station. So, you see, I had, first of all, to recover from college. I had to build up, so to speak. And my chiefest desire was to write plainly and unmistakably, so that all men (and some women) might read and understand. That to my mind is good writing. There is a great deal of labor connected with literature. I think that is the hardest thing about it. There is nothing to respect in art save one's own opinion of it. [. . .]

The one thing that deeply pleases me in my literary life—brief and inglorious as it is—is the fact that men of sense believe me to be sincere. "Maggie," published in paper covers, made me the friendship of Hamlin Garland and W. D. Howells, and the one thing that makes my life worth living in the midst of all this abuse and ridicule is the consciousness that never for an instant have those friendships at all diminished. Personally I am aware that my work does not amount to a string of dried beans—I always calmly admit it. But I also know that I do the best that is in me, without regard to cheers or damnation. When I was the mark for every humorist in the country I went ahead, and now, when I am the mark for only 50 per cent of the humorists in the country, I go ahead, for I understand that a man is born into the world with his own pair of eyes and he is not at all responsible for his quality of personal honesty. To keep close to my honesty is my supreme ambition. There is a sublime egotism in talking of honesty. I, however, do not say that I am honest. I merely say that I am as nearly honest as a weak mental machinery will allow. This aim in life struck me as being the only thing worth while. A man is sure to fail at it, but there is something in the failure.

from "A Remarkable First Success"

I have heard a great deal about genius lately, but genius is a very vague word; and as far as I am concerned I do not think it has been rightly used. Whatever success I have had has been the result simply of imagination coupled with great application and concentration. It has been a theory of mine ever since I began to write, which was eight years ago, when I was sixteen, that the most artistic and the most enduring literature was that which reflected life accurately. Therefore I have tried to observe closely, and to set down what I have seen in the simplest and most concise way. I have been very careful not to let any theories or pet ideas of my own be seen in my writing. Preaching is fatal to art in literature. I try to give to readers a slice out of life; and if there is any moral or lesson in it I do not point it out. I let the reader find it for himself. As Emerson said, "There should be a long logic beneath the story, but it should be kept carefully out of sight."

Before "The Red Badge of Courage" was published I often found it difficult to make both ends meet. The book was written during this period. It was an effort born of pain, and I believe this was beneficial to it as a piece of literature. It seems a pity that this should be so,—that art should be a child of suffering; and yet such seems to be the case. Of course there are fine writers who have good incomes and live comfortably and contentedly; but if the conditions of their lives were harder, I believe that their work would be better.

Personally, I like my little book of poems, "The Black Riders," better than I do "The Red Badge of Courage." The reason is, I suppose, that the former is the more ambitious effort. In it I aim to give my ideas of life as a whole, so far as I know it, and the latter is a mere episode,—an amplification. Now that I have reached the goal for which I have been working ever since I began to write, I suppose I ought to be contented; but I am not. I was happier in the old days when I was always dreaming of the thing I have now attained. I am disappointed with success. Like many things we strive for, it proves when obtained to be an empty and fleeting joy.

FROM *THE BLACK RIDERS AND OTHER LINES*

Many red devils ran from my heart
And out upon the page,
They were so tiny
The pen could mash them.
And many struggled in the ink.
It was strange
To write in this red muck
Of things from my heart.

Paul Laurence Dunbar

(1872–1906)

Born in Dayton, Ohio, the son of two former slaves—his father was a Civil
War veteran who had served in the 55th Massachusetts Volunteers, one of
the early regiments of black troops—at a young age Paul Dunbar submitted his poetry to the local Ohio papers, and, encouraged by his success, he
published a collection of fifty-six poems, *Oak and Ivy* (1893), at his own
expense. Frederick Douglass, for whom he worked as a clerk during the
World's Columbian Exposition in Chicago, called Dunbar "one of the sweetest songsters his race has produced." Publishing a second volume, *Majors and
Minors* (1895), funded by friends, Dunbar was then praised by the reigning
dean of American letters, William D. Howells, who wrote the laudatory introduction to Dunbar's next book, *Lyrics of Lowly Life* (1896). After being hired
as a clerk by the Library of Congress, Dunbar continued to compose prolifically: novels, short stories, plays, essays, and libretti; allegedly he composed
the book and lyrics for the Broadway musical *Clorindy; or, The Origin of the
Cakewalk* (1898) in one night.

   The first African American writer to attain international stature, he
continued to write well-perfected dialect poems and to experiment with
prosody, point of view, and verse form, and for many years schoolchildren
memorized his poem "Sympathy": "I know why the caged bird sings, ah me /

When his wing is bruised and his bosom sore / When he beats his bars and he would be free." In 1895 he had begun corresponding with Alice Ruth Moore, a writer from New Orleans and later an activist and educator who had just published her first volume, *Violets and Other Tales*. Moore and Dunbar married in 1898 and separated four years later largely because of his abusive, violent alcoholism. And they differed on the matter of his using the so-called plantation school dialect (white regionalist writing nostalgic for the antebellum South), which for him represented conflicting, competing, and diverse communities (and anticipated W. E. B. DuBois's notion of double consciousness). But his early letters to Moore suggest he sought an artistic fellow-traveler partly because, as his poetry also implies, all writers, and particularly African Americans, "wear the mask."

FROM *The Paul Dunbar Reader*

To Alice Ruth Moore

April 17, 1895

I too believe that a story is a story and try to make my characters "real live people." But I believe that characters in fiction should be what men and women are in real life,—the embodiment of a principle or idea.

There is no individuality apart from an idea. Every character who moves across the pages of a story is to my mind—and a very humble mind it is— only an idea, incarnate.

"We Wear the Mask"

We wear the mask that grins and lies,
It hides our cheeks and shades our eyes,—
This debt we pay to human guile;
With torn and bleeding hearts we smile,
And mouth with myriad subtleties.

Why should the world be over-wise,
In counting all our tears and sighs?
Nay, let them only see us, while
We wear the mask.

We smile, but, O great Christ, our cries
To thee from tortured souls arise.
We sing, but oh the clay is vile
Beneath our feet, and long the mile;
But let the world dream otherwise,
We wear the mask!

Permissions

Bibliography

HENRY ADAMS, excerpt (1) from letter to Charles Milnes Gaskell, in *Henry Adams, Selected Letters*, ed. Ernest Samuels. Cambridge, Mass.: Belknap Press of Harvard University Press, 1992. Excerpt (2) from *The Education of Henry Adams: An Autobiography*. Boston and New York: Houghton Mifflin Company, 1918. Excerpt (3) from "Chats with Henry Adams," by Jacob E. Cooke. *American Heritage* 7.1 (Dec. 1955).

LOUISA MAY ALCOTT, excerpt from *Little Women*, in *Little Women; Little Men; Jo's Boys*. New York: Library of America, 2005.

AMBROSE BIERCE, excerpt (1) from *The Devil's Dictionary*. New York: A. and C. Boni, 1925. Excerpts (2, 3, 4, and 5) from *A Much Understood Man: Selected Letters of Ambrose Bierce*, ed. S. T. Joshi and David E. Schultz. Columbus: Ohio University State Press, 1993.

WILLIAM WELLS BROWN, excerpt from introduction to *Clotel; or, The President's Daughter: A Narrative of Slave Life in the United States*. London: Partridge and Oakey, 1853.

WILLIAM CULLEN BRYANT, "Green River," in *Philip Freneau to Walt Whitman*, vol. 1 of *American Poetry: The Nineteenth Century*, ed. John Hollander. New York: Library of America, 1993.

JOHN BURROUGHS, excerpt from "The Vital Touch in Literature," in *The Atlantic Monthly* 83. Boston and New York: Houghton Mifflin, 1899.

GEORGE WASHINGTON CABLE, excerpt (1) from "The Speculations of a Story-Teller," in *The Atlantic Monthly* 78. Boston and New York: Houghton, Mifflin, 1896. Excerpt (2) from "After-thoughts of a Story-Teller," in *The North American Review* 158 (1894).

JOHN JAY CHAPMAN, excerpt (1) from *John Jay Chapman and his Letters*, ed. M. A. De Wolfe Howe. Boston and New York: Houghton Mifflin, 1937. Excerpt (2) from

Learning and Other Essays. New York: Moffat, Yard, 1910. Excerpt (3) from *Memories and Milestones*. New York: Moffat, Yard, 1915. Excerpt (4) from *Emerson and Other Essays*. London: D. Nutt, 1898.

MARY BOKYIN CHESNUT, excerpts from *Mary Chesnut's Civil War*, ed. C. Vann Woodward. New Haven: Yale University Press, 1981.

CHARLES CHESNUTT, excerpt (1) from *The Journals of Charles W. Chesnutt*, ed. Richard Brodhead. Durham, N.C.: Duke University Press, 1993. Excerpts (2 and 3) from letters to George Washington Cable and Houghton Mifflin editors, in *"To Be an Author": The Letters of Charles W. Chesnutt*, ed. Joseph R. McElrather Jr. and Robert C. Leitz III. Princeton: Princeton University Press, 1997.

LYDIA MARIA CHILD, excerpt (1) from letter to Convers Francis, in *Letters of Lydia Maria Child: With a Biographical Introduction by John G. Whittier*. Boston: Houghton, Mifflin, 1882. Excerpt (2) from *Letters from New York*. New York: C. S. Francis, 1845.

KATE CHOPIN, excerpts from "On Certain Bright Days," "As You Like It," and "In the Confidence of a Story-Writer," in *The Complete Works of Kate Chopin*, ed. Per Seyersted. Baton Rouge: Louisiana State University Press, 2006.

JAMES FENIMORE COOPER, excerpt (1) from *Notions of the Americans; Picked up by a Travelling Bachelor*. New York: Frederick Ungar, 1963. Excerpt (2) from *Home as Found*. Philadelphia: Lea and Blanchard, 1838.

STEPHEN CRANE, excerpt (1) from "Stephen Crane," by John N. Hilliard, in the *New York Times*. 14 July 1900. Excerpt (2) from "A Remarkable First Success," in *Demorest's Family Magazine* 32 (May 1896). Excerpt (3) from *The Black Riders and Other Lines*. Boston: Copeland and Day, 1895.

JOHN DE FOREST, excerpt from "The Great American Novel," in *The Nation* (9 Jan. 1868).

EMILY DICKINSON, excerpts (1, 2, 4, 5, 7, and 8) from letters to Thomas Higginson and excerpt (6) from letter to Elizabeth Holland, in *Letters of Emily Dickinson*, vol. 2, ed. Thomas H. Johnson. Cambridge, Mass.: Belknap Press of Harvard University Press, 1997. Excerpts (3, 9, 10, 11, 12, and 13) from Fr 278, Fr 512, Fr 665, Fr 772, Fr 930, and Fr 1491, in *The Poems of Emily Dickinson: Reading Edition*, ed. R. W. Franklin. Cambridge, Mass.: Belknap Press of Harvard University Press, 2005.

FREDERICK DOUGLASS, excerpts from *The Narrative of the Life of Frederick Douglass*. New York: Oxford University Press, 1999.

PAUL LAURENCE DUNBAR, excerpt (1) from letter to Alice Ruth Moore, in *The Paul Laurence Dunbar Reader*, ed. Jay Martin and Gossie H. Hudson. New York: Dodd, Mead, 1975. Excerpt (2), "We Wear the Mask," in *Black Voices: An Anthology of African-American Literature*. New York: Signet Classic, 2001.

RALPH WALDO EMERSON, excerpt (1) from *The Journals and Miscellaneous Notebooks of Ralph Waldo Emerson, 1835–1838*, vol. 5, ed. Merton M. Sealts Jr. Cambridge, Mass.: Belknap Press of Harvard University Press, 1965. Excerpt (2) from "Tantalus," in *Uncollected Writings: Essays, Addresses, Poems, Reviews and Letters*. New York:

The Lamb Publishing Company, 1912. Excerpts (3 and 4) from "Circles" and "Poet," in *Emerson: Essays and Lectures*, ed. Joel Porte. New York: Library of America, 1983.

FANNY FERN (SARA WILLIS PARTON), excerpt (1) from "A Practical Bluestocking," in *Fern Leaves from Fanny's Portfolio*. Auburn and Buffalo: Miller, Orton and Mulligan, 1854. Excerpt (2) from "Literary People," in *Folly as It Flies*. New York: G. W. Carleton; London: S. Low, Son and Company, 1868.

HAROLD FREDERIC, excerpt (1) from "An American Journalist in London: A Chat with Mr. Harold Frederic," in *The Sketch*. 13 March 1895. Excerpt (2) from the *New York Times*. 26 Jan. 1896.

MARGARET FULLER, excerpt (1) from "American Literature; Its Position in the Present Time, and Prospects for the Future," in *Papers on Literature and Art*. New York: John Wiley, 1848. Excerpt (2) from *Memoirs of Margaret Fuller Ossoli*. Boston: Roberts Brothers, 1884.

HAMLIN GARLAND, excerpt from *Crumbling Idols*. Chicago and Cambridge: Stone and Kimball, 1894.

ULYSSES S. GRANT, excerpt from preface to *Personal Memoirs of U. S. Grant*, vol. 1. New York: Century Company, 1903.

FRANCES ELLEN WATKINS HARPER, excerpt from "Learning to Read," in *Sketches of Southern Life*. Philadelphia: Ferguson, 1891.

FRANCIS (BRET) HARTE, excerpt (1) from "A Morning with Bret Harte," by Henry J. W. Dam, in *McClure's* 4 (December 1894–May 1895). New York and London: S. S. McClure, 1895. Excerpt (2) from "The Rise of the 'Short Story.'" *Cornhill Magazine* (July 1899).

NATHANIEL HAWTHORNE, excerpt (1) from "The Devil in Manuscript," in *Hawthorne: Tales and Sketches*. New York: Library of America, 1982. Excerpt (2) from "The Elixir of Life," manuscript, in *Centenary Edition of the Works of Nathaniel Hawthorne*, vol. 13, ed. Edward H. Davidson, Claude M. Simpson, and L. Neal Smith. Columbus: Ohio State University Press, 1978.

LAFCADIO HEARN, excerpts from letters to Basil Hall Chamberlain, in *The Japanese Letters of Lafcadio Hearn*, ed. Elizabeth Bisland. Boston and New York: Houghton Mifflin, 1910.

THOMAS WENTWORTH HIGGINSON, excerpts (1, 2, and 4) from "Water-Lilies," "My Out-Door Study," and "The Procession of the Flowers," in *Out-Door Papers*. Boston: Lee and Shepard; New York: Charles T. Dillingham, 1886. Excerpt (3) from "Letter to a Young Contributor," in *The Atlantic Monthly* 9. Boston: Ticknor and Fields, 1862. Excerpt (5) from "Literature as an Art," in *The Atlantic Monthly* 20. Boston: Ticknor and Fields, 1867.

JULIA WARD HOWE, excerpt (1) from "Mother Mind," in *Passion-flowers*. Boston: Ticknor, Reed and Fields, 1854. Excerpt (2) from *The Story of the Battle Hymn of the Republic*, by Florence Howe Hall. New York and London: Harper and Brothers, 1916.

WILLIAM DEAN HOWELLS, excerpt (1) from *Criticism and Fiction*. New York: Harper and Brothers, 1891. Excerpt (2) from "Novel-Writing and Novel-Reading," in *Selected Literary Criticism: 1898–1920*. Bloomington: Indiana University Press, 1993. Excerpt (3) from chapter 14 of *The Rise of Silas Lapham*. Boston: Houghton Mifflin, 1937. Excerpt (4) from "The Editor's Relations with the Young Contributor," in *Literature and Life: Studies*. New York and London: Harper and Brothers, 1902. Excerpts (5 and 7) from letters to James Parton and Hugo Erichsen, in *Selected Letters*, vol. 3, 1882–1891. Boston: Twayne, 1980. Excerpt (6) from "Fears Realists Must Wait," by Stephen Crane, in the *New York Times*. 28 Oct. 1894. Excerpts (8 and 9) from letters to Charles Eliot Norton and Henry James, in *Selected Letters*, vol. 5, 1902–1911. Boston: Twayne, 1983.

HELEN HUNT JACKSON, excerpt (1) from *Letters of Emily Dickinson*, vol. 3, ed. Thomas H. Johnson. Cambridge, Mass.: Belknap Press of Harvard University Press, 1997. Excerpt (2) from *Contemporaries*, by Thomas Wentworth Higginson. Cambridge: Riverside Press, 1899.

HARRIET JACOBS, excerpt (1) from autograph letter, signed; Isaac and Amy Post Family Papers, University of Rochester Library. July 21, 1857, www.yale.edu/glc/harriet/07.htm. Excerpt (2), "Preface by the Author," in *Incidents in the Life of a Slave Girl*. Boston: Published for the Author, 1861. Excerpt (3) from Autograph letter, signed; Isaac and Amy Post Family Papers, University of Rochester Library. August 13, 1860, www.yale.edu/glc/harriet/08.htm.

ALICE JAMES, excerpts from *The Diary of Alice James*, ed. Leon Edel. New York: Dodd, Mead, 1934.

HENRY JAMES, excerpt (1) from unpublished letter to Grace Norton in *Henry James: The Young Master*, by Sheldon M. Novick. New York: Random House, 1996. Excerpt (2) from letter to William James, in *William and Henry James: Selected Letters*, ed. Ignas K. Skrupskelis and Elizabeth M. Berkeley. Charlottesville: University Press of Virginia, 1997. Excerpt (3) from "Ivan Turgénieff," in *French Poets and Novelists*. London: Macmillan, 1884. Excerpt (4) from preface to *The Spoils of Poynton*. Boston and New York: Houghton, Mifflin, 1897. Excerpt (5) from "The Art of Fiction," in *The Art of Fiction: And Other Essays*. Oxford: Oxford University Press, 1948. Excerpt (6) from *The Middle Years*. New York: C. Scribner's Sons, 1917.

WILLIAM JAMES, excerpts (1 and 3) from letters to Henry James, in *The Selected Letters of William James*, ed. Elizabeth Hardwick. Boston: David R. Godine, 1980. Excerpt (2) from letter to Henry James, in *William and Henry James, Selected Letters*, ed. Ignas K. Skrupskelis and Elizabeth M. Berkeley. Charlottesville: University Press of Virginia, 1997.

SARAH ORNE JEWETT, excerpt (1) from letter to Laura Bellamy, in *Sarah Orne Jewett Letters*, ed. Richard Cary. Waterville, Maine: Colby College Press, 1967. Excerpts (2 and 3) from letters to Rose Lamb and Willa Cather, in *The Letters of Sarah Orne Jewett*, ed. Annie Fields. Boston: Houghton Mifflin, 1911.

SIDNEY LANIER, excerpt (1) from letter to Virginia Hankins and excerpts (2 and 3) from letters to Bayard Taylor, in *The Centennial Edition of the Works of Sidney*

Lanier. Baltimore: Johns Hopkins Press, 1945. Excerpt (4), "Marsh Song—At Sunset," in *Hymns of the Marshes.* New York: Charles Scribner's Sons, 1907.

EMMA LAZARUS, excerpt (1), "Long Island Sound," in *Selected Poems,* ed. John Hollander. New York: Library of America, 2005. Excerpt (2) from letter, 24 Feb. 1883, quoted in *The Poems of Emma Lazarus,* vol. 1. Boston and New York: Houghton Mifflin, 1899.

ABRAHAM LINCOLN, excerpts from *Speeches and Writings 1859–1865: Speeches, Letters, and Miscellaneous Writings, Presidential Messages and Proclamations.* New York: Library of America, 1989.

HENRY WADSWORTH LONGFELLOW, excerpt from *Kavanagh: A Tale.* Boston: Ticknor, Reed, and Fields, 1849.

JAMES RUSSELL LOWELL, excerpt from *A Fable for Critics.* Boston and New York: Houghton, Mifflin, 1848.

HERMAN MELVILLE, excerpts (1 and 2) from letters to Nathaniel Hawthorne, in *The Correspondence of Herman Melville,* ed. Harrison Hayford. Evanston and Chicago: Northwestern University Press and the Newberry Library, 1993. Excerpt (3) from *Pierre.* New York: Harper and Brothers, 1852.

JOHN NEAL, excerpt from preface to *Rachel Dyer: A North American Story.* Portland: Shirley and Hyde, 1828.

FRANK NORRIS, excerpts from "The Novel with a 'Purpose'" and "A Plea for Romantic Fiction," in *Complete Works of Frank Norris: The Responsibilities of the Novelist.* New York: Doubleday, Page, 1903.

FRANCIS PARKMAN, preface to the first edition of *The Conspiracy of Pontiac,* in *The Oregon Trail; The Conspiracy of Pontiac,* ed. William R. Taylor. New York: Library of America, 1991.

EDGAR ALLAN POE, excerpt (1) from "Marginalia," in *The Brevities: Pinakidia, Marginalia, Fifty Suggestions, and Other Works,* ed. Burton R. Pollin. New York: Gordian Press, 1985. Excerpt (2) from "Thomas Moore," in *Essays and Reviews,* ed. Gary Richard Thompson. New York: Library of America, 1984. Excerpt (3) from "The Literati of New York," in *The Works of Edgar Allan Poe,* vol. 4, ed. John H. Ingram. London: A. and C. Black, 1901. Excerpt (4) from "The Philosophy of Composition," in *Graham's Magazine* (April 1846). Excerpt (5) from letter to F. W. Thomas, in *The Works of Edgar Allan Poe,* vol. 17. New York: Thomas Y. Crowell, 1902.

EDWIN ARLINGTON ROBINSON, excerpt from "Walt Whitman," in *The Children of the Night: A Book of Poems.* New York: Charles Scribner's Son, 1914.

HARRIET BEECHER STOWE, excerpt from *The Life of Harriet Beecher Stowe, Compiled from Her Letters and Journals,* by Charles Edward Stowe. Boston: Houghton Mifflin, 1889.

CELIA THAXTER, excerpt (1) from letter to James T. Fields, excerpts (2 and 3) from letters to Annie Fields, and excerpt (4) from letter to Sarah Orne Jewett, in

The Letters of Celia Thaxter, ed. Annie Fields and Rose Lamb. Boston: Houghton Mifflin, 1896.

HENRY DAVID THOREAU, excerpt (1) from *Early Spring in Massachusetts: from the Journal of Henry D. Thoreau*, ed. H. G. O. Blake. Boston: Mifflin, 1884. Excerpt (2) from *Summer: from the Journal of Henry D. Thoreau*, ed. H. G. O. Blake. Boston: Mifflin, 1884. Excerpt (3) from *Autumn: from the Journal of Henry D. Thoreau*, ed. H. G. O. Blake. Boston: Mifflin, 1884. Excerpt (4) from *The Writings of Henry David Thoreau*, vol. 3, ed. Bradford Torrey. Boston: Houghton Mifflin, 1904. Excerpts (5, 6, 7, and 10) from *The Writings of Henry David Thoreau*, vol. 6, ed. Bradford Torrey. Boston: Houghton Mifflin, 1904. Excerpts (8 and 12) from *Winter: From the Journal of Henry D. Thoreau*, ed. H. G. O. Blake. Boston: Mifflin, 1884. Excerpt (9) from *The Journal of Henry D. Thoreau*, vol. 2, ed. Bradford Torrey and Francis H. Allen. New York: Dover, 1962. Excerpts (11 and 13) from *The Writings of Henry David Thoreau*, vol. 11, ed. Bradford Torrey. Boston: Houghton Mifflin, 1904. Excerpts (14 and 15) from *A Week on the Concord and Merrimack Rivers* and from the conclusion of *Walden, or Life in the Woods*, in *Thoreau*, ed. Robert F. Sayre. New York: Library of America, 1985. Excerpt (16) from "A Plea for Captain John Brown." Boston: David R. Godine, 1969. Excerpt (17) from *Walking*. Bedford, Mass.: Applewood, 1862 (original publication date).

HENRY TIMROD, excerpts (1 and 3) from "Literature in the South" and "A Theory of Poetry," in *The Essays of Henry Timrod*, ed. Edd Winfield Parks. Athens: University of Georgia Press, 2007. Excerpt (2) from "Dreams," in *Poems of Henry Timrod: With Memoir and Portrait*. Richmond, Va.: B. F. Johnson, 1901.

MARK TWAIN, excerpt (1) from letter to his brother, in *Mark Twain's Letters: Stormfield Edition*. New York: Harper and Brothers, 1929. Excerpts (2, 3, and 5) from letters to W. D. Howells, in *Mark Twain–Howells Letters: The Correspondence of Samuel L. Clemens and William D. Howells*, ed. Henry Nash Smith and William Gibson. Cambridge, Mass.: Belknap Press of Harvard University Press, 1960. Excerpt (4) from *Mark Twain: The Complete Interviews*, ed. Gary Scharnhorst. Tuscaloosa: University of Alabama Press, 2006. Excerpt (6) from "William Dean Howells," in *The Complete Essays of Mark Twain*, ed. Charles Neider. New York: Doubleday, 1963. Excerpt (7) from *"Is Shakespeare Dead?"* in *Is Shakespeare Dead? From My Autobiography*. New York and London: Harper and Brothers, 1909. Excerpt (8) from "Fenimore Cooper's Literary Offenses," in *Humorous Stories and Sketches*. Mineola, N.Y.: Dover, 1996.

EDITH WHARTON, excerpts (1, 2, and 3) from letters to William Crary Brownell, Dr. Morgan Dix, and Corinne Roosevelt Robinson, in *The Letters of Edith Wharton*, ed. R. W. B. and Nancy Lewis. New York: Collier, 1988. Excerpt (4) from *A Backward Glance*. New York: Scribner, 1985. Excerpt (5) from *The Writing of Fiction*. New York: Touchstone, 1997.

WALT WHITMAN, excerpts (1 and 2) from preface to the first edition of *Leaves of Grass* and conclusion of *Specimen Days*, in *Walt Whitman: Complete Poetry and Col-*

lected Prose, ed. Justin Kaplan. New York: Library of America, 1982. Excerpts (3 and 6) from *With Walt Whitman in Camden*, by Horace Traubel. New York: Mitchell Kennerley, 1915. Excerpts (4 and 5) from *With Walt Whitman in Camden: July 16–October 31, 1888*, by Horace Traubel. New York: D. Appleton, 1908.

JOHN GREENLEAF WHITTIER, excerpt from *The Tent on the Beach*. Boston and New York: Houghton, Mifflin, 1867.

CONSTANCE FENIMORE WOOLSON, excerpts (1 and 2) from letters to Arabella Carter Washburn and Harriet Benedict Sherman, excerpts (3 and 4) from "Reflections Upon Art, Music, and Literature," in *Constance Fenimore Woolson*, ed. Clare Benedict. London: Ellis, 1930.

Writers/Works Index

TRINITY UNIVERSITY PRESS strives to produce its books using methods and materials in an environmentally sensitive manner. We favor working with manufacturers that practice sustainable management of all natural resources, produce paper using recycled stock, and manage forests with the best possible practices for people, biodiversity, and sustainability. The press is a member of the Green Press Initiative, a nonprofit program dedicated to supporting publishers in their efforts to reduce their impacts on endangered forests, climate change, and forest dependent communities.